Donna M. Wulff

DRAMA AS A MODE OF RELIGIOUS REALIZATION

The *Vidagdhamādhava* of Rūpa Gosvāmī

Scholars Press
Chico, California

DRAMA AS A MODE OF RELIGIOUS REALIZATION
The *Vidagdhamādhava* of Rūpa Gosvāmī

by
Donna M. Wulff
Ph.D., 1977, Harvard University
Cambridge, Massachusetts

Library of Congress Cataloging in Publication Data

Wulff, Donna Marie, 1943–.
Drama as a mode of religious realization.

(American Academy of Religion academy series ; no. 43)
Bibliography: p.
1. Rūpagosvāmī, 16th cent. Vidagdhamādhava. I. Title.
II. Series.
PK3798.R83V538 1983 294.5'512 82–23128
ISBN 0–89130–608–0

Printed in the United States of America

TABLE OF CONTENTS

LIST OF ABBREVIATIONS

B	Satyendranāth Bāsu edition of the *Vidagdhamādhava*
BAU	*Bṛhadāraṇyaka Upaniṣad*
BhG	*Bhagavadgītā*
BhP	*Bhāgavata Purāṇa*
BRS	Rūpa Gosvāmī, *Bhaktirasāmṛtasindhu*
CB	Vṛndāvanadāsa, *Caitanyabhāgavata*
CC	Kṛṣṇadāsa Kavirāja, *Caitanyacaritāmṛta*
DKK	Rūpa Gosvāmī, *Dānakelikaumudī*
DR	Dhanañjaya, *Daśarūpaka*
GVA	Haridās Dās, *Gauḍīya Vaiṣṇava Abhidhān*
HOS	Harvard Oriental Series
HR	*History of Religions*
HSP	S. K. De, *History of Sanskrit Poetics*
HV	*Harivaṁśa*
JAAR	*Journal of the American Academy of Religion*
JAOS	*Journal of the American Oriental Society*
JASB	*Journal of the Asiatic Society of Bengal*
JRAS	*Journal of the Royal Asiatic Society*
KM	Kāvyamālā edition of the *Vidagdhamādhava*
LM	Rūpa Gosvāmī, *Lalitamādhava*
MBh	*Mahābhārata*
NC	Rūpa Gosvāmī, *Nāṭakacandrikā*
NŚ	*Nāṭyaśāstra*
P	Purīdās edition of the *Vidagdhamādhava*
SBE	Sacred Books of the East
SD	Viśvanātha, *Sāhityadarpaṇa*
UNM	Rūpa Gosvāmī, *Ujjvalanīlamaṇi*
VFM	S. K. De, *Early History of the Vaiṣṇava Faith and Movement in Bengal*
VM	Rūpa Gosvāmī, *Vidagdhamādhava*
VP	*Viṣṇu Purāṇa*
ZDMG	*Zeitschrift der deutschen morgenländischen Gesellschaft*

ACKNOWLEDGMENTS

In my research on the works of Rūpa Gosvāmin and their wider cultural and religious contexts, I have received the generous help and advice of many persons, both here and in India. I remember with special pleasure the delightful hours spent reading and discussing the *Vidagdhamādhava* with Dr. Prem Latā Sharma in Banaras. To Paṇḍit Ambika Datta Upādhayāya, also of Banaras, whose encouragement, wit, and expertise illumined many an hour as we read portions of the *Nāṭyaśāstra* and Kālidāsa's *Śakuntala*, I am likewise deeply grateful. In Calcutta I read and discussed Rūpa's works with two scholars, Dr. Umā Ray and Professor Janardan Chakravarty; I wish here to thank them for their generosity in giving of their time and their considerable knowledge of Gauḍīya Vaiṣṇava tradition. To others in India who offered their advice and helped me in my reading of certain Bengali materials, especially Professor Śukdeb Siṅha of Banaras and Tridib Ghosh of Calcutta, I am also grateful.

Although my work in India was largely textual, I was fortunate to have fruitful contacts with Vaiṣṇava devotees both in Gengal and in Brindavan. Chief among these are Prān Kiśor Gosvāmī of Calcutta, Puruṣottam Gosvāmī of the temple Rādhā Raman in Brindavan, and the late Dīnśaran Dās, also of Brindavan. The inspiration of their devotion and their generosity in discussing with me various facets of their religious life immeasurably enriched my textual study. The several *līlās* and the performances of Bengali *kirtan* that I witnessed during a visit with Puruṣottam Gosvāmī's family brought the material that I was reading vividly to life. Puruṣottam's son Śrīvatsa Gosvāmī, whose thesis is on Rūpa's nephew Jīva, has also been of assistance in many ways.

Among scholars in this country, I am grateful for the advice and encouragement of Professor Edward C. Dimock, Jr., of the University of Chicago, and Professor Joseph T. O'Connell of St. Michael's College of the University of Toronto, both of whom have done excellent work on various aspects of the Gaudīya

Vaiṣṇava movement. I would also like to thank each member of my committee, Professors Daniel H. H. Ingalls, John B. Carman, and J. L. Mehta. I wish to express sincere appreciation to Professor Ingalls, my advisor, whose patient help at many points went far beyond what a student has a right to expect. I am especially grateful for his careful attention to my working translation of the play; many of his suggestions have been incorporated into the present version. To Professor Carman, who took time from his busy schedule as Director of the Center for the Study of World Religions to read portions of my thesis and discuss them with me, I am likewise indebted. Some of his penetrating comments and questions have inspired further reflection and research, which in incorporated in these pages; others remain as intriguing issues for me to pursue at some future time. To Professor Wilfred Cantwell Smith, the director of my program and my mentor during most of my first years at Harvard, I owe a profound debt of gratitude, especially for the inspiration that has sustained me through this long and at times arduous program. I trust that he will recognize the reflection of some of his own ideas in these pages. I am also deeply grateful to Elizabeth Kirk and Jack Hawley, who read portions of an early draft and offered helpful suggestions and vital encouragement.

I wish also to thank Grazina Kulawas, Elaine Haste and the late Dody Giletti, who typed the original thesis, and Joann Burnich, who typed the present version. I am especially grateful for the meticulous care and considerable patience of Joann Burnich through the protracted period of revision. Finally, I wish most profoundly to thank my husband, David, who has twice taken time from his teaching to accompany me to India and whose support and help at every stage of this project have been inestimable.

INTRODUCTION

"Beauty is truth, truth beauty,"--that is all
Ye know on earth, and all ye need to know.

--Keats, "Ode on a Grecian Urn"

raso vai saḥ

--Taittirīya Upaniṣad II.7

To one nurtured in the modern Western intellectual tradition, in which the aesthetic and the religious or metaphysical are typically conceived as disparate categories, the lines of Keats quoted above come at first as something of a shock. Similarly, a representative of what is usually considered the dominant school of Upaniṣadic interpretation in India, that of Advaita Vedānta, would not be likely to interpret this famous statement from the Taittirīya Upaniṣad in a way that identifies these two realms. Yet it is in precisely this way that the words *raso vai saḥ* have been understood in the Gauḍīya[1] or Bengali Vaiṣṇava school: *rasa*, the aim of artistic creation, is identified with the Lord, the ultimate goal of religious striving, Reality or Truth itself.[2] Although Rūpa Gosvāmī (fl. ca. 1500-1550) appears not to have quoted this passage, his works form a virtual commentary on it, for in his writings the aesthetic and the religious are inseparably intertwined. The context of this union was a highly emotional form of devotion to Kṛṣṇa that had its roots in the *Bhāgavata Purāṇa* and drew nourishment from later Kṛṣṇa poetry, but flowered throughout much of eastern India largely in response to the powerful religious inspiration of the sixteenth-century Vaiṣṇava revivalist Caitanya.

Rūpa was not the first in India to perceive and articulate the intimate relation of aesthetics and religious realization. Working within the sophisticated philosophical tradition of Kashmir Śaivism, the renowned eleventh-century writer Abhinavagupta compared the highest aesthetic experience to the supreme bliss of "tasting" the Absolute (*brahmāsvādasahodara*).[3]

Moreover, throughout the history of religion in India there have been countless examples of aesthetic forms that have had profound religious significance. In addition to those of dance and drama, certain examples of which we shall consider briefly in the first chapter, there are striking instances in the realms of sculpture and music, including the magnificent figure of the dancing Śiva, cast in bronze by numerous South Indian craftsmen from the eleventh century onward, as well as the deeply moving devotional songs in both the Karnatak and the Hindusthani musical idioms. Nowhere else, however, has the aesthetic been so prominent as in Kṛṣṇa devotion, for Kṛṣṇa has from at least the time of the *Harivaṁśa* been represented as supremely alluring, and each of the arts has been employed to make his beauty manifest. Among the traditions of Kṛṣṇa worship, it is in the Gauḍīya Sampradāya, specifically in the writings of Rūpa Gosvāmī, that the relation of the aesthetic and the religious has been most explicitly elaborated.

In this thesis I explore Rūpa's integral vision primarily as it manifests itself in one of his Sanskrit dramas, the *Vidagdhamādhava*, in the light of his theory of *bhaktirasa*, devotion conceived as an aesthetic "mood." The broader question of the relation of aesthetics and religion becomes here the more specific one of the relation of drama and devotion. However, because drama has long been regarded in India as the quintessential art, in the context of which general theories of aesthetics, most notably the *rasa* theory, have been evolved, this delimitation is not so severe as it might at first appear. The analysis of a single devotional drama thus has implications for the broader issue of the relation of aesthetics and devotion, both in the worship of Kṛṣṇa generally and in the Gauḍīya Vaiṣṇava movement in particular. Furthermore, the significance of our understanding of Rūpa's *Vidagdhamādhava* and his theory of *bhaktirasa* is wider still. In the astute judgment of Edwin Gerow,

> The medieval refraction of *rasa* in the Vaiṣṇava theologies not only constitutes the chief distinctive contribution of Bengal to Indian intellectual history, but has determined the cultural milieu down to and even throughout the imposition of European culture by the British.[4]

Among Rūpa's works, the *Vidagdhamādhava* in particular rewards sustained attention. Of his two *nāṭaka*s,[5] it has been the one more highly treasured by members of the Gauḍīya Vaiṣṇava community. Evidence of the great esteem in which it has been held is provided by the numerous translations of the work into the Indian vernaculars, beginning with the Bengali verse rendering by Yadunandanadāsa, which appeared as early as the first part of the seventeenth century.[6] The *Lalitamādhava*, by contrast, was not translated into Bengali until the last quarter of the nineteenth century.[7] An Oriya version of the *Vidagdhamādhava* based on the poetry of Abhimanyu Sāmanta Siṅgāra, the *Vidagdhacintāmaṇi*, was seen in 1921 in Puri by the late Dīnśaraṇ Dās of Brindavan.[8]

My own judgment of the relative merits of Rūpa's two *nāṭaka*s accords with that of the Vaiṣṇava community. There are, to be sure, some passages in the *Lalitamādhava* of considerable power and beauty, notably the extensive portrayal in Act III of Rādhā's extreme anguish at Kṛṣṇa's departure, and the subsequent depiction in Act IV of Kṛṣṇa, after his arrival in Mathurā, as irresistibly attracted to the heavenly actor playing the role of the Kṛṣṇa of Vṛndāvana. Yet the obvious theological purpose behind the elaborate plot of that drama--the identification of Kṛṣṇa's queens at Dvārakā with the *gopī*s or cowherd women of Vraja--renders it more cumbersome and artificial than Rūpa's simpler, more spontaneous representation of the Vṛndāvana *līlā* in his *Vidagdhamādhava*.

In spite of these differences between the two dramas, one of them may serve to illustrate the nature of Rūpa's dramatic compositions. The two have a number of common themes and similar verses. Moreover, although the plot of the *Vidagdhamādhava* is far simpler than that of the *Lalitamādhava*, the reader will discover that its complexities alone afford sufficient challenge. Giving equal attention to both dramas would necessitate a significant sacrifice of depth. Finally, the *Vidagdhamādhava*, even more than its longer and more elaborate sequel, provides a concrete picture of Rūpa's vision of the religious life that is far more vivid and accessible than the rather abstract reflections found in his theoretical works.

Although we shall review the main features of Rūpa's theory, our primary concern will be with the characters, structure, and ultimately the devotional significance of the *Vidagdhamādhava*. Toward this end I include a relatively full summary of each of the drama's seven acts, together with a translation of the last of these. From the outlines of the plot the reader will be able to discern certain devotional elements, but nothing short of a complete translation of a substantial portion of the drama can begin to convey its rich flavor, complex texture, and measured movement. For a full appreciation of the play's subtleties, of course, one must turn to the original, for the lyrical qualities of the verses, especially their varied rhythms and the alliteration and assonance with which they are filled, cannot be even remotely approximated in English. The many puns are likewise untranslatable: reading two meanings in sequence yields a different experience from that of perceiving them simultaneously in the same group of syllables. In spite of these limitations, however, I have found the translation to be the most effective way of communicating Rūpa's intention.

Although the precise dates of Rūpa's birth and death are not known, the approximate period of his literary activity (ca. 1500-1550)[9] is well established. His two *nāṭaka*s, apparently originally conceived as a single drama, were begun fairly early in that period but not completed until some years later. The second of the concluding verses found in the three printed editions of the *Vidagdhamādhava* that I have consulted contains the date Saṁvat 1589 (= 1532-1533 A.D.), and the corresponding verse in the *Lalitamādhava* gives the date Śaka 1459 (= 1537 A.D.).[10] Rūpa's theoretical treatises, which quote from his plays, must be somewhat later; of these, only the *Bhaktirasāmṛtasindhu* contains a date (Śaka 1463 = 1541-1542 A.D.).[11] It is significant that it was only after Rūpa expressed his vision of the *līlā* of Kṛṣṇa in several literary works, including two long dramas, that he turned to the task of delineating the forms and stages of devotion. Yet it is chiefly his later, more systematic writings that have been studied; his plays have been virtually ignored by scholars of Gauḍīya Vaiṣṇava thought and practice. The present study is intended to fill this gap.

One who is unacquainted with the literary tradition of dramatic composition in India, especially as represented by the later Sanskrit dramas, would naturally assume that plays such as Rūpa's would have been written for the stage. Yet it is possible that Rūpa's dramas have never been performed in their original versions. In particular, it is not known whether they were enacted in Vṛndāvana during his lifetime--even informally, without elaborate costumes or make-up. My questioning of scholars in Bengal and Brindavan elicited surprisingly strong opinions on both sides of this issue but no knowledge of any direct evidence either way. There are, so far as I have been able to determine, no references in the Sanskrit or Bengali biographies of Caitanya to such a performance, not even in the voluminous *Caitanyacaritāmṛta* of Kṛṣṇadāsa, who was a disciple of the *gosvāmīs*[12] and lived for much of his life in Vṛndāvana. What Kṛṣṇadāsa does give us is an account of two occasions in Puri on which verses from Rūpa's dramas were allegedly read or recited. The first was by Caitanya himself, who is described as having read aloud a verse of the *Vidagdhamādhava* (I.15) just after Rūpa had finished writing it. The second was by Rūpa who, at the urging of Caitanya and Rāmānanda Rāya, is said to have recited a number of verses from both plays for them and a group of Caitanya's disciples. On each occasion the response of Caitanya and the others to Rūpa's poetry was one of great joy.[13]

Whether or not this account describes actual historical events, it may be presumed to reflect the attitude of Kṛṣṇadāsa and later generations of Kṛṣṇa devotees toward Rūpa's poetry. The words ascribed by Kṛṣṇadāsa to Rāmānanda Rāya at the conclusion of Rūpa's recitation epitomize this attitude:

> This is no poetry, this is a stream of nectar; it has the marks of a drama [but] is the essence of the ultimate truths. This is a wonderful description of the varieties of prema, and when I listen to it my ears and mind whirl in delight.[14]

According to Sukumar Sen, Rūpa's dramas have indeed been read through the years by Vaiṣṇavas, not simply as works of literature, but as vehicles of religious truth.[15] Yet although they have been plumbed for their theological principles, their significance has not been primarily didactic. The way in which the

Vidagdhamādhava has served as an avenue of religious realization will be a primary focus of our investigation.

Rūpa's dramas, like his theoretical works, are accessible in the original only to learned devotees and scholars who know Sanskrit well. Their influence, however, has not been limited to the circles of the highly educated. It is chiefly through Bengali works, especially the widely read *Caitanyacaritāmṛta* of Kṛṣṇadāsa, as well as Yadunandanadāsa's verse renderings and later devotional poetry, that Rūpa's theoretical and literary works have come to permeate Bengali culture. Bengali verses inspired by Rūpa's Sanskrit ones have for centuries been sung throughout Bengal in the semi-dramatic form called *kīrtan*.[16] In these and other settings Rūpa's works continue to be important for Vaiṣṇava devotion even today.

To a Western reader unfamiliar with the Kṛṣṇa devotion expressed in the later *purāṇa*s, the erotic aspects of the *Vidagdhamādhava* may be disturbing or at least puzzling. Such a reader may be comforted to learn that Indians since the time of the *Bhāgavata Purāṇa* (ca. ninth century A.D.) have shared his bewilderment. At the end of the five chapters in that *purāṇa* on Kṛṣṇa's amorous relations with the *gopī*s, King Parikṣit poses to Śuka a question that must have been in many a hearer's mind: how is it that Kṛṣṇa, who is the Lord and the preceptor of *dharma* (righteousness), openly violated *dharma* by making love with married women? In his reply, Śuka draws an important distinction: it is the words of the gods that are to be heeded; their actions, by contrast, are not to be imitated.[17] Rūpa can presume that his audience or readers will know this passage, with which he clearly concurs: in his theoretical works he nowhere advocates imitation of Kṛṣṇa. The question of which characters in the drama *are* fit objects for imitation, or whether imitation is even a proper mode of relating to Kṛṣṇa's close associates, will form part of our larger exploration of the religious significance of the *Vidagdhamādhava*.

CHAPTER I

THE CENTRALITY OF DRAMA IN KṚṢṆA DEVOTION

With the notable exception of S. K. De's monumental treatise, classic studies of Kṛṣṇa *bhakti*, including those that deal substantially with Gauḍīya Vaiṣṇavism, make little or no mention of drama.[1] Most of these works do not even include terms such as *nāṭaka*, *līlā* (in the sense of a dramatic representation), *yātrā*, or "drama" in their indices or tables of contents, nor do many of them cite specific Vaiṣṇava dramas. Yet even a cursory survey of the development of the Kṛṣṇa tradition in its various forms, especially those that center upon his childhood and youth in Vraja, reveals a large number of dramatic elements that are highly significant for devotion. By reviewing certain prominent examples of such elements, we shall see how pervasive drama--both as a concept and as a religious practice--has been in Kṛṣṇa worship generally. We shall then undertake a more sustained exploration of the religious significance of drama and dramatic analysis in one school of Vaiṣṇavism, the Gauḍīya Sampradāya, especially through the works of one of its foremost exponents, Rūpa Gosvāmī. In our preliminary survey, we shall note features of earlier and subsequent texts and dramatic forms that have a direct bearing on our study of Rūpa's plays. As we consider the importance of drama in Kṛṣṇa devotion generally and in Gauḍīya Vaiṣṇavism in particular, we shall attempt to discern the role of drama in the life of the Vaiṣṇava devotee. The question of the precise way in which the devotee relates to the eternal drama of Kṛṣṇa and Rādhā, as well as to concrete representations of that *līlā*, is a subtle and intricate one to which we shall return many times in subsequent chapters.

In a brilliant piece of historical detective work, Norvin Hein has put forward and convincingly defended the thesis that there was a flourishing tradition of vernacular Kṛṣṇa dramas in ancient Mathurā as early as the second century B. C.[2] The evidence supporting this view and documenting a continuing history of related dramatic forms down to the present day has been extracted from a remarkable collection of diverse sources, including the celebrated passage in Patañjali's *Mahābhāṣya* that has confounded scholars of the Indian drama for more than a century. Hein's investigations are by no means limited to Mathurā and the surrounding region of Braj (Sanskrit Vraja),[3] but range over much of the Indian subcontinent at the same time that they span a period of more than two thousand years. His extensive research thus substantiates my fundamental claim that drama has long been central in the worship of Kṛṣṇa. Moreover, some of the materials that he has assembled may serve as the basis for further observations that grow chiefly out of my own research into an important component of the religious life of Braj that he has not explored in detail, the Bengali contribution of the Vṛndāvana *gosvāmī*s. Indeed, the dramas of Rūpa may provide a missing link in the chain that Hein has so ingeniously pieced together, for although they are conceived on the model of classical Sanskrit dramas, they show striking affinities in certain of their features to the *rās līlā*s that Hein describes in the second half of his book.

Hein is careful not to discount the possibility that comparable dramatic forms may have evolved among other ancient and medieval religious communities--in fact, he cites evidence for the existence of Jain dance dramas in both ancient and medieval times[4]--but his discovery of several different theatrical styles that have grown up around the figures of Rāma and Kṛṣṇa leads him to make the intriguing suggestion "that fondness for the stage was a special Vaishṇava characteristic."[5] It is indeed puzzling--given the frequent representation of Śiva as Naṭarāja, "Lord of the dance," in dance itself as well as in sculpture, and his close association with the theater, as attested by the invocations to him that open most classical Sanskrit dramas--that there has, so far as is known, been no parallel development of religious drama in Śaiva circles.[6] One prominent characteristic of Viṣṇu that is not shared to any appreciable extent by Śiva may help to account for this fact: his practice of "descending" in *avatāra*s, embodied forms in which he effects the welfare of the world and protects his devotees. The loveliness and charm of certain of these *avatāra*s, notably that of Kṛṣṇa,[7] further differentiate them from the hideous, frightening forms often assumed by Śiva. These strong aesthetic qualities may thus also be linked to the prevalence of drama--regarded from ancient times in India as the aesthetic form *par excellence*--in Kṛṣṇa devotion. Because of the fluid and mutually imitative quality of the purāṇic materials, however, such distinctions can never be absolute, and the connections inferred from them must therefore remain speculative.

Kṛṣṇa is represented as assuming a gracious guise in numerous passages from Vaiṣṇava texts, including those that Hein has assembled in support of his central thesis. Hein's intention of documenting the history of dramatic representations of Kṛṣṇa's deeds has led him to focus on two levels of acting found in these texts, that of the *gopīs*, who mime Kṛṣṇa's gestures and exploits, and that of ordinary human *bhaktas*, who are enjoined to do the same.[8] There is, however, also a third level that is no less significant for our discussion: the "acting" of the Lord himself. Let us review the relevant passages with this level in mind.

We begin with the famous lines in the *Bhagavadgītā* (4:5-9) that provide the earliest account of Kṛṣṇa's many births (*janmāni*, 4.5). The forms that the Lord assumes are there said to be fundamentally different from his true nature, for he is eternal and unborn (*avyayātman*, *aja*, 4.6).[9] The parallel with actors who assume roles for a specified time--a parallel that is merely suggested here--is strengthened by the dramatic scene described in the eleventh chapter, in which Kṛṣṇa first reveals to Arjuna his awesome cosmic form (*paramaṁ rūpam aiśvaram*, 11.9) and then assumes once more his gentle appearance (*saumyavapuḥ*, 11.50) as Arjuna's charioteer. Before Kṛṣṇa resumes his human guise, however, Arjuna apologizes profusely for treating him as a friend, that is, for mistaking Kṛṣṇa's temporary semblance for his true reality (11.41-42).[10]

The idea that the Lord periodically assumes a role in order to enter the earthly arena is developed further in the major Vaiṣṇava *purāṇas*. A term found recurrently throughout these accounts is *līlā*,[11] which designates the Lord's "play," the spontaneous, unfettered activity manifest in each of his *avatāras* but expressed most fully in the playfulness of Kṛṣṇa. Because *līlā*, like the English word "play," refers to dramatic representations as well as to joyous activity free of any utilitarian purpose, its frequent use to designate Kṛṣṇa's actions suggests that they themselves constitute a divine drama in which Kṛṣṇa has the principal role. It is therefore noteworthy that this term is the generic one used in each of the three purāṇic passages in which the *gopīs* are described as imitating Kṛṣṇa's actions.[12]

Still more explicit in their representation of Kṛṣṇa as an actor are certain other passages in the *Viṣṇu Purāṇa*. In describing the worship of Mount Govardhana, advocated by the child Kṛṣṇa in place of the former festival of Indra, this *purāṇa* portrays Kṛṣṇa as presenting himself on the summit with the words "I am the mountain" and partaking of the food offerings at the same time that he ascends the mountain in his familiar form to offer worship (to himself!) along with the other cowherds (V. 10.46-47). The Lord's assumption of the form of the mountain is paralleled by the imitation of him by the *gopīs*, two of whom are represented in that text as saying "I am Kṛṣṇa"[13]; and the *gopīs* in turn are taken as the exemplars of the tradition of enacting Kṛṣṇa's *līlās* by the directors of the modern troupes of Braj.[14]

Later passages in the same *purāṇa* represent Kṛṣṇa's entire earthly existence as a form of pretense. In a hymn of praise to Viṣṇu, Akrūra refers to his illusory and incomprehensible adoption of earthly relatives and friends (V. 17.13), and the same point is subsequently made in more personal terms by Kṛṣṇa's earthly father. In a brief moment of insight when Kṛṣṇa touches his feet immediately after slaying Kaṁsa, Vasudeva, recognizing Kṛṣṇa as the Lord, wonderingly acknowledges that his affection for Kṛṣṇa, and that of his wife Devakī, *as if he were their child*, is but delusion (V.20.85).

It is in the *Bhāgavata Purāṇa*, however, that the theme of Kṛṣṇa's paradoxical assumption of roles is developed most fully. The author of the *Bhāgavata* continually juxtaposes Kṛṣṇa's cosmic reality with his human form, and indicates at various points that Kṛṣṇa is wholly conscious of his true nature (e.g., X.10.42). His human actions are thus necessarily represented as play-acting. When Yaśodā catches her infant son stealing butter, for example, Kṛṣṇa is portrayed as running away "like one afraid" (*bhītavat*, X.9.9). Although genuine indignation is ascribed to him when his mother abandons him in order to rescue her boiling milk from the fire, the very same verse describes him as merely pretending to cry (*mṛṣāśruḥ*, X.9.6). At times it is not only Kṛṣṇa but also the other inhabitants of Vraja who are represented as playing roles: one verse describes Kṛṣṇa's companions as gods in the guise of cowherd boys, who extol Kṛṣṇa and Balarāma--similarly disguised--just as one actor (*naṭa*) praises another (X.18.11).[15] The term *naṭa* is used more generally in relation to all the Lord's *avatāra*s in the first book of the Bhāgavata, where he is compared to an actor in his practice of taking on and discarding successive forms (I.15.35).

The traditions surrounding Kṛṣṇa thus have drama at their very center, for the evolving conception of the Lord in relation to his devotees, as represented in texts from the *Bhagavadgītā* to the *Bhāgavata Purāṇa*, is a fundamentally dramatic one. In certain passages in these texts, moreover, the experience of those characters in the accounts who witness--and in some cases imitate--Kṛṣṇa's actions is expressly linked with that of devotees who hear or tell of these *līlā*s. Already in the *Gītā* we find a clear relationship expressed between the emotional response of Arjuna to the supernal vision of Kṛṣṇa, and that of Sañjaya as he narrates the story to the blind king. The term *adbhuta*, "wondrous,"[16] is used of Kṛṣṇa's cosmic form in both the eleventh chapter (11.10) and the eighteenth (*rūpam atyadbhutaṁ hareḥ*, 18.77), and the corresponding term *vismaya*, "amazement, wonder,"[17] is predicated of Arjuna as he sees that form (11.14) and of Sañjaya as he recalls it (18.77). Even more specific is the parallel between the closely related terms *hṛṣṭaromā*, "with hair standing on end" (11.14), and *romaharṣaṇam*, "causing one's hair to stand on end" (18.74), which expresses the thrilling effects on Arjuna of the vision itself and on Sañjaya of the dialogue bearing witness to that vision.[18] The hearing or telling of the tale becomes, then, a re-presentation, the effect of which is comparable to that of the original event. We shall soon see the extent to which such a relation is understood to obtain in the case of the *līlā*s enacted in present-day Braj.

At the other end of the approximate millenium spanned by these texts, we find in the *Bhāgavata* a comparable relation between the response of the *gopī*s to Kṛṣṇa, whose graceful actions they behold and imitate and with whom they engage in amorous play, and that of devotees who hear an account of these *līlās*. In this text the link is established from both ends. First of all, the *gopīs* are themselves portrayed as *bhaktas* whose intense longing for Kṛṣṇa is expressed in part through their fervent desire to serve him.[19] At the same time, those who hear a recitation of Kṛṣṇa's amorous *līlās* with the *gopīs* are explicitly said to attain loving devotion to the Lord (BhP X.33.37). Moreover, just as the *gopīs* desire nothing but Kṛṣṇa (BhP X.29.30-31), so the supreme devotion of one who hears the account of their love is said to banish all earthly desire (*kāma*, BhP X.33.40). Finally, as the complete absorption of the *gopīs* in their beloved Lord expresses itself in their impassioned words and elaborate imitation of his actions when he disappears from their midst, so *bhatas* separated from Kṛṣṇa in their worldly existence are encouraged to console one another by reciting and enacting stories of his deeds.[20] Both for the *gopīs* and for devotees who hear or read this account, Kṛṣṇa is experienced as a youth of unsurpassed beauty, and the response of *gopī* and devotee alike is an intensely emotional one. The close relation suggested in these texts between the emotions of the characters in the accounts and those of devotees for whom the texts were composed is critical for later developments in the conception of *bhakti*, notably those articulated in the theoretical works of Rūpa Gosvāmī.

Sanskrit Kṛṣṇa Dramas

When we turn from purāṇic accounts to dramatic works portraying Kṛṣṇa's deeds, we find a large number that appear to be conceived on the model of classical Sanskrit dramas. The sheer number of such works, however, is no guarantee of the importance of this form in Kṛṣṇa devotion. One would have to examine each play with some care in order to determine whether and in what ways it is devotional in nature. In addition, it would be invaluable to have information about the circumstances of its composition and performance. Unfortunately, the lists of such dramas given by Konow and others[21] are based largely on manuscript catalogues and provide almost no information about the plays. For many, even the approximate date is unknown, and some are of anonymous authorship. Even in cases where a brief summary is available, it is usually disappointingly uninformative: the outlines of a plot give little clue to a drama's religious significance, which must be ascertained from its context and from such subtle indications as the attitudes of other characters toward the hero or heroine. To appreciate the extent to which this is the case, one has only to read the comparatively full summaries of Rūpa's two full-length dramas given by S. K. De.[22]

If summaries are of little help in our attempt to determine the devotional significance of Sanskrit Kṛṣṇa dramas, we can conclude even less in cases where only the title and general subject matter are known. Yet because Kṛṣṇa's later life in Dvārakā has in general not inspired the religious fervor that has grown up around the stories of his early years in Vraja,[23] we may doubt that all plays representing the heroic exploits surrounding his marriages to Rukmiṇī and Satyabhāmā[24] would necessarily be devotional in nature. Even if we leave these out of account entirely, however, we are left with a significant number of extant dramas depicting Kṛṣṇa's life among the cowherds and his love for Rādhā. In addition to his initial list of six Kṛṣṇa plays, several of which seem to center upon this theme,[25] Konow lists twelve more, two of which contain the compound *kṛṣṇalīlā*,[26] a term that we have seen in the devotional context of the *purāṇa*s and that we shall soon meet again as a designation for a form of devotional drama that has persisted down to the present day. Among the twelve is also an anonymous *Rādhāmādhava* in seven acts, and Rūpa's own *Vidagdhamādhava*.[27] Although the evidence is by no means conclusive, Konow's enumeration suggests that the theme of Kṛṣṇa's *līlā* in Vraja, especially the love between Kṛṣṇa and Rādhā, has found devotional expression in a number of Sanskrit dramas in addition to those of Rūpa.[28]

Several of these are worthy of special mention. The first is the single extant Sanskrit Kṛṣṇa drama that is almost certainly early, the *Bālacarita* atrributed to Bhāsa.[29] Its five acts narrate and portray the wondrous deeds of Kṛṣṇa's childhood familiar to us from the *purāṇas*; however, its representations differ in certain details from all of these, and it contains whole episodes not known from any other source. It is the heroic element that prevails in this work; there is considerable violence, and the gentle beauty that permeates the purāṇic descriptions of Kṛṣṇa's amorous relations with the *gopīs* seems wholly lacking. Yet the play contains passages that are clearly devotional, such as the scene in Act I in which the heavenly sage Nārada, seeing the baby Kṛṣṇa in his mother's arms, utters a hymn of praise to him that extols his divine power and majesty.[30] Winternitz, who has studied the work in detail, considers it to be from the hand of a pious Kṛṣṇa *bhakta* who never allows the audience to forget that its hero is none other than the supreme Lord. He comments that the work goes farther in this direction than either the *Harivaṁśa* or the *Viṣṇu Purāṇa*, and that it is at many points reminiscent of more recent works of Kṛṣṇa devotion.[31] In this juxtaposition of the divine and the human the text may be compared to the *Bhāgavata* account, which is roughly contemporaneous with the period to which John Hawley, arguing from iconographic evidence, tentatively assigns the work.[32]

Similar in certain respects to the *Bālacarita* is the much later *Kaṁsavadha* of Śeṣakṛṣṇa, also called Kṛṣṇakavi (early seventeenth century?),[33] which contains emotional elements and conversations that afford considerable scope for devotion. These include the conversation between Akrūra and his charioteer on their way to Gokula to carry out Kaṁsa's command that they bring Kṛṣṇa and his brother to Mathurā, the leavetaking from Nanda and Yaśodā, who express grief at the loss of their foster son, the interruption of the journey by the arrival of a messenger from Rādhā, who prevails upon Kṛṣṇa to spend some time in Vṛndāvana, and the final scene in which the two boys are reunited with their real parents, Vasudeva and Devakī. Although the major events in this drama are also found in the *Bālacarita*, the quality of the devotion appears to be rather different: the *Bālacarita* emphasizes the awe of the other characters at the superhuman strength and heroic prowess of Kṛṣṇa, whereas the *Kaṁsavadha* gives more attention to the tender emotions of grief expressed by Krsna's foster parents and to the longing felt by Rādhā. The intensely emotional scene of Kṛṣṇa's departure for Mathurā, the rich devotional possibilities of which are exploited by Rūpa throughout an entire act (III) in his *Lalitamādhava*, is entirely absent from the *Bālacarita*.

A drama about the love of Rādhā and Kṛṣṇa that may well have served as the prototype for Rūpa's *Vidagdhamādhava* is the

Jagannāthavallabha Nāṭaka of Rāmānanda Rāya,[34] quoted twice by Rūpa in his *Ujjvalanīlamaṇi*.[35] Called a *saṅgīta-nāṭaka*, or "musical drama," the play contains twenty-one songs clearly modelled in their meter, alliteration, assonance, and meaning on those of Jayadeva's *Gītagovinda*.[36] Far shorter and simpler in its conception than Rūpa's, the play nevertheless contains in brief form some of the basic elements of the *Vidagdhamādhava*.[37] Among these are Kṛṣṇa's pretense of indifference when Rādhā's friend delivers a love letter from Rādhā, the depiction of each of the lovers suffering in separation, and the description by Rādhā's friends of the nocturnal love-making of Rādhā and Kṛṣṇa. A verse in which her friend tells Kṛṣṇa of Rādhā's emotional state[38] utilizes some of the same conventional elements that Rūpa develops more elaborately: her indifference to her elders' abuse as well as to the sweet words of her friends hints at the parallel with a *yogī* that Rūpa draws explicitly. In spite of its brevity, Rāmānanda's play affords opportunities for emotional participation by the devotee in fundamental phases of the love of Rādhā and Kṛṣṇa, from love at first sight, as it literally is here, through first union.

A dramatic work of a somewhat different sort, said to have been composed in Gujarat for a group of Kṛṣṇa devotees assembled for a festival, is Rāmakṛṣṇa's *Gopālakelicandrikā*.[39] Written entirely in Sanskrit, rather than in a combination of Sanskrit and Prakrit, the work contains narrative passages in both prose and verse, which were to be directed to the audience by a *sūcaka*, or "narrator," who may have been identical with the stage manager (*sūtradhāra*) mentioned in the prologue. Because of these narrative elements, Winternitz calls the work "ein Mittelding zwischen Drama und Epos."[40] Its explicitly devotional nature is evident from the opening scene, in which an actress adores the cowherd Kṛṣṇa by tracing a series of circles before him with a lamp, a form of worship known in India today as *āratī*. During this scene the narrator informs the audience that this is the Lord who has personally appeared to show grace to his devotees, and describes the spectators as standing with reverently folded hands and bowed heads.[41] In the final act, during the representation of the *rāsa* dance, the narrator again emphasizes that it is the Lord himself, in the exquisite form of a dancer, who reveals his play (*keli*, a synonym for *līlā*) in their midst.[42]

The *sūtradhāra* then ends the spectacle with a statement of the impossibility of representing the majesty of the all-powerful Lord. Depicted at great length between these two scenes are numerous episodes involving Kṛṣṇa, Rādhā, and their friends, including Kṛṣṇa's theft of the *gopīs*' clothes, represented here as a test of their devotion. Of special interest for our study of Rūpa's plays are the characters Vṛndā, Paurṇamāsī, and Śāradī: Vṛndā explains the ultimate identity of Rādhā and Kṛṣṇa, calling Rādhā the Lord's *śakti*,[43] and Paurṇamāsī and Śāradī urge Kṛṣṇa to fulfill his vow by performing the *rāsa* dance. Paurṇamāsī and Vṛndā, we shall soon see, have prominent roles in the *Vidagdhamādhava*, and Śarad (autumn personified), from which is derived the form Śāradī (the full-moon day in the autumn month of Kārtika, here likewise personified), figures in Rūpa's *Lalitamādhava*.

The idiosyncratic, semi-narrative character of the *Gopālakelicandrikā* has led scholars to compare it with a number of regional dramatic forms, including the Mathura *līlā*s as described by Growse,[44] the Bengali *yātrā*s, and the *svāng* of Northwest India.[45] Although Winternitz designates it "ein Werk der vollendeten Kunstdichtung,"[46] he acknowledges the strong possibility that it is dependent on such popular mystery plays, and concludes that it is itself "eine Art Mysterienspiel."[47] These vernacular dramatic representations, which are more clearly devotional than most Sanskrit Kṛṣṇa dramas, and decidedly more accessible to the general populace, have flourished for centuries in virtually every region of India, and provide eloquent testimony, through their number, variety, and vitality, to the importance of drama in Kṛṣṇa devotion.

Popular Forms of Kṛṣṇa Drama

It is only relatively recently that the spectacular regional dramas and dance dramas of India have begun to receive the attention they deserve.[48] Even from the sketchy material that is available for most of these, it is evident that they have long been significant avenues of devotion. Although the styles of presentation vary widely, many of these devotional forms have the Kṛṣṇa story, in one or more of its phases, as their chief or even their exclusive subject. Such dramas and dance dramas have often been associated with religious festivals or performed in temple or monastery compounds,[49] sometimes explicitly as an offering to the deity.[50] From opposite ends of the Indian subcontinent come two quite different illustrations of dramatic forms conceived at least in part as religious offerings: the *aṅkīyā nāṭs*, one-act plays almost exclusively on Kṛṣṇa themes that have been performed as offerings to the Lord in the monasteries of Assam since the sixteenth century,[51] and the *kuchipuḍi* dance drama of the village by that name in Andhra Pradesh. According to Balwant Gargi, every brahman of Kuchipuḍi village is expected once in his life, as an offering to Kṛṣṇa, to play the emotionally demanding role of the jealous Satyabhāmā.[52] Other regional forms of drama and dance drama that express devotion to Kṛṣṇa are the *kūṭiyāṭṭam*, the *kathakali*, and the *kṛṣṇanāṭṭam* of Kerala;[53] the Kṛṣṇa *līlā* of the Ganges Valley;[54] such dance forms as the *kathak* of the northern plains[55] and *manipuri* in Assam, which focus on the love of Kṛṣṇa and Rādhā;[56] a powerful semi-dramatic musical form of Bengal and Orissa known as *kīrtan*, *pālākīrtan*, or simply *pālā*,[57] which likewise celebrates their love; and finally the two dramatic forms on which we shall focus our attention, the Bengali *yātrā* and the *rās līlā* of Braj.

The *yātrā*

Although one frequently encounters references to "the well-known *yātrā*s of Bengal," there is a surprising dearth of good descriptive or analytical material on this important regional form. It is not known how ancient it is, or whether the Kṛṣṇa theme that appears to have dominated it during the eighteenth and nineteenth centuries was equally prominent in the earliest phases of its development.[58] What is clear, however, is that Kṛṣṇa *yātrā*s, enacted with relatively simple means and improvised dialogue, but filled with lyrical songs, were in certain periods immensely popular,[59] and that these vernacular representations evoked strong emotions in those who witnessed them, many of whom would doubtless have been devotees of Kṛṣṇa.[60] Although an early form of Kṛṣṇa *yātrā* was called generically *kāliyadaman yātrā*, plays included under this rubric depicted episodes of Kṛṣṇa's amorous relations with Rādhā and the other *gopī*s as well as the title episode, Kṛṣṇa's feat of subduing the many-headed serpent Kāliya.[61] That this was still the case at the beginning of the last century is attested by William Ward, whose list of sixteen Kṛṣṇa *yātrās* contains eight titles that designate incidents in the love of Kṛṣṇa and the *gopīs*, especially Rādhā,[62] as well as five representing his heroic deeds, including his defeat of Kāliya. It is thus probable that the generic name *kāliyadaman yātrā* reflects an earlier fascination with Kṛṣṇa's wondrous childhood feats as narrated in the *purāṇas*, and that the emphasis gradually shifted in the direction of his role as lover of Rādhā, a theme represented in Bengal at least as early as the twelfth century in Jayadeva's Sanskrit *Gītagovinda*, and developed in the Bengali lyrics of Caṇḍīdāsa (ca. 1400) and later poets. Such a development also parallels the shift from the heroic, violent *Bālacarita*, in which the episode representing Kṛṣṇa's heroic defeat of Kāliya figures prominently, to the more lyrical Sanskrit dramas on the love of Rādhā and Kṛṣṇa that began to appear at least as early as the first part of the sixteenth century.

Commanding our attention in their own right as prominent examples of devotional dramas with widespread popular appeal, the Kṛṣṇa *yātrās* of Bengal are also of interest to us because of the possibility that they may have had historical connections with Rūpa's Sanskrit Kṛṣṇa dramas. The considerable influence of Rūpa's works on subsequent devotional poetry in Bengali has been discussed by Śukdeb Siṁha in a recent book.[63] That Rūpa's dramas may well have been major sources of the episodes and manner of treatment of the nineteenth-century *yātrās* of Kṛṣṇakamala Gosvāmī, an ardent Kṛṣṇa *bhakta*, is suggested by a comparison of an excerpt from Kṛṣṇakamala's *Divyonmāda*, also called *Rāi Unmādinī*,[64] with the third act of Rūpa's *Lalitamādhava*. Still more striking is Niśikānta Chaṭṭopādhyāya's summary of a popular legend--presumably enacted in *yātrās*[65]--that is an unmistakable variant of the climactic scene in the last act of Rūpa's *Vidagdhamādhava*. Yet the differences between the two forms of the story are puzzling.[66] Is the folk legend a later, rather radically transformed version of a story created by Rūpa, or might the folk version itself have an independent history of oral or enacted representations that antedate and possibly influenced Rūpa's work? An answer to this question would be sheer conjecture. I would only point out that the absence of older literary sources for the episode represented by Rūpa in the seventh act of the *Vidagdhamādhava* does not necessarily mean that he fashioned the tale out of whole cloth. It is possible that earlier versions of the story existed in popular legends that have not been recorded, and Rūpa may have encountered one such version, whether simply narrated, sung in *kīrtan*, or dramatized in the form of a Bengali *yātrā*.

The *rās līlā*

The most fully and carefully documented vernacular dramas portraying Kṛṣṇa's childhood and youth are the *rās līlā*s of Braj.[67] The devotional, even ritual quality of this highly evolved dramatic form is readily sensed by one who witnesses a *rās līlā* performance in one of its characteristic settings--a temple compound or a devotee's home--in the midst of an audience of devout Vaiṣṇavas. Although a sensitive and informed observer can discern religious dimensions throughout, it is in the first of its two principal divisions, the *rās*, that the ritual elements are most apparent. An invariable component of a *rās līlā*, the *rās* represents the climactic event of the autumnal full-moon night described in the *Bhāgavata* (X.33), on which Kṛṣṇa graciously acquiesced to the impassioned pleas of the *gopī*s and danced with them the circular *rāsa* dance, multiplying himself in such a way that each *gopī* found him at her side. The dynamic spectacle of this wondrous event is preceded by a more serene vision of Rādhā and Kṛṣṇa seated together on a throne at the back of the stage area, receiving the worshipful gaze of the spectators, the praise or invocation sung by the *svāmī* who directs the troupe, and the worship of a *gopī*, who performs *āratī* by gracefully waving toward them a tray bearing a lighted oil lamp.[68] Such reverence on the part of participants and audience alike is based on a religious perception of the young brahman boys who play the principal roles, once they have donned the *mukuṭ*s or tiara-like headdresses that indicate their identity, as no mere representations of divinity, but *svarūp*s, forms in which the Lord himself and his beloved Rādhā are fully, if temporarily, manifest. This conviction is also expressed more actively by the devotees witnessing the performance, who reverently and joyfully touch the feet of the *svarūp*s and find numerous ways to serve them, such as carrying them on their shoulders or fanning them to relieve them from the intense summer heat. The close parallel with image worship is unmistakable.[69] Gestures like these also reveal the combination of reverent service and intimacy that is so characteristic of this form of Kṛṣṇa devotion.

In contrast to the sacramental re-enaction of the *rās*, which forms the first portion of every performance, the *līlā* chosen for a given occasion may represent any of a large number of different episodes in Kṛṣṇa's early life.[70] Although the repertoire of the troupes includes numerous *līlā*s dramatizing Kṛṣṇa's heroic slaying of demons, it is not primarily these *līlā*s portraying Kṛṣṇa's lordly power (*aiśvarya*), but those depicting his sweetness and charm (*mādhurya*[71])--whether as adorable child or irresistible lover--that are the favorites of players and audiences alike.[72] Often during a *līlā* the devotees are visibly affected, expressing their emotional participation in the events being enacted by laughing, shouting formulas of praise, thrusting their right arms upwards in moments of joy, or weeping openly during scenes of separation. In a performance of the *līlā* representing Yaśodā's grief at Kṛṣṇa's departure for Mathurā, which I saw in Brindavan in 1972 during the 40-day festival of Kṛṣṇa's birth (*Kṛṣṇajanmāṣṭamī*), the emotional response of the audience grew so intense that the *līlā* was somewhat abruptly cut short. Afterwards I was informed that the *gosvāmī* presiding over the occasion feared that the devotees watching the *līlā*, who had been weeping profusely throughout, would not be able to bear any more grief. It is such an experience of total absorption in the eternal *līlā* of Kṛṣṇa, of complete self-forgetfulness through communal participation in intense emotions toward the Lord like those expressed on the stage, that is the cherished goal of this form of Kṛṣṇa devotion; and this, at least for a few brief hours, the *līlā*s make possible.

Several sharp contrasts strike us initially when we juxtapose these *līlā*s with Rūpa's dramas. Both forms use a combination of prose and verse, but the language of the *līlā*s is a vernacular called Brajbhāṣā, a dialect of Western Hindi still spoken in the region of Braj, whereas Rūpa's plays are written brated dramatic poem,[84] was sung and danced from at least end of the fifteenth century in the temple of Jagannātha in ., not far distant from Rūpa's family's home, is known from Oriya inscription of 1499 that is found in that temple.[85] conjecture that Rūpa was exposed to popular forms of Kṛṣṇa ıa is supported by evidence of the prominent role of drama :he earliest phase of the Bengali or Gauḍīya Vaiṣṇava move- : inspired by Caitanya.

in the highly complex style of late medieval Sanskrit, a classical language known well only by *paṇḍit*s and scholars. Both in language and in style, the *līlā*s are thus far more accessible than Rūpa's plays, which employ such abstruse literary devices as elaborate puns extending over entire verses and other recondite figures of speech. In Rūpa's dramas, moreover, there are no prose paraphrases following difficult verses, as there are in the *līlā*s.[73] If Rūpa's plays were intended to be performed at all, it was for an elite audience utterly fluent in Sanskrit. Moreover, the complexities of Rūpa's two *nāṭaka*s do not end with their language and style: unlike the *līlā*s, each of which explores the emotional possibilities of one relatively simple incident, Rūpa's plays have highly intricate plots comprised of elaborate sequences of interconnected episodes.

Together with these contrasts, however, we find certain strong similarities in both subject matter and treatment. Many *līlā*s center upon the love of Rādhā and Kṛṣṇa, which is the theme of Rūpa's dramas, and all the *līlā*s, like the *Vidagdhamādhava* (and ultimately the *Lalitamādhava* as well), emphasize Kṛṣṇa's lovable "human" qualities rather than his divine majesty. Moreover, they do so for the same reason: to draw his earthly devotees--and finally all persons--to him in love. In cultivating and intensifying this love, both explore minutely the emotional nuances of basic human situations.

The difference between these two forms is primarily that the repetition of fundamental situations in the *līlā*s is between one separately enacted episode and another, whereas Rūpa employs repetition within a single complex plot. However, if we consider one way in which Rūpa's plays have been appreciated, through communal reading of one or more scenes at a time by groups of *bhakta*s literate in Sanskrit, we see at once that the effect would be akin to that of a series of interconnected *līlā*s performed on successive days. Both cases allow devotees to be steeped for some time in the emotion of a single incident, embroidered through elaborate verses in Rūpa's dramas and likewise extended, though through simpler means, in a *līlā*. Moreover, the juxtapositions that puns express on a sophisticated literary level are represented in the *līlā*s by such devices as disguise, or graphically illustrated through the enactions of such episodes as the *Bhāgavata* story in which Yaśodā vainly tries to bind Kṛṣṇa with a rope. The radical difference in form thus does not preclude a continuity of function, of emotional effect. Indeed, when I inquired of the late Dīnśaraṇ Dās of Brindavan, who had just finished reading the *Vidagdhamādhava* with a friend, about his response to the play, he said with deep feeling that he had wept as they read it.

Among the many specific parallels between themes in the *līlā*s and those in Rūpa's dramas, one in particular stands out. A recurrent element in both is the adoption of an ingenious disguise by one of the characters, usually Kṛṣṇa, or less often Rādhā, each of whom employs this means to gain access to the other's presence. There is an entire class of such *līlā*s, many of them written in the eighteenth century by Cācā Vṛndāvanadāsa,[74] and others presumably inspired by his example. One that is especially reminiscent of Rūpa's dramas is *Siddheśvarī Līlā*, in which Rādhā, disguised as a doctor, is the only person able to cure Kṛṣṇa, who has become "ill" at her sharp words.[75] Of the *līlā*s of Cācā Vṛndāvanadāsa, Hein writes, "His radically innovating stories about Krishṇa's disguises are obviously new literary creations having no roots in the Bhāgavata or in any older literature."[76] It is conceivable that Rūpa's dramas, filtering into the vernacular languages through partial translations or paraphrased in Bengali or Brajbhāṣā by those who had read or heard them in Sanskrit, may have been a source of this disguise motif in the *līlā*s of Braj. However, Rūpa may well not have been its originator. Disguise is a familiar story motif in India from ancient times,[77] and Rūpa may himself have been drawing on earlier popular traditions represented in tales or vernacular dramas in Braj or in Bengal or both.[78] Moreover, the most general form of this theme, that of a play within a play, is already adumbrated in the purāṇic passages describing the *gopī*s' imitation of Kṛṣṇa, and it may even be viewed as a further development of the fundamental notion of the Lord's disguising himself by taking on embodied forms, a conception that found expression as early as the *Bhagavadgītā*.

What the numerous highly diverse popular Kṛṣṇa dramas that we have surveyed have in common is the power to awaken profound

religious emotions in the devotees who witness
tain and deepen these emotions not only during
single performance, but through repeated perfor
course of a devotee's entire lifetime. During
Brindavan, for example, especially at the time
festival of *Kṛṣṇajanmāṣṭamī*, a pilgrim may atte
formances daily for a month or more. Many devo
pilgrimages yearly, and others come regularly a
frequent intervals. The shared emotional parti
*līlā*s of Kṛṣṇa lies at the heart of the religio
the pilgrims that I encountered in Brindavan.
activities engaged in by these pilgrims and by
of Braj, as well as by Vaiṣṇavas elsewhere--not
to *kīrtan* performances,[79] participating in grou
singing (*saṅkīrtan*), visiting the sacred sites
Kṛṣṇa and Rādhā, and serving their images--also
dramatic elements, some of which we shall note
We must first, however, return to the intriguin
question of Rūpa's relation to earlier dramatic
forms.

We shall soon see the extent to which dram
Rūpa's theoretical works as well as in his lite
The chief textual models for his two treatises
in which devotion is analyzed in aesthetic term
sical works on Sanskrit poetics,[80] and his play
patterned after classical Sanskrit dramas. Yet
especially from his plays and poetry that Rūpa
only out of his immense śāstric[81] learning, but
own profound religious experience. This experi
been shaped in part by the devotional fervor of
those Kṛṣṇa *bhakta*s, including Rūpa's older bro
that Caitanya inspired. Might it also have bee
dramatic forms vividly portraying the emotions o
*gopī*s, especially Rādhā? As Hein's research has
have been possible for Rūpa to witness early ve
*līlā*s in the region of Braj, where he lived and
last decades of his life. It is likewise probab
from Kṛṣṇa's childhood and youth were enacted in
the Bengal of Rūpa's day.[83] That the *Gītagovind*

ce
th
Pu
th
Ou
dr
in
me

CHAPTER II

DRAMA IN THE GAUḌĪYA VAIṢṆAVA MOVEMENT

We have seen that drama, both as a concept and as a concrete form of religious expression and participation, has been integral to Kṛṣṇa devotion from the time of the *Bhagavadgītā* or even earlier to the present day. It is therefore no surprise that dramatic forms and conceptions are found in abundance in the Gauḍīya Vaiṣṇava movement from its very inception. Yet our previous findings hardly prepare us for the remarkable extent to which drama has permeated Gauḍīya Vaiṣṇava thought and practice, both in Brindavan and in Bengal. In this school, drama has served as the very paradigm according to which devotion has been understood and expressed. We therefore find dramatic elements in every major genre of Gauḍīya Vaiṣṇava literature: in the Sanskrit and Bengali biographies of Caitanya as well as in the theoretical treatises of the Vṛndāvana *gosvāmīs*, in the intensely lyrical Bengali *padas*[1] as well as in the more stylized Sanskrit poems and dramas. Underlying all these writings is a fundamentally dramatic conception of devotion that found its most systematic and authoritative exposition in the two major theoretical works of Rūpa Gosvāmī, the *Bhaktirasāmṛtasindhu*[2] and its detailed supplement on *madhura bhaktirasa*, the *Ujjvalanīlamaṇi*.[3] Although it is impossible to give here an exhaustive analysis of these elaborate works,[4] we must consider briefly certain salient features of Rūpa's theory of devotion, for his theory provides cludes for interpreting his dramas as well as for understanding other prominent aspects of Gauḍīya Vaiṣṇava religious life.

Rūpa's Theory of *Bhaktirasa*

In three of the four divisions of his magnum opus on *bhakti*, Rūpa expresses his vision of the devotional life in the terminology of Sanskrit aesthetics, using as his specific framework the *rasa* theory based on the classical Sanskrit drama.[5] The term *rasa* is difficult to render in English: its ordinary meanings of "flavor," "essence," "liquid extract" are blended and transformed in its specialized poetic meaning of a relishable "mood" produced in the spectator through the combination of elements in a given drama. The standard analogy is that of a blend of a basic foodstuff, such as yoghurt, with a number of spices; the resulting decoction has a unique flavor (*rasa*) identical with none of the single elements that comprise it.[6]

Rūpa's general analysis of *bhaktirasa* follows the classical model quite closely. In the ideal devotee, the *sthāyibhāva* or permanent emotion of *rati*, love for Kṛṣṇa[7] in one of its forms, is gradually transformed into a *rasa*, a refined "mood" or attitude that can, like Kṛṣṇa himself, be perpetually relished. Involved in this process of transformation are the remaining "ingredients" of *rasa* in the classical theory: the *vibhāva*s or causes of the emotion, here primarily Kṛṣṇa and his close associates, and secondarily such stimulants (*uddīpana*s) as Kṛṣṇa's flute and the beauty of Vṛndāvana, which serve to heighten the emotion; the *anubhāva*s and *sāttvika bhāva*s, words, gestures, and involuntary physical reactions through which the emotion is expressed; and finally the *vyabhicāribhāva*s or transient emotions, which may temporarily accompany and to a certain extent color the permanent emotion.

In spite of such strong continuities, however, there are several important ways in which Rūpa's analysis differs formally and substantively from those of the major classical writers on aesthetics. First, the process that he outlines is not limited to a single dramatic performance lasting only a few hours, but is conceived as extending through a devotee's entire lifetime. Related to this first difference is a second, that of the *rasa*s enumerated and emphasized in each theory. Among the five *bhaktirasa*s that Rūpa designates as primary (*mukhya*), he includes only one of the original eight given by Bharata, the *rasa* of erotic love (*śṛṅgāra*, here called *madhura*), together with a ninth, *śānta*, the "peaceful" *rasa*, which was later added to the eight and elevated by the great philosopher Abhinavagupta to a position of supremacy.[8] Underlying these two differences is a more fundamental one: Rūpa's theory refers not simply to earthly dramas, but to a cosmic play: the eternal *līlā* of Kṛṣṇa with Rādhā and the other inhabitants of Vṛndāvana.[9] It is in a state of constant absorption in this eternal drama, which is ultimate reality for the Gauḍīya Vaiṣṇava, that the devotee is to live each day. The subject of Rūpa's work is thus not primarily *aesthetic* experience--even in the sense in which that experience is understood by Abhinavagupta and others to prefigure by analogy the ultimate experience of liberation (*mokṣa*)[10]--but rather *religious* experience in an aesthetic mode, *bhakti* toward the Lord conceived largely through the categories of dramatic analysis.

Because Rūpa is interested in the development of enduring relations of love between devotees and the Lord, he subordinates seven of the eight *rasa*s of the classical theory to five *rasa*s that designate such ideal relations. These he further differentiates from the seven--which he declares to be ephemeral,[11] thus effectively demoting them to the position of transient emotions--by asserting that they are in reality a single *rasa* because of the unity of *rati*, the love that inheres in all of them as their *sthāyibhāva*.[12] He then presents the five in a graded series (BRS II.5.26, 88) and illustrates them with examples drawn primarily from the *Bhāgavata Purāṇa*.

The lowest and for Rūpa the least important of the five primary *bhaktirasa*s, *śānta* (literally, "peaceful"), seems in some respects to be a preparatory stage rather than a full relation with Kṛṣṇa. Unlike the others, it involves no enjoyment of his charming *līlā*s, but only a realization of his exalted nature (*īśasvarūpa*) as manifest in his four-armed form (BRS III.1.6-7). Although the joy that a *śānta bhakta* experiences is compared to that of a *yogī*, this state is not utterly devoid of love, for its *sthāyibhāva* is called *śāntirati* (BRS III.1.4).

A sense of the Lord's majesty is also a prominent characteristic of the second *bhaktirasa*, *prīta*, better known--as are the remaining three--by the name of its *sthāyibhāva*, *dāsya* ("servitude"). Here the relation is one of a servant to a master, expressed through attitudes of humility and obedience (BRS III.2.13). Among those said to have realized this *rasa* are the deities Brahmā, Śiva, and Indra, as well as the brahman Uddhava, whose overwhelming love wins Rūpa's highest praise (BRS III.2.15, 20-22). *Dāsya bhakta*s are subdivided by Rūpa into three types, those devoted to Kṛṣṇa and his beloved women, those devoted to one of these women, and those who serve Kṛṣṇa alone. That devotion to Kṛṣṇa may take the indirect form of service to Rādhā or one of the other *gopī*s will be particularly pertinent to the question of the devotee's relation to the figures of the Vraja *līlā*.

The relation of the third *bhāva*, *sakhya* ("friendship"), culminating in the *rasa* called *preyas*, is of a radically different sort, for Kṛṣṇa and his friends are on the same level, and their emotions are thus comparable. Rūpa contrasts this *rasa* not only with the preceding one but also with *vatsala*, the next to be discussed, for the relations of *dāsya* and *vātsalya* both involve inequality, so that in each the emotions of Kṛṣṇa and devotee are different. It is precisely because of its mutuality that Rūpa attributes a special delight to the *rasa* arising from *sakhya bhāva* (BRS III.3.62-64). Of Kṛṣṇa's friends, those in Vraja are said to be the best, for they experience Kṛṣṇa as their very life, becoming dejected at even a moment's separation from him (BRS III.3.10).

Kṛṣṇa's majesty is likewise unmanifest in the fourth *bhāva*, *vātsalya* ("parental affection"), which becomes transformed into *vatsala rasa*. To devotees of pure *vātsalya*, Kṛṣṇa is always experienced as a child, even after he becomes an adolescent. The persons who exemplify this *bhāva* most perfectly are Yaśodā and Nanda, Kṛṣṇa's foster parents in Vraja (BRS III.4.4., 7, 19, 25). Terming this *rasa*, together with the preceding two, *paramādbhuta*, "most wondrous," Rūpa states that these three may be combined in individual *bhakta*s, as they are, for example, in Kṛṣṇa's elder brother Balarāma (BRS III.4.30-31).

The fifth and highest[13] of the five primary *bhaktirasa*s, *madhura*, is treated only briefly by Rūpa in the *Bhaktirasāmṛtasindhu*; although he here speaks of its incomprehensible and secret nature,[14] he subsequently devotes an entire treatise, the *Ujjvalanīlamaṇi*, to its detailed exposition. Its importance for Rūpa may likewise be ascertained from his three dramas, all of which center upon *madhura*. This *rasa*, with *madhurā rati* as its *sthāyibhāva*, is a transfiguration of *śṛṅgāra rasa*, the "mood" of erotic love, which is the most important *rasa* of classical Sanskrit poetry and drama. The women depicted in the *Bhāgavata* and elsewhere who love Kṛṣṇa passionately, especially the *gopī*s of Vraja, are the *bhakta*s of this *rasa*, and of these Rūpa explicitly designates Rādhā as supreme (BRS III.5.3, 5, 9).

Because Rūpa illustrates the various aspects of his theory with verses drawn largely from the *Bhāgavata* and from his own poetry and dramas, in which Kṛṣṇa's close associates are portrayed in their relations with him, it is difficult to determine precisely how ordinary *bhakta*s are expected to realize these *rasa*s. Not surprisingly, therefore, Rūpa's theory has been interpreted in fundamentally different ways. According to S. K. De, the process is one of imaginative identification with one of the principal characters in the Vraja *līlā*.

> One desirous of this way of realisation [*rāgānugā bhakti*, discussed below] will adopt the particular Bhava (e.g. Rādhā-bhāva, Sakhī-bhāva, etc.) of the particular favourite of Kṛṣṇa according to his or her Līlā, Veśa, and Svabhāva, and live in the ecstasy of that vicarious enjoyment. The emotion . . . is engendered . . . by elaborately imitating the action and feeling of those connected with Kṛṣṇa in Vraja. . . . The devotee by his ardent meditation not only seeks to visualise and make the whole Vṛndāvana-līlā of Kṛṣṇa live before him, but he enters into it imaginatively, and by playing the part of a beloved of Kṛṣṇa, he experiences vicariously the passionate feelings which are so vividly pictured in the literature.[15]

Edward Dimock, whose approach follows De's, asserts that the *bhakta* "becomes, by a mental-training process . . . , one or another of the people in the *Bhāgavata* stories in his relation to the Lord."[16]

Other interpreters of the tradition have taken a rather different position. Drawing on the work of Bimanbehari Majumdar and others, Joseph O'Connell has argued in his thesis that the primary models whose feelings and actions toward the Lord are imitated by the devotee are not the close associates of Kṛṣṇa in Vraja, but the *mañjarī*s or maidservants who humbly serve Rādhā and the other prominent *gopī*s.[17] The practice of *mañjarīsādhana* is attested in a significant number of poems and other writings from at least the time of the immediate followers of the six *gosvāmī*s as well as in the oral tradition represented by several contemporary Vaiṣṇavas with whom I discussed the matter.[18] Between these two views lies the position articulated by Shashibhusan Dasgupta:

> The attitude of the Vaiṣṇava poets was *Sakhi-bhāva* rather than *Rādhā-bhāva*. Śri-Caitanya placed himself in the position

> of Rādhā . . . but the Vaiṣṇava poets, headed by Jayadeva, Caṇḍīdāsa and Vidyāpati, placed themselves, rather in the position of the Sakhis, or the female companions of Rādhā and Kṛṣṇa, who did never long for their union with Kṛṣṇa,-- but ever longed for the opportunity of witnessing from a distance the eternal love-making of Rādhā and Kṛṣṇa in the supranatural land of Vṛndāvana. . . .[19]

An interpretation of the devotional significance of Rūpa's dramas turns in large measure on the way in which the devotee relates to their principal characters, and especially to Rādhā and Kṛṣṇa. This question is a more specific version of the issue addressed by the writers just quoted and cited. De elsewhere compares the *bhakta* to the appreciative spectator (*sahṛdaya*) described in the classical aesthetic theory.[20] To what extent is the devotee a spectator of the eternal *līlā* of Kṛṣṇa and his intimate associates in Vraja, and to what extent may he become a participant in this *līlā*? And if he becomes a participant, what role or roles does he assume? Although we cannot answer this question in general, for the experience of each devotee will be in some respects different, we can attempt to ascertain Rūpa's views on this issue. The remaining chapters of the thesis will explore the *Vidagdhamādhava* with this fundamental question in mind. Here we shall concentrate on the first part of the *Bhaktirasāmṛtasindhu*, in which Rūpa gives his most systematic exposition of the forms and stages of *bhakti*.

In his discussion of *sādhanabhakti*, devotion attained through concrete practical disciplines, Rūpa distinguishes two fundamental types, *vaidhī* and *rāgānugā*. Whereas *vaidhī bhakti* follows the injunctions of scripture, such as those found in the *Bhāgavata*, *rāgānugā bhakti* follows the deep love (*rāga*) of those persons most closely associated with Kṛṣṇa in Vraja, whose *bhakti* Rūpa terms *rāgātmikā*, "having *rāga* as its very essence."[21] What is unclear, however, is precisely what Rūpa understands by the term *anuga*, "following," and it is on this point that differences of opinion have arisen. Let us then look more closely at the passages in which Rūpa spells out his understanding of this form of devotional practice.

Much has been made of the fact that the term used by Rūpa as a synonym for *anuga* is not *anukara*, "imitating," but *anusāra*, "following, going after (both literally and figuratively)." Rūpa defines *rāgānugā bhakti* as following (*anusṛtā*) the *rāgātmikā bhakti* manifested clearly by the inhabitants of Vraja,[22] and later he employs the compound *vrajalokānusāra*, "following the people of Vraja" (BRS I.2.89). Yet *anusāra*, with its figurative sense, is hardly more specific than *anuga* and would not seem to exclude imitation. Indeed, imitation in some form seems to be prescribed by Rūpa in his discussion of *sambandhānugā*, a type of *rāgānugā*, in which he instructs devotees who desire to practice this form of *bhakti*, in the mode, for example, of *vātsalya*, to do so according to the feelings, actions, and gestures of such persons as Nanda and Yaśodā (BRS I.2.97).

The verse just noted and the commentaries on it provide an illuminating illustration of the direction of the evolving tradition. Although Rūpa himself seems content to leave the matter open, both of his major commentators, Jīva Gosvāmī and Viśvanātha Cakravartī, hedge his injunction about with restrictions. Jīva, for example, specifically excludes identification in the usual sense, drawing a clear distinction between the conceit of identifying with Nanda or one of Kṛṣṇa's other intimate associates (*vrajendrāditvābhimāna*) and a more general identification--for example, with a fatherly role (*pitṛtvādyabhimāna*) --and insisting that Rūpa is not advocating the former. Viśvanātha not only explicitly proscribes identification,[23] but goes a step further and limits imitation to the realm of the imagination. Asserting unequivocally that *bhakti* is service (*sevā*), he argues that service with the emotions and actions of such associates of Kṛṣṇa as Nanda or Subala should be performed mentally, with one's *siddhadeha* or realized body, and not with one's *sādhakadeha*, or ordinary physical form.[24] The commentators, then, are more concerned than Rūpa to maintain distance, not only between the devotee and the Lord, but also between the devotee and Kṛṣṇa's close associates, who are elsewhere classified by Jīva as parts of Kṛṣṇa himself. The development in this direction may in fact have been in part a response to this metaphysical distinction of Jīva's between Kṛṣṇa's *antaraṅgā* or *svarūpa-śakti*, which is composed of ordinary human *bhakta*s.[25] For Rūpa, the dividing line is not so sharp.

Other terms and phrases used by Rūpa provide important clues to his meaning, although they are hardly less ambiguous than *anuga* and *anusāra*. Rūpa speaks, for example, of living in Vraja; if one interprets this phrase, as does the commentator Viśvanātha, to include dwelling there mentally (*manasā*),[26] the *rāgānuga bhakta* could imaginatively participate in, and not merely witness, the Vraja *līlā*. Rūpa further characterizes these *bhakta*s as possessed by the desire for the emotions of the people of Vraja (*tadbhāvalipsu*, BRS I.2.89), and he elsewhere uses the still stronger term *lobha*, "greed,"[27] to refer to their longing to experience these emotions. The heart of this discipline Rūpa asserts to be *smaraṇa*, "remembering": the *sādhaka* dwelling in Vraja (presumably either imaginatively or physically) should always remember Kṛṣṇa and the dear associates whose *bhāva* he desires and talk of them constantly (BRS I.2.88).

In accordance with Rūpa's clear emphasis on aspiring to and cultivating within oneself the feelings toward Kṛṣṇa of one or another of the inhabitants of Vraja, we might render *anusāra* as "conforming (oneself) to" rather than "following." One could express one's ardent longing for the love toward Kṛṣṇa shown by his closest associates and gradually develop corresponding emotions toward the Lord either through imaginative identification with the mode of one of the principal characters, as De and Dimock assume, or by realizing oneself to be a *mañjarī* who accompanies, serves, and therby imbibes the emotion of one of the primary figures in the *līlā*. The analogy of a lifelong apprentice suggests itself especially in the latter case, but it is also not inappropriate to the former: one may never, or at least not in the course of a single lifetime, attain to the heights of emotion of one's master or mistress or of the character whose *bhāva* one assumes, but either repeated association or imaginative identification would allow for ever greater approximation.

As is so often the case in the history of religions, Rūpa's own theory seems to be more flexible than the interpretations of his successors. The ambiguity that allows scope for such conflicting interpretations stems in part from Rūpa's use of the same term, *bhakta*, to refer both to *rāgātmikā* devotees, those close associates of Kṛṣṇa who are depicted most fully in the tenth book of the *Bhāgavata* and in dramas such as Rūpa's, and to *rāgānugā* devotees, ordinary mortals who yearn for the direct, natural love shown by these intimate associates. In this ambiguity Rūpa follows the lead of the *Bhāgavata* itself, which, as we have noted earlier, portrays the *gopī*s as *bhakta*s and links their emotions with those of subsequent devotees who hear of Kṛṣṇa's *līlā*s with these most fortunate women.

The relatively fluid nature of Rūpa's scheme is most evident in the *anubhāva*s or outward expressions of *bhakti* that he enumerates in the *Bhaktirasāmṛtasindhu* in three major contexts. In each of the first two divisions of this work, Rūpa gives a general list of *anubhāva*s, and he subsequently gives more specific lists for the primary *bhaktirasa*s when he discusses them individually. The first of the general lists, found in the section on *bhāvabhakti*, seems to be written with the ordinary human *bhakta* in mind, for it includes such signs as *kṣānti* ("patience," defined by Rūpa as unperturbability), *virakti* ("distaste," i.e., for the objects of sense), *samutkaṇṭhā* (eagerness), *nāmagāne sadā ruci* (perpetual delight in singing the names of the Lord), and *tadguṇākhyāne āsakti* (fondness for the recitation of the Lord's excellent qualities) (BRS I.3.14-15). By contrast, the second list, given in the context of Rūpa's general exposition of *bhaktirasa*, is ambiguous in its applicability. Although the examples given by Rūpa of persons manifesting these *anubhāva*s are characters in such texts as the *Bhāgavata* rather than ordinary devotees, the *anubhāva*s in this list are also appropriate if unusual expressions of earthly devotion. They include *nṛtya* (dancing), *viluṭhita* (rolling on the ground), *gīta* (singing), *krośana* (crying), and *lokānapekṣitā* (disregarding the opinions of worldly persons) (BRS II.2.2).

As an example of one of these, *viluṭhita*, Rūpa quotes a verse from the *Bhāgavata* that describes the ecstatic actions of Akrūra as he reaches Vraja: he rolls in the dust of the path marked by the feet of Kṛṣṇa, wholly overcome with love.[28] In the prologue of Rūpa's own *Vidagdhamādhava* he similarly describes the actions of an entire group of *bhakta*s: drawn to Vṛndāvana by their great love for Kṛṣṇa, they too roll in the dust of the holy sites (I.2.8-10; I.3). Such continuity between the expression of emotion by characters in the accounts that Rūpa cites and his description of devotees contemporary with him suggests that he conceives the differences between them to be matters of degree rather than of kind. This continuity is clearest in the case of such intermediate figures as Akrūra, who is not one of Kṛṣṇa's associates in Vraja, but comes there to take him to Mathurā, and is thus in some ways analogous to a pilgrim as he approaches the sacred scenes of Kṛṣṇa's childhood.

Such continuity, however, is not evident in Rūpa's discussion of individual *bhaktirasa*s, the third context in which he enumerates *anubhāva*s, for those especially of the three highest *rasa*s (*preyas*, *vatsala*, and *madhura*) are clearly the expressions and actions of the people of Vraja and not those of earthly *bhakta*s. In relation to these *bhāva*s the devotee would seem to be conceived in the role of a spectator rather than that of a participant who likewise manifests such *anubhāva*s. Not surprisingly, the discontinuity is most apparent in the highest and most intimate mode of relating to Kṛṣṇa, the *bhāva* that is exemplified by the *gopī*s and realized most fully by Rādhā. It is this *bhāva* that is central to Rūpa's dramas and to the Vaiṣṇava lyrics in Bengali and Brajabuli,[29] as well as to much Sanskrit Kṛṣṇa poetry. Moreover, it is in the context of the love between Rādhā and Kṛṣṇa that the devotional stances of *sakhībhāva* and *mañjarībhāva* have been elaborated. Our analysis of the *Vidagdhamādhava* will help us to determine the extent to which these alternatives are anticipated by Rūpa himself.

The fact that Rūpa is not wholly explicit about the way in which the devotee is to realize the *bhaktirasa*s exemplified by the *gopī*s and others who enjoyed Kṛṣṇa's immediate presence affords scope for diverse interpretations. As we have noted, the Vaiṣṇava community represents a spectrum of viewpoints and types of experience.[30] Such diversity should not, however, obscure the salient point for the argument of the present chapter, for in each of its major interpretations, Rūpa's theory places drama at the very center of devotion. Regardless of whether the devotee remains ever a spectator of the eternal *līlā* of Kṛṣṇa or assumes in his devotional life the role of a major or minor character in that *līlā*, he is to live, ideally, in perpetual awareness of the divine drama.

In view of the fundamentally dramatic structure of Rūpa's theory of *bhaktirasa*, one would expect him to give great importance to dramas representing the eternal *līlā*. It is therefore startling to discover his only explicit statement about the devotional value of drama and poetry:

> When love (*rati*) has newly dawned in a devotee of Hari, poetry and drama are efficacious in making [Kṛṣṇa and all associated with him] the *vibhāva*s [and other dramatic elements that combine to produce *rasa*]. Good devotees, [however,] taste *rasa* at the slightest mention of Hari; for this, the power of their love (*rati*) alone is sufficient cause.[31]

Taken at face value, this statement seems to minimize or even deny the devotional value of drama and poetry for all but the beginner on the path of *bhakti*.[32] Yet such an interpretation is contradicted by the sheer weight of the evidence for Rūpa's valuing of both poetry and drama.

We have already observed that Rūpa's exposition of *bhaktirasa* in three of the four divisions of his *Bhaktirasāmṛtasindhu* is based squarely on the dramatic theory of the classical Sanskrit theater. Rūpa's *Ujjvalanīlamaṇi* is likewise permeated with dramatic and poetic elements. In addition to these two works, Rūpa wrote an entire treatise on dramaturgy, the *Nāṭakacandrikā*, as well as two full-length dramas and a smaller dramatic work in one act (the *Dānakelikaumudī*) on various aspects of Kṛṣṇa's *līlā*, especially his love for Rādhā. His contributions in the realm of poetry, two sustained *kāvya*s, a large number of briefer *stotra*s, and the collecting and arranging of verses on Kṛṣṇa into a major anthology, the *Padyāvalī*, are likewise impressive.[33]

Moreover, Rūpa's poetic and dramatic works are not primers for beginning students, but highly elaborate literary productions presupposing vast knowledge of such earlier devotional texts as the *Bhāgavata* as well as of the subtle intricacies of Sanskrit poetics. Nor is it novices who read these works; Rūpa's dramas are considered suitable only for advanced devotees. Indeed, this conception of *adhikāritva* or "eligibility" to read such texts proved to be an obstacle in my efforts to discuss Rūpa's dramas with devotees in Bengal: how was it that I--not only a non-Vaiṣṇava, but a foreigner and a mere neophyte in the study of Gauḍīya Vaiṣṇava literature--was reading these highly esoteric works? One monk, who showed me around the library of the Sri Chaitanya Research Institute in Calcutta, said that he had been studying Gauḍīya Vaiṣṇava texts for many years, but he had not yet read Rūpa's two *nāṭaka*s. He made it clear that he expected to read these dramas at a later stage, but that he still considered them to be too advanced for him.[34]

The devotional significance ascribed by Rūpa himself to his two *nāṭaka*s is clearly indicated in their prologues. The opening verse of the *Vidagdhamādhava* succinctly expresses Rūpa's purpose in composing such a play:

> Redolent with the camphor of Rādhā's love
>   and the love of the other *gopī*s
> And sweeter than even the moon's ambrosia
> Is a draught of Hari's *līlā*:
> May it slake your thirst,
> Born of the tortuous journey of *saṁsāra*,
> Where troubles are met at every turn. (I.1)

That Rūpa is referring not only to the eternal *līlā* of Kṛṣṇa with Rādhā and the other *gopī*s, but simultaneously, through deliberate ambiguity, to a dramatic enactment of this *līlā*, is indicated by the *sūtradhāra* (here identified as Rūpa himself) in his opening lines. Śiva, he reports, appeared to him in a dream and described the eagerness of a large assembly of *rasika*s ("connoisseurs")[35] who had been drawn to Vṛndāvana by their great love for Kṛṣṇa. These devotees, he said, had been rolling in the dust of the blessed sites of the Lord's activity and weeping as they listened again and again to stories of his deeds. Because their intense grief at being separated from their Lord had become unbearable, Rūpa was requested to revive these devotees with a river of nectar in the form of Kṛṣṇa's amorous sports. In addition to such evidence of their fervent devotion, hardly to be expected from mere novices, Rūpa indicates their advanced status by calling them *bhagavaddharmajñagoṣṭhīgurūṇām*, "elders in the assembly of persons learned in the *dharma* of the Lord (i.e., in *bhakti*)" (I.5.1-2). Although Rūpa here as elsewhere exemplifies characteristic Vaiṣṇava humility, he asserts in the next verse that his play, because it is composed of the excellent qualities of Kṛṣṇa,[36] can lead the audience to their desired goals (I.6).

It is clear from the prologues of both Rūpa's *nāṭakas* that they are intended, not for a secular audience, but for ardent devotees of Kṛṣṇa. Furthermore, according to the commentator on the *Vidagdhamādhava*,[37] the actors were also to be *bhaktas*; this accords with the practice followed in the enaction of *rās līlās* in present-day Braj.[38] Far from simply adapting epic or purāṇic material to the secular stage, Rūpa thus clearly had a thoroughly devotional context in mind: his was a play about Kṛṣṇa's *līlā* intended, from all appearances,[39] to be performed by Kṛṣṇa *bhaktas* for *rasika* devotees, those sensitive to aesthetic embodiments of the divine play.

The nature of the devotion of the ideal audience envisioned by Rūpa and the relation of dramas representing Kṛṣṇa's *līlā* to that devotion may be ascertained from the passages of the *Vidagdhamādhava* that we have surveyed. The initial metaphor of thirst and the subsequent description of devotees on the point of expiring from the grief of separation from Kṛṣṇa communicate vividly a religious longing of remarkable intensity. The form of this strong religious emotion is further specified by the description of the actions of the devotees in Vṛndāvana, whose desire for proximity to their Lord is so great that they embrace even the particles of dust that may have been touched by his feet. Finally, it is highly significant that the *līlās* of Kṛṣṇa and Rādhā, as represented in the *Vidagdhamādhava*, are said to quench the thirst of devotees in *saṁsāra* and to revive those whose suffering, caused by separation from their Lord, has become unbearable. This is a form of spirituality in which the passionate desire for the divine presence is satisfied in some measure by the dramatic representations of Kṛṣṇa's *līlās*.

The satisfaction, however, is never complete; at the same time that they alleviate the pain of separation, such representations also enhance the devotee's thirst for the blessed vision of the eternal *līlā*. Vṛndā asks rhetorically in the final act:

> Could ever a person become sated
> Whose eyes, like avid bees,
> Feast on the pure sweet nectar
> Of the love-play of Rādhā and Mādhava? (VII.41)

Indeed, it is the enhancement of the devotee's love and desire for the Lord and his beloved, and for the privilege of witnessing their divine love, rather than the satisfaction of such desire, that is the primary aim not only of such dramatic representation, but also of much else in the Gauḍīya Vaiṣṇava tradition.

The Centrality of Drama in Gauḍīya Vaiṣṇavism

Although the importance of drama in Gauḍīya Vaiṣṇava devotion is most obvious in the writings of Rūpa, dramatic conceptions and modes of expression are found throughout the tradition. These are especially prominent in the life of its central figure, Caitanya, as he has been represented in the numerous Sanskrit and Bengali biographies that appeared within a century after his death, some even within two decades.[40] The highly emotional quality of Caitanya's devotion has been adequately attested. It is, however, difficult to determine the degree to which this emotion was experienced and expressed through dramatic modes, for his biographers, especially Kṛṣṇadāsa, interpret his life through the prism of Rūpa's theory of *bhaktirasa*.

Just as Kṛṣṇa has often been viewed as an *avatāra* in the earlier literature,[41] so Caitanya is represented as an *avatāra* of Kṛṣṇa both by his orthodox biographers and in scattered verses of homage (*namaskriyā*) in the writings of the Vṛndāvana *gosvāmīs*.[42] In the second of the two *nāndī* verses that introduce the *Vidagdhamādhava*, Rūpa identifies Caitanya with Hari (Viṣṇu or Kṛṣṇa), who has become incarnate (*avatīrṇa*) in this degenerate *kali* age in order to confer upon the world a supreme treasure, a new form of *bhakti* known as *ujjvalarasa*.[43] A charming story, found in several variants, tells how this incarnation came about. According to one version, it was Kṛṣṇa's longing to experience the emotion of his beloved Rādhā toward him that impelled him to take the form of Caitanya, who had Rādhā's fair complexion as well as her great love (*bhāva*).[44]

There were theological disagreements about the nature of Caitanya: was he fully identical with Kṛṣṇa, a *bhaktāvatāra* of Kṛṣṇa, or a dual incarnation of Kṛṣṇa and Rādhā, who are themselves ultimately one?[45] Regardless of the position that one takes on this question, however, the conception remains a fundamentally dramatic one, for in each case Kṛṣṇa (or Rādhā-Kṛṣṇa) is conceived as assuming a role in the figure of Caitanya. The notion that he does so in order to experience Rādhā's unparalleled love for him indicates the significance of Rādhā for Gauḍīya Vaiṣṇava devotion at the same time that it attests to the fervor of Caitanya's own religious longing. This longing is itself understood through the categories of dramatic analysis.

It is in the early seventeenth-century *Caitanyacaritāmṛta* of Kṛṣṇadāsa Kavirāja, a devotee greatly influenced by the writings of Rūpa (which he frequently quotes and paraphrases), that we find the most consistent interpretation of Caitanya's devotion in terms of the dramatic theory elaborated by Rūpa. We have already seen that Caitanya's emotion is conceived to be the very *bhāva* of Rādhā. His longing is thus the longing of a woman in a state of separation from her lover; his madness, the mad frenzy of Rādhā after Kṛṣṇa's departure for Mathurā. The signs of his intense inner experience--laughing, weeping, dancing, singing--are like the outward expressions of emotion shown by an actor who is possessed by the character that he is representing. Indeed, in at least one passage such signs are explicitly called *sāttvika*s,[46] the term used in dramaturgy to designate the involuntary manifestations of emotion displayed by an actor. More comprehensively, Caitanya's actions, like Kṛṣṇa's, are called *līlā*s by Kṛṣṇadāsa,[47] and Caitanya is described by Murāri Gupta, his first biographer, as one who dances or enacts the manifold *bhaktirasa*.[48]

In addition to stanzas identifying Caitanya as an *avatāra* and passages that interpret his devotional longing and his ecstasies as expressions of *madhura bhaktirasa*, specifically identifying his emotional states with those of Rādhā, there are scattered through the biographical-hagiographical literature several indications of Caitanya's concrete involvement with drama. Besides such extraordinary accounts as those of his appearances to his disciples in the forms of several of Viṣṇu's *avatāra*s, including the boar, the man-lion, and Balarāma,[49] there is the description in three of his biographies of his "coronation" (*abhiṣeka*) as the Lord in the house of Śrīvāsa,[50] as well as repeated mention of his "acting." On the festival of Kṛṣṇa's birth, Kṛṣṇadāsa tells us, he donned cowherd's garb and carried a pot of yoghurt and a staff.[51] At Purī, during a festival honoring Rāma, he took part in a dramatic performance, assuming the role of Hanumān while his disciples played the parts of the army of monkeys.[52] Finally, there is the frequently mentioned performance of the *Rukmiṇīharaṇ* at Candraśekhara's house, in which elaborate costumes and make-up were used and Caitanya's impersonation of Rukmiṇī was allegedly so authentic that no one was able to recognize him.[53] The accumulated testimonies of his biographers to such episodes suggest that Caitanya himself took pleasure in acting.

Rūpa's plays and his theoretical works on *bhaktirasa*, together with the biographies of Caitanya, some of which incorporate elements of Rūpa's theory, are not the only genres of Gauḍīya Vaiṣṇava literature in which we find prominent dramatic qualities. Like many of the verses of Jayadeva's Sanskrit *Gītagovinda*, to which terms like "dramatic" have frequently been applied,[54] the lyrical Bengali and Brajabuli verses known collectively as *padāvalī* characteristically represent dramatic moments in the love of Rādhā and Kṛṣṇa.[55] Even the Sanskrit *stotra*s or hymns of praise of this school typically present dynamic rather than static pictures of Kṛṣṇa. One especially vivid hymn depicts Kṛṣṇa crying as he runs away from Yaśodā, who is attempting to tie him to a mortar; the devotee who recites this *stotra* then joins the author in asking that Kṛṣṇa appear in his mind in the form of a cowherd boy.[56] In Rūpa's *Stavamālā* ("Garland of Praises") are found a number of dramatic verses, including one that describes Rādhā as she goes out to meet Kṛṣṇa on a moonlit night.[57] Such verses portray dramatic situations in such a way that they can be readily visualized, and they evoke corresponding emotions in the devotee.

Forms of Gauḍīya Vaiṣṇava devotional practice likewise contain an abundance of dramatic elements. A survey of Rūpa's own list of sixty-four *bhaktyaṅgas* or constituents of *vaidhī bhakti*, practices undertaken because they are enjoined by scripture, reveals a number that have strong dramatic qualities. These include listening to the names, qualities, and *līlā*s of the Lord;[58] relishing the meaning of the *Bhāgavata* stories together with other *rasika* devotees;[59] hearing, remembering, and (if possible) living in the region of Mathurā;[60] communal singing of the names of the Lord;[61] celebration of festivals (*mahotsava*s) by the community of devotees according to its means;[62] and lovingly serving the image in various ways, such as touching and viewing it and dancing before it.[63] The fact that even these practices--which are only preliminary by Rūpa's account--are basically dramatic in nature suggests the degree to which the entire Gauḍīya Vaiṣṇava tradition is permeated with elements of the drama. Nor does Rūpa's list exhaust the "dramatic" practices found in this tradition, for in many of its devotional forms we find a transformation of time and space in ways that are typical of drama. Nowhere is this transformation more clearly illustrated than in Braj.

The Braj region[64] is for the Vaiṣṇava a giant stage on which Kṛṣṇa's earthly or *prakaṭa* (literally, "manifest") *līlā* with Rādhā and the other inhabitants was enacted once, *in illo tempore*,[65] and continues to be reenacted both physically and mentally. There is, for example, an event known as the *banjātrā*,[66] which is observed annually in an especially elaborate way by members of the Vallabha Sampradāya. The pilgrims who make this tour of the sacred sites witness every evening a reenaction of the *līlā* for which the site is remembered.[67] Pilgrims also circumambulate the area, or portions of it, such as the town of Brindavan, in order to sense the special enchantment of these holy places, an enchantment that is closely bound up with the specific events associated with each. Other observances connected with these sites in Braj likewise have dramatic qualities. I was told, for instance, that there should be no loud noises in Gokula after sunset, for the baby Kṛṣṇa is said to be sleeping there.

This last example illustrates the fact that not only space, but also time, is transformed in the Vaiṣṇava religious vision. For those Vaiṣṇavas who dwell either physically or mentally in Vraja,[68] time is structured in relation to Kṛṣṇa's Vraja *līlā*. Not only are there special annual festivals, such as *Dolayātrā*, the swing festival,[69] but each day is also ordered in accordance with Kṛṣṇa's activities. In the elaboration of the *aṣṭakālīya-līlā*, a minute description is given of the activities of Kṛṣṇa and Rādhā during each of the eight three-hour periods of the day. Literary works describing these activities[70] serve as a guide for *rāgānugā* devotees, who contemplate during each period of their own day what Kṛṣṇa and Rādhā are doing during the corresponding period. This is clearly an extension of Rūpa's theory: with the aid of such writings the devotee as a spectator may witness imaginatively successive phases of the divine drama.

In addition to such visualization, certain of the daily events in the lives of Kṛṣṇa and Rādhā are reenacted through the service of their images. We have seen that a *rās līlā* performance opens with a tableau of Rādhā and Kṛṣṇa, seated side by side on a raised throne in order to afford *darśan* to their eager devotees, and worshipped in song and with oil lamps and fans. Such a spectacle is clearly a variation of image worship; like images, the *svarūp*s are forms (*mūrti*s) in which the Lord and his beloved have graciously condescended to dwell. Conversely, the elaborate rituals performed daily in certain temples, in which the deities in their image forms are bathed, dressed, and fed, may be viewed as a kind of drama, in which roles are assumed and various modes of service to the Lord and his beloved are eagerly carried out.

In an example from the *Skanda Purāṇa* that he gives in the *Bhaktirasāmṛtasindhu*, Rūpa explicitly links image worship with the form of *rāgānugā bhakti* called *sambandhānugā*, in which the devotee models his devotion on that of the friends or the foster parents of Kṛṣṇa. He points out that in that *Purāṇa* the aged king of Kurupurī, who had no son, is said to have worshipped the Lord in the image of Nandasuta (the son of Nanda, i.e., Kṛṣṇa, probably represented as a child), regarding him as hiw own son, and that he thus attained perfection in *vātsalya bhakti* (BRS I.2.98). Although Rūpa includes the service of Kṛṣṇa's image form among the *bhaktyaṅga*s or preliminary practices comprising *vaidhī bhakti*, it is clear from this example that he saw a close relation between image worship and the assumption of an emotional relation (*bhāva*) toward the Lord.

Presupposed by all these "dramatic" devotional practices is a fundamental characteristic of the Gauḍīya Vaiṣṇava movement that has frequently been noted: its communal nature.[71] In the *Bhaktirasāmṛtasindhu*, Rūpa advocates the association with other Kṛṣṇa *bhakta*s, especially those who have similar devotional leanings. He further counsels the *bhakta* to avoid the company of persons who are hostile to Kṛṣṇa (BRSI.2.26[11]). In the second portion of that work, he describes devotees with *rati* (love) for Kṛṣṇa as delighting in the company of other *rasika*s and he adds that the great joy of their devotion to Kṛṣṇa has become their very life (BRS II.1.9-10). Several of the practices listed above, especially hearing and chanting the names, qualities, and *līlā*s of the Lord, and tasting the essence of the *Bhāgavata* in the company of other *rasika bhakta*s, are explicitly communal in nature.

Intimately linked with the communal quality of Gauḍīya Vaiṣṇava devotion is its highly emotional character. We have already noted this quality in the religious ecstasies of Caitanya as well as in the somewhat more restrained theoretical formulations of Rūpa, which emphasize the development of strong, even passionate emotions toward the Lord. The means of manifesting these emotions in the company of other devotees--words, gestures, and such involuntary expressions as weeping--are closely akin to those of an actor,[72] and the emotions so expressed are similarly infectious. The relations of ardent Vaiṣṇavas to one another thus also embrace elements of the drama. The importance of such outward manifestation of emotion, which we shall soon see illustrated in the *Vidagdhamādhava*, is emphasized with the aid of a typical Bengali analogy in a little book by a well-known Vaiṣṇava leader. He points out that one can see sweets displayed in a sweet shop without having a desire to eat them. If, however, one sees someone obviously *enjoying* such delicacies, one's own desire will inevitably be stimulated.[73] For Gauḍīya Vaiṣṇavas, there is nothing on earth that is sweeter than the *līlās* of Kṛṣṇa and Rādhā.

In the light of the material that we have just surveyed, which demonstrates unequivocally that drama lies at the very heart of Gauḍīya Vaiṣṇava devotion, especially as that devotion has been interpreted and shaped by Rūpa's theory, it seems utterly inconceivable that Rūpa would limit the significance of drama to mere beginners. How, then, can we interpret his puzzling statement about the lack of causal efficacy of poetry and drama? I would suggest that what he means to say is not that these forms are insignificant for advanced devotees, but rather that they are not what brings about their *rati* for Kṛṣṇa initially, nor are they necessary for its further development and manifestation.[74] This is hardly, however, because drama itself is not central, but rather because these advanced devotees, inspired in part by the expressions of devotion of those with whom they associate intimately, live in the perpetual awareness of the eternal *līlā* of the Lord and his beloved. Rūpa says that for them merely hearing about Kṛṣṇa is sufficient: so small a stimulus is enough to cause the entire Vṛndāvana *līlā* to appear vividly before their eyes. How much more profoundly, then, would they respond to the drama in which Rūpa lovingly elaborates the manifold details of this eternal *līlā:* his *Vidagdhamādhava.*

CHAPTER III

THE *VIDAGDHAMĀDHAVA:* A SUMMARY

The seven acts of the *Vidagdhamādhava* portray the *līlā*s of Rādhā and Kṛṣṇa in the pastoral setting of Vṛndāvana. Their unique love unfolds in an intricate nexus of relationships in which most of their friends and relatives facilitate their trysts; challenge and opposition are furnished primarily by Jaṭilā, Rādhā's mother-in-law, who is naturally quite concerned at the repeated rumors of Rādhā's liaison with Kṛṣṇa, that "snake toward young women,"[1] and Candrāvalī, Rādhā's chief rival for Kṛṣṇa's attention.

Act I. The Seductive Sound of the Flute

Prastāvanā (Prologue)

As in most classical Sanskrit dramas, the play is introduced by the *sūtradhāra* or stage manager, who here, contrary to usual practice, speaks as the author of the drama.[2] Talking with his assistant, he relates that his inspiration for this performance was a dream in which a voice[3] told him to produce such a drama in order to resuscitate a group of devotees who were expiring because they were separated from their Lord. In a punning verse, he states the theme of the drama: the union of Rādhā and Kṛṣṇa brought about through the efforts of Paurṇamāsī. After introducing her, he and his assistant leave as she appears with her granddaughter Nāndīmukhī.

Viṣkambhaka (Introductory Scene)

In the course of her conversation with Nāndīmukhī, Paurṇamāsī informs the audience that Rādhā has been taken from Gokula to Bhānutīrtha[4] out of fear of King Kaṁsa, who has surely heard of her extraordinary[5] beauty. The two discuss the problem that Rādhā's husband Abhimanyu poses for the realization of Paurṇamāsī's purpose, but reach no decision. Their main concern is that Abhimanyu may take Rādhā away from the cowherd village,[6] thereby preventing her union with Kṛṣṇa.

After these deliberations, Nāndīmukhī describes Rādhā's *pūrvarāga*. the first blossoming of her love for Kṛṣṇa, which has been occasioned by the mere mention of Kṛṣṇa's name. The sweet "nectar" of these two syllables furnishes the subject for a beautiful devotional verse by Paurṇamāsī.[7] After they discuss the spontaneous quality of Rādhā's love for Kṛṣṇa, Paurṇamāsī details her developing strategy: Nāndīmukhī is to instruct Viśākhā to paint a picture of Kṛṣṇa that will delight Rādhā's eyes, and Paurṇamāsī herself will contrive to entrance Kṛṣṇa with the sweet sounds of Rādhā's name.[8] Before they leave, they describe Kṛṣṇa's radiant beauty[9] as he comes toward Vṛndāvana surrounded by his brother and friends and caressed by his loving parents.

The main portion of the act begins with the appearance of Kṛṣṇa together with his foster parents Nanda and Yaśodā, whose great affection for him is revealed through their words and gestures. However, into this idyllic childhood scene there intrudes an incongruous element that hints at what is to come. Madhumaṅgala, Kṛṣṇa's humorous companion and confidant, begins an apparently innocuous verse (I.20) about Kṛṣṇa, who smiles approvingly. In the second and third *pādas*,[10] though, the verse takes an ominous turn with the appearance of certain feminine plural adjectives[11] and other hints suggesting Kṛṣṇa's dalliance with the *gopīs*. Fearing discovery, Kṛṣṇa signals his friend to stop, but Madhumaṅgala proclaims openly that he intends to make his disclosure immediately in front of Kṛṣṇa's mother. Kṛṣṇa's mounting apprehension, however, soon changes to relief as Madhumaṅgala's verse concludes as innocently as it began: a feminine pluralizer[12] is added to the masculine *suhṛd*, "friend," and the verse thus merely describes Kṛṣṇa's rowdy pastimes with his fellow cowherds.

Using as an excuse the fact that the hungry cows are waiting for him to take them out to pasture, Kṛṣṇa asks his parents to return to the village, and he and his young companions proceed toward the verdant fields and groves of Vṛndāvana. Kṛṣṇa puts his flute to his lips, and his elder brother Rāma[13] and Madhumaṅgala describe the marvellous effects of its sounds on the cows and even upon the rocks and streams. A voice in the sky points out the cosmic repercussions of Kṛṣṇa's flute-playing, and the gods who approach at the sound are mistaken for demons by the terrified Madhumaṅgala.

After this humorous incident, Kṛṣṇa and the others again move on, and shortly afterward Paurṇamāsī appears with a plate of sweets. When queried about the source and the occasion of this unexpected gift, Paurṇamāsī answers that the sweets come from Mukharā, whose granddaughter Rādhā has just been married to Abhimanyu. At the name "Rādhā," Kṛṣṇa begins to tremble[14] and shyly endeavors to conceal his agitation by changing the subject, but Paurṇamāsī cleverly brings the conversation back to the *gopī*s and again mentions Rādhā. Madhumaṅgala, too, noticing Kṛṣṇa's loss of composure, teases Kṛṣṇa about Rādhā, and Paurṇamāsī leaves them, satisfied that her purpose in coming has been accomplished.

After Kṛṣṇa and his friends have left, Paurṇamāsī walks on ahead and sees Rādhā talking with her close friend Lalitā. As the two girls approach Vṛndāvana, Lalitā tells Rādhā that this is the place of Kṛṣṇa's *līlā*. When she hears Kṛṣṇa's name, Rādhā, visibly affected, asks Lalitā to repeat it. Suddenly hearing the sound of his flute, she is utterly captivated by its enchanting beauty. Just then, Viśākhā enters with the picture of Kṛṣṇa that she has painted, and the three go into a grove to look at it.

Act II. The Love-letter

At the request of Paurṇamāsī, Nāndīmukhī goes in search of Mukharā in order to investigate the rumor that Rādhā is seriously ill. She finds Mukharā weeping because of Rādhā's intense suffering, and infers from Mukharā's description of Rādhā's "madness" that Rādhā has fallen prey to Kṛṣṇa's fascination.

As they leave, Rādhā enters with her two closest friends, who are pressing her to reveal the cause of her consternation. Rādhā blames her suffering on Viśākhā, who showed her the picture, and, half-crazed with intense desire, describes a meeting with Kṛṣṇa as if it has already taken place. In despair, she expresses her intention to take her own life, for she thinks that she is in love with three men: the bearer of the name "Kṛṣṇa," the player of the flute, and the radiantly handsome youth in the picture. Her friends, who have tried in vain to convince her that the object of her desire is not wholly unattainable, now console her with the message that these are not three men, but one. For how, they ask, could the *gopīs* love anyone except Kṛṣṇa?[15]

At this point Nāndīmukhī, who has been sent by Mukharā to the bamboo grove to see Rādhā, enters and immediately guesses from Rādhā's appearance that she has been affected by "the Kāma of Vṛndāvana."[16] She is informed by Viśākhā of all that has transpired,[17] and expresses her wonder at this transformation in one who is hardly more than a child. When she leaves to bring Paurṇamāsī, Rādhā expresses a new struggle going on within her: the conflict between the *dharma*[18] of respectable women and the irresistible attraction of that "prince of *nāgaras*."[19]

Nāndīmukhī soon returns with Paurṇnamāsī and Mukharā, and the latter, somewhat bewildered by Rādhā's behavior, suggests that it may be caused by an evil spirit.[20] Paurṇamāsī seizes upon this explanation and links it with Kaṁsa and his fellow demons, who, she says, have been searching for Rādhā. This interpretation gives her an opportunity to propose a radical solution: Rādhā should be treated by exposure to the glance of the enemy of demons, that is, Kṛṣṇa.[21] In response to Mukharā's apprehensiveness that Jaṭilā will not be happy with this remedy, Paurṇamāsī promises to create a Kṛṣṇa by her spiritual power.[22] Mukharā leaves, and Paurṇamāsī and Nāndīmukhī discuss Rādhā's deep love for Kṛṣṇa, agreeing that it is ultimately incomprehensible.[23] Having tested further the quality of Rādhā's emotion[24] by feigning disapproval and noting the intensity of her response, Paurṇamāsī, satisfied that "the tree of her love is firmly rooted,"[25] encourages her to write a love-letter to Kṛṣṇa.

Elsewhere, Kṛṣṇa expresses in soliloquy his own incessant preoccupation with Rādhā, but when Madhumaṅgala arrives he attempts to conceal his feelings. When pressed by his suspecting companion, however, he admits that Rādhā is the object of his longing, and describes her beauty and grace as glimpsed by him from afar.

As Kṛṣṇa and Madhumaṅgala are talking about Rādhā, Lalitā and Viśākhā appear with the love-letter and present it to Kṛṣṇa, whose initial delight is increased when Madhumaṅgala reads aloud its contents. Again hiding his true feelings, Kṛṣṇa acts insulted at the insinuation that he would have anything to do with a woman, and he does not desist from his pretense even when Lalitā asks how he, who gives delight to all the inhabitants of Gokula, can cause Rādhā alone sorrow. Viśākhā nevertheless puts Rādhā's necklace of *guñjā* berries[26] around Kṛṣṇa's neck, with a punning verse conveying the singlemindedness of Rādhā's devotion.[27] Kṛṣṇa rejoins with another punning verse denying his desire for either the necklace or the love of young maidens (II.39). At the same time, as if by mistake, he takes off his own *raṅgana* garland[28] and gives it to Viśākhā, who hides it gleefully and departs with Lalitā.

As soon as they have left, Kṛṣṇa repents, fearing that his show of indifference will cause Rādhā to withdraw from the world or even to take her own life. The two friends deliberate, decide that Kṛṣṇa should send a love-letter to Rādhā in return, and immediately set out to find flowers to make the ink.

Viśākhā, returning to inform Rādhā of their encounter with Kṛṣṇa, attempts to console her distressed friend by means of the *raṅgana* garland. Rādhā continues to talk of suicide, and in response to Viśākhā's reminder of her characteristic steadiness she says that she has been robbed of all her good qualities by "that villain."[29]

In the course of their search for flowers, Kṛṣṇa and Madhumaṅgala come upon Rādhā and Viśākhā and hide in order to overhear their conversation. Rādhā's statements indicating her steadfast devotion bring Kṛṣṇa to tears, and when she closes her eyes to meditate upon his form after learning that his picture is not presently at hand, he emerges to stand in front of her. However, her delight, when she realizes that she is not dreaming, proves to be short-lived, for the humorous banter of Kṛṣṇa, Madhumaṅgala and Viśākhā is soon interrupted by the untimely appearance of Jaṭilā, who has come to ask Viśākhā about the preparations for *pūjā*.[30] Surprised to find Kṛṣṇa there, she challenges him, seemingly hardly affected by Madhumaṅgala's insults and Kṛṣṇa's insolence. Kṛṣṇa and Viśākhā manage through verses with double meanings to communicate surreptitiously about Kṛṣṇa's love for Rādhā, and Jaṭilā, who concludes that this Kṛṣṇa is an apparition brought about by Paurṇamāsī's magic, admits to herself that his glance is indeed powerful, for she can see that Rādhā is greatly improved. She then takes Viśākhā and

Rādhā to the pavilion of Sūrya to perform *pūjā*, and Kṛṣṇa and Madhumaṅgala set out to find Paurṇamāsī.

Act III. The Meeting with Rādhā

As Paurṇamāsī and Lalitā are discussing Kṛṣṇa's reluctance to meet Rādhā, Paurṇamāsī spies Kṛṣṇa talking with Madhumaṅgala and guesses that Rādhā is the object of his preoccupation.[31] When Kṛṣṇa greets her, she teases him about his relations with the *gopīs*, and in the course of their joking conversation, the mutual love of Kṛṣṇa and Rādhā and their utter distraction become manifest. Paurṇamāsī asks Kṛṣṇa why he rejects Rādhā's love when she has overcome for his sake three obstacles, *dharma*, her husband, and the elders,[32] and Madhumaṅgala responds with a cryptic remark[33] indicating that Kṛṣṇa's opposition to a meeting with Rādhā is only feigned. They arrange a tryst, and Paurṇamāsī and Lalitā go in search of Rādhā.

At that moment, Rādhā enters, describing to Viśākhā her desperate state, brought about by unbearable longing for union with Kṛṣṇa. Paurṇamāsī, after indicating to Lalitā that she wants to induce Rādhā to express her love, tells Rādhā that Kṛṣṇa refuses to meet her, and emphasizes the gulf that separates an ordinary mortal from "Viṣṇu who roams through the heavens."[34] Seeing the intensity of Rādhā's emotion and her complete devotion, as indicated by her wish to die and be reborn as a bee on Kṛṣṇa's forest garland, solely intent upon the fragrance of his face, Paurṇamāsī confesses that she has misled Rādhā in order that her emotional state might become manifest.[35] She then reveals to Rādhā her incomparable good fortune: whereas Śiva and the other gods perform penance just to have a glimpse of Kṛṣṇa, this very Kṛṣṇa has himself become emaciated from pining to see Rādhā (III.17). Hardly able to believe her ears, Rādhā accompanies Lalitā to the grove to await Kṛṣṇa.

Viśākhā returns to the mango tree, where she finds Kṛṣṇa expressing his apprehension because night has come and no *sakhī*[36] has arrived to take him to Rādhā. Resolving to play a trick on him, Viśākhā intimates with feigned sorrow that Abhimanyu has taken Rādhā to Mathurā. When Kṛṣṇa responds in utter consternation that he cannot bear even an instant without Rādhā, Viśākhā alleges that she was only joking, and at Krsna's request she describes to him the manifestations of Rādhā's love (III.23).

Meanwhile, Rādhā is likewise tormented by doubts because of Viśākhā's delay in bringing Kṛṣṇa, and as they near the grove the two tarry just long enough to observe her eagerness for the meeting. At Kṛṣṇa's approach, Rādhā is wonder-struck and faints from joy, but Lalitā urges her to be bold in meeting him. Lalitā and Viśākhā then engage in a playful exchange with Kṛṣṇa, accusing him of stealing Rādhā's heart and demanding that he prove his innocence in a singularly difficult test: he must touch the central jewel of Rādhā's necklace without being affected. Rādhā protests and tries to flee, but Lalitā restrains her, and as Kṛṣṇa approaches her, Lalitā stops him with a description of the obvious signs of his excitement. When Kṛṣṇa subsequently takes Rādhā's hand, Rādhā, protesting that his action is not proper, disappears among the trees. The two friends urge Rādhā to cooperate in playing a trick on "that jokester Kṛṣṇa,"[37] and Lalitā tells Kṛṣṇa that Rādhā is afraid to transgress *dharma* by meeting him. Kṛṣṇa is disappointed, but he does not give up without an argument, and in the course of their exchange he realizes that Rādhā's resistance is largely pretense. Rādhā, however, continues to be shy, and her friends alternate between urging her to satisfy Kṛṣṇa's desire and protecting her from Kṛṣṇa's advances.

When Kṛṣṇa enumerates the ways in which he will serve her in their love-making, Rādhā, pretending to be shocked, again attempts to leave. At that very moment Mukharā comes in search of her. Distressed to find Kṛṣṇa there, she asks how she can have any peace so long as his flute continues to lure the *gopīs* from their homes. Told by Mukharā to leave, Kṛṣṇa feigns departure, but he soon emerges from his hiding place and pulls Rādhā's sari. When Mukharā remarks on this impropriety, Lalitā convinces her that she is seeing the *tamāla* tree on the banks of the Yamunā, and Makharā, suddenly feeling dizzy, goes home to sleep.

Rādhā's friends continue to joke with her, and at Viśākhā's mention of the *raṅgana* garland, Kṛṣṇa expresses his envy of this fortunate garland, which is close to Rādhā's bosom. When Rādhā asks for her *guñjā* necklace, Kṛṣṇa lovingly puts it around her neck, and Lalitā and Viśākhā tease her about Kṛṣṇa's touch. Seeing Rādhā's sidelong glances at Kṛṣṇa, the two friends, delighted, find a pretext to slip away.[38] Kṛṣṇa overcomes Rādhā's shyness with verses professing his ardent response to her great love, and the two enter the bower together.

Act IV. Stealing the Flute

Nāndīmukhī enters, intent on fulfilling Lalitā's request that she ask Subala to remind Kṛṣṇa of Rādhā at every opportunity, for Lalitā has seen Kṛṣṇa setting out toward the area in which Candrāvalī lives. Padmā, arriving at that moment, asks Nāndīmukhī how she can console Candrāvalī, who is distraught because Kṛṣṇa no longer frequents their southern region. Nāndīmukhī tells Padmā to comfort Candrāvalī with the news, heard from offstage, that Kṛṣṇa is approaching Mount Govardhana, and she herself hurries off to find Subala. Padmā identifies the voice from the wings as that of Vṛndā, and complains that this forest goddess, at the behest of Candrāvalī's grandmother Karālā, is keeping Candrāvalī from meeting Kṛṣṇa. Just as Vṛndā's voice is heard again, warning Candrāvalī not to go out, lest she fall prey to Kṛṣṇa's bewitching sidelong glances and become mad as Rādhā has done, Candrāvalī appears. Seeing that she is unhappy at not finding Kṛṣṇa, Padmā reassures her with the news that the lord of the Yadus[39] is nearby.

Just then Kṛṣṇa arrives, remarking to Subala that he has come here filled with desire because he was suddenly reminded of Candrāvalī. When he puts the flute to his lips, the flustered Candrāvalī observes that Kṛṣṇa's flute is always able to cause surprise, as if its tones have never before been heard. After requesting Subala's help in securing Candravālī's favors, Kṛṣṇa approaches her with respectful affection[40] and flattery, and makes excuses for nights he has spent elsewhere. To her accusation that he is as fickle as a bee, ever seeking new companionship, Kṛṣṇa replies that Candrāvalī is herself always new. However, his attempt to describe his taking recourse to a stream to cool the heat of his separation from her ends in disaster: he accidentally transposes the syllables of the word *dhārā*, "stream," saying instead, "Rādhā"![41] Candrāvalī's jealousy is immediately aroused, although Kṛṣṇa quickly denies having misspoken, and Padmā counsels Candrāvalī to accept her fate, for Kṛṣṇa is in love with Rādhā. Too deeply hurt, for the moment at least, to do more than pretend to forgive Kṛṣṇa, Candrāvalī soon leaves with Padmā.

Kṛṣṇa is despondent, and consults with Subala about a means to appease Candravālī. An inadvertent pun,[42] however, provides an opportunity for Subala to mention Rādhā, and Kṛṣṇa immediately sends Subala to Lalitā to arrange a tryst. At this point, Padmā and Madhumaṅgala arrive on the scene, plotting a way to arrange a union between Kṛṣṇa and Candrāvalī. They overhear Kṛṣṇa's words of joyful anticipation, but mistakenly assume that it is Candrāvalī whom he is eagerly awaiting. In an aside to Madhumaṅgala, Padmā expresses confidence that Candrāvalī will quickly get over her anger,[43] and Madhumaṅgala tells the delighted Kṛṣṇa that he will bring his beloved soon.[44]

Padmā and Madhumaṅgala leave and return shortly with Candravālī. When Kṛṣṇa hears the jingling of her anklets, he thinks that Rādhā has come, and rushes to her side with a verse in praise of Rādhā, whom he mentions by name. However, Candrāvalī's renewed jealousy is quickly cut short by Madhumaṅgala, who splits the words of Kṛṣṇa's verse differently, thus yielding a neutral sense,[45] and the startled Kṛṣṇa hastily completes his verse in such a way that it refers explicitly to Candrāvalī. As soon as Padmā and Madhumaṅgala leave, Kṛṣṇa, fearing that Rādhā will be coming momentarily, takes Candrāvalī elsewhere.

A short time later, Rādhā, and Lalitā come to find Kṛṣṇa. Lalitā comments on Rādhā's distracted state: in the confusion of her great eagerness to meet Kṛṣṇa, she has put all her ornaments on wrong.[46] When they fail to find Kṛṣṇa in the grove, Lalitā grows apprehensive, but Rādhā suggests that he has hidden in order to play a joke on them. After an eager but unsuccessful search, they prepare the love bower and continue to wait. When Kṛṣṇa still does not appear, Rādhā expresses her fear that he has been detained by Padmā, and the two leave.

As dawn approaches, Kṛṣṇa comes to the grove where Rādhā and Lalitā were waiting, concerned that Rādhā may be terribly upset because of his failure to meet her. However, he hits upon a strategem: he decides to pretend that he meant the *nāgakesara* bower instead of the *kesara* bower, and he gathers *nāgakesara* flowers so that he can claim that he has been waiting there all night for Rādhā. When Rādhā, Viśākhā and Lalitā arrive and see Kṛṣṇa, Lalitā counsels Rādhā to be "hard like a gold statue."[47] To Kṛṣṇa's accusation that Lalitā has caused him to spend a sleepless night in the *kesara* grove,[48] Lalitā retorts that this is impossible, for Rādhā spent the night waiting for him in the grove. In the course of the ensuing exchange, Kṛṣṇa insinuates that Rādhā's love is not enduring, and Rādhā's friends accuse Kṛṣṇa of being hard-hearted and fickle. Kṛṣṇa offers Rādhā the *nāgakesara* flowers to adorn her hair, and in his distracted state, infatuated by her bewitching sidelong glance, he inadvertently puts his flute into the *añcal*[49] of her sari along with the flowers. As Rādhā and her friends whisper to one another of their utter delight at this unprecedented coup, Madhumaṅgala enters and attempts to console Rādhā with a verse about the power of her glance upon Kṛṣṇa. He and Rādhā exchange ironies, and Madhumaṅgala misinterprets Rādhā's verse (IV.37), taking it to mean that she saw Candrāvalī in the grove with Kṛṣṇa. He decides to acknowledge that Kṛṣṇa spent the night with Candrāvalī, but abruptly realizes his mistake when Kṛṣṇa stops him in the middle of his verse. Although Kṛṣṇa facilely completes the verse in such a way that it suggests that the moon served to console him in his separation from Rādhā, the damage has already been done: Lalitā points to the signs of enjoyment on Kṛṣṇa's limbs, and Rādhā is compelled to realize that she has been deceived. Kṛṣṇa then tries to appease her, maintaining that he is utterly subservient to her and offering her the jasmine garland brought by Madhumaṅgala.[50] However, despite Viśākhā's urging and Kṛṣṇa's repeated prostrations, Rādhā refuses to be conciliated.

At this tense moment, Mukharā arrives, remarking that even her innocent granddaughter Rādhā has fallen prey to the villainous Kṛṣṇa. When Madhumaṅgala responds, brashly comparing her vapidness to that of Kṛṣṇa's flute, Kṛṣṇa suddenly realizes that it is missing. In a punning verse,[51] he accuses Rādhā of stealing it, but Rādhā protests her innocence. They continue to bicker, and Mukharā finally orders Kṛṣṇa to go. Threatening to have Kaṁsa punish him for his insolence, she then departs with Rādhā and her two friends, leaving Kṛṣṇa to reflect upon the manifold expressions of Rādhā's ambivalent feelings toward him.[52]

Act V. The Appeasing of Rādhā

Paurṇamāsī, pondering the relation of love and pain, sees Madhumaṅgala approaching with Vṛndā. When they question her about the cause of her grief, she tells them that Rādhā's husband is angry because he has seen on her body the marks of love-play with Kṛṣṇa, and he therefore wishes to move to Mathurā, taking his family with him. His mother Jaṭilā compounds the difficulty, tormenting Rādhā whenever his jealousy flares up. Vṛndā tells Paurṇamāsī of Kṛṣṇa's dejection, caused by Rādhā's *māna*,[53] and Madhumaṅgala blames Rādhā's obstinacy on Lalitā. As they are talking, Subala, whom Vṛndā has earlier deputed to find Rādhā and her friends, arrives, and he and the others arrange for Rādhā's *abhisāra*.[54] When Lalitā subsequently encounters Paurṇamāsī and tells her of Rādhā's eagerness to meet "that villain,"[55] Paurṇamāsī counsels her to stop blaming Kṛṣṇa unfairly. The two then draw near the mango tree in order to listen to Rādhā's expression of her love.

Rādhā is filled with regret because she did not accept Kṛṣṇa's apology. In her demented state, she regards the bees and other creatures of Vṛndāvana as Kṛṣṇa's messengers, and addresses words to an imaginary Kṛṣṇa, who she thinks is forcefully embracing her. When Lalitā approaches Rādhā and asks her what she is muttering to herself, she realizes abruptly that Kṛṣṇa is not there. Viśākhā then enters with the letter given to Subala by Vṛndā, which suggests that Kṛṣṇa is amusing himself elsewhere because Rādhā has rejected him. Rādhā is utterly distressed, fearing that he no longer loves her. Happily, Nāndīmukhī appears at that moment with the news that Kṛṣṇa is conducting himself like a *yogī*, ever concentrating upon her beautiful face.[56] At this, Rādhā is elated. Reminded of Kṛṣṇa's flute, and informed by Viśākhā that it sounds by itself if held toward the wind, she decides to test its wonderful powers. When it emits a sweet sound, Lalitā warns her not to let Kṛṣṇa's followers hear it.

Roused by the sound of the flute and thinking to find Kṛṣṇa there, Jaṭilā comes rushing up and snatches it from Rādhā. The friends are horrified, but Vṛndā assures Paurṇamāsī that she will soon recover it. Subala warns Jaṭilā that the old female monkey is going toward her house, greedy for yogurt. Jaṭilā leaves on a run, and Paurṇamāsī reflects that the monkey must have been sent as a distraction by Vṛndā. Jaṭilā impulsively throws the flute at the monkey, who takes it and climbs a tree. She asks Subala to get it, and he tells her to fetch her nephew Viśāla, who lives some distance away. Hardly has this obstacle been removed, and the coast thereby cleared for Rādhā's tryst, when a new difficulty emerges: Mukharā arrives with a message from Abhimanyu, who summons Rādhā to join him immediately in worshipping Caṇḍī.[57] There seems to be no way out of this new dilemma, and Paurṇamāsī accordingly advises Subala to go with Vṛndā to console Kṛṣṇa. Subala worries that Kṛṣṇa will be disconsolate, and Vṛndā suggests that they disguise themselves in order to amuse him.

When the two have left, Kṛṣṇa enters, expressing to Madhumaṅgala his complete obsession with Rādhā. Madhumaṅgala tells him not to despair, for he hears the tinkling of anklets. Glimpsing Subala and Vṛndā dressed as Rādhā and Lalitā, Kṛṣṇa is delighted, but he remains somewhat apprehensive, for they do not approach too closely.[58] Just then Sāraṅgī, Viśāla's sister, appears with a message from Mukharā, who wants to know why Kṛṣṇa is blaming Rādhā for taking his flute, for she saw it in the old monkey's possession. Kṛṣṇa, having spied his flute in Subala's hands, replies that he has found it. Subala, impersonating Rādhā, says something from backstage, and Sāraṅgī, thinking the voice is Rādhā's, asks why she has not heeded Abhimanyu's summons. The insulting reply from Vṛndā, impersonating Lalitā, angers Sāraṅgī, and she goes to tell Jaṭilā. Vṛndā as Lalitā then grabs the flute from Subala/Rādhā and flings it toward Kṛṣṇa, and Madhumaṅgala picks it up.

At this point Jaṭilā arrives in a great rage, and, mistaking Subala and Vṛndā for Rādhā and Lalitā, drags them off. Kṛṣṇa, apprehensive, sends Madhumaṅgala after them in order to learn what transpires. Madhumaṅgala returns before long, and tells Kṛṣṇa that Rādhā must be a magician, for when Jaṭilā brought her before the elders among the village women,[59] she threw back her veil and emerged as Subala. At the roar of laughter that arose, Jaṭilā fled in embarrassment. Kṛṣṇa guesses at once that Vṛndā concocted the deception for his amusement, and expresses his eagerness to see Vṛndā and Subala in their disguises. He plays on his flute, but this time it is the real Rādhā and Lalitā who appear. Kṛṣṇa marvels at their excellent disguise and asks Rādhā, whom he takes to be Subala, to embrace him in order that he may experience for a moment the same delight that he receives when he touches Rādhā. When Vṛndā arrives subsequently and urges Rādhā to give Kṛṣṇa what he desires, Kṛṣṇa expresses his joy and wonder that it is Rādhā who stands before him. Not yet fully appeased, however, she and Lalitā continue to accuse him of unfaithfulness and deceit. When Rādhā begins to cry, Kṛṣṇa wipes away her tears, confessing that he is indeed desirous of dalliance with the other *gopī*s, but emphasizing that she is especially dear to his heart.

At Kṛṣṇa's wish to frolic with Rādhā in the forest, Vṛndā causes all the flowering creepers to bloom. With puns inspired by the different blossoms, Madhumaṅgala and Lalitā initiate a teasing argument. Vṛndā and Kṛṣṇa join in, and their punning rivalry is continued by two parrots: the (male) *śuka*, who criticizes the *gopī*s and praises Kṛṣṇa, and the (female) *sārī*, who takes Rādhā's part.[60] Vṛndā brings lotuses from the river to adorn Kṛṣṇa, and he places them behind Rādhā's ears. A bee emerging from a lotus bud alights on one of these lotuses, frightening Rādhā, and Madhumaṅgala drives it away with his stick. Rādhā misinterprets his remark about the bee's disappearance, taking Madhusūdana[61] (lover of honey = bee) to mean Kṛṣṇa (slayer of the demon Madhu). Utterly bewildered, she enumerates the reasons he might have for abandoning her, thinks of all the things they have not yet done, reacts with alarm to the very elements of nature that have previously been most pleasing, and finally loses all control. Kṛṣṇa, who has been right in front of her all the time, takes her hand, and she quickly regains her composure. After the two of them display their literary skill in a series of verses, Madhumaṅgala points out Jaṭilā's staff, which she has left there earlier, and at that very moment Jaṭilā enters to reclaim it. Rādhā, frightened, hastily departs with Lalitā and Vṛndā, but Jaṭilā, thinking she is Subala once again disguised as Rādhā, leaves this time without causing any more trouble. Kṛṣṇa and Madhumaṅgala then return to Gokula.

Act VI. The Amusement of *Śarad*[62]

Hearing that Rādhā is wearing a garment of yellow, the color worn by Kṛṣṇa, Jaṭilā decides to investigate. Arriving in the compound, she finds Viśākhā, exhausted from the *rāsa*[63] dance of the previous night, reeling and staggering around the courtyard. At Jaṭilā's command, Viśākhā calls Rādhā, who emerges rubbing her eyes and wearing Kṛṣṇa's yellow upper garment. Jaṭilā is aghast, and it is only Viśākhā's cleverness in attributing the yellow color to turmeric-water thrown by the young *gopīs* during the festival that saves Rādhā from Jaṭilā's wrath.

Shortly after Jaṭilā has gone, Lalitā arrives with Padmā, who gives her a letter from Kṛṣṇa. Lalitā immediately understands the coded message, but she must wait until Padmā leaves to fulfill Kṛṣṇa's request that she bring Rādhā to him. Before going, Padmā engages Lalitā and Visākhā in a contest of braggadocio, each asserting the superiority of her heroine's love for Kṛṣṇa and of his corresponding favors. As soon as Padmā departs, Lalitā takes Rādhā to Kṛṣṇa under the pretext of gathering flowers for the worship of Sūrya.

Kṛṣṇa and Madhumaṅgala then enter, conversing about the beauty of Vṛndāvana after the monsoon rains; Kṛṣṇa, however, points out that it does not afford him even a drop of delight because Rādhā is not there. He gives a signal with his flute, and shortly thereafter Rādhā appears with Lalitā and Viśākhā. The two friends tease Rādhā about her eagerness, which she endeavors to conceal, and she in turn accuses them of dalliance with Kṛṣṇa. Suddenly seeing a dark tree at a distance, and mistaking it for Kṛṣṇa, Rādhā shyly tries to flee: as Viśākhā points out, the whole world has become Kṛṣṇa for her.[64] Again hearing the flute, she reels about dizzily, finally catching hold of a *kadamba* tree. Lalitā is grateful to the flute for inducing Rādhā to reveal her deep love for Kṛṣṇa, but Rādhā curses it for causing her so much agony.

Kṛṣṇa sees Rādhā from a distance and eulogizes her radiant beauty, which appears to him as the moon without its mark.[65] So moved is he at the sight of her that Madhumaṅgala has to support him as he draws closer. Rādhā likewise marvels at the intoxicating effect of Kṛṣṇa's beauty on her, but, feeling apprehensive at the same time, she takes refuge in Lalitā's protection. Lalitā teasingly prevents Kṛṣṇa from approaching too closely, and Rādhā, continuing the play of opposition, suggests that they take the flowers they have gathered and go to the banks of the Yamunā. Kṛṣṇa blocks their path, asking Rādhā how she can be so cruel as to leave with the *bandhūka* flowers (the life of [her] friend, i.e., Kṛṣṇa).[66] Rādhā likewise addresses Kṛṣṇa in a verse with two senses, simultaneously telling him not to behave like a snake in her path, and to take her into his arms.[67] Yet when Kṛṣṇa, taking the second meaning, tries to comply with her request, Lalitā again shields her.

Madhumaṅgala and Kṛṣṇa then decide on a price for the flowers that the girls are taking from Kṛṣṇa's Vṛndāvana: an equal number of gems from the girls' necklaces.[68] Before Kṛṣṇa can collect, however, he is warned to keep away by Viśākhā with words about Rādhā's readiness for battle that have as an alternate meaning her eagerness for union.[69] Again repelled by Lalitā as he tries to approach Rādhā, Kṛṣṇa in desperation offers Lalitā a bribe: he will cheat Rādhā and spend the night with *her*! Having angrily rejected this offer, and then been asked what bribe *would* satisfy her, Lalitā, hinting at Rādhā's desire, tells him to adorn Rādhā with flowers. However, as Kṛṣṇa reaches for Rādhā's necklace, Lalitā smiles mischievously, telling him not to touch Rādhā, who has taken a purificatory bath in preparation to worship Sūrya. Kṛṣṇa replies that he too has had a ceremonial bath[70] in the perspiration caused by his intense emotion. When Lalitā softens and Rādhā reminds her of their intention to worship Sūrya, Madhumaṅgala rejoins that he and Kṛṣṇa too perform worship, for they stay awake at the altar formed by the grove of trees, gather fragrant flowers, and concentrate single-mindedly on the jingling of anklets.[71] At this they all smile.

After praising Rādhā in elaborate verses with double meanings, Madhumaṅgala and Kṛṣṇa leave to gather peacock feathers to make a crest for Rādhā. While they are out of sight, Rādhā hides in a nearby grove of trees, and when they return Lalitā tells them that Rādhā has gone home. In his great distraction, Kṛṣṇa mistakes first a land-lotus golden with pollen, and then a yellow flower, for the golden-hued Rādhā. Following a deliberate false lead from Lalitā, he proceeds to the grove of *kadamba* trees, but finds it empty. Madhumaṅgala, too, claims to have found Rādhā, and promises to deliver her into Kṛṣṇa's hand. Instead of Rādhā herself, however, he gives Kṛṣṇa a leaf inscribed with the two syllables *Rā-dhā*; yet this time Kṛṣṇa is not disappointed, for the very name of his beloved gives him deep satisfaction.[72]

At last Kṛṣṇa finds Rādhā in a grove of *aśoka* trees, and their sportive rivalry continues. At Lalitā's boasting of Rādhā's superiority, Kṛṣṇa proposes that he hide in order to see whether they can continue to brag when he is out of their sight. Rādhā and her friends immediately begin searching for him, and Rādhā ascertains from the behavior of the animals and trees the direction that Kṛṣṇa has taken.[73] When she reaches the *tamāla* grove where Kṛṣṇa is hiding, Kṛṣṇa freezes with the hope of escaping detection. Rādhā pretends not to recognize him, but her reference to a row of moons (Candrāvalī) reflected in the refulgent sapphire pillar in front of her gives her away. Kṛṣṇa suggests that they put an end to their teasing, which only serves to separate them, and retire instead to the grove of *saptaparṇa* trees. Their footprints reveal to Lalitā and Viśākhā that they have been united; this inference is confirmed by Rādhā's disheveled appearance when they find her some time later in the grove. Kṛṣṇa then emerges, explaining that he has hidden in the forest in order to escape the ravages of Rādhā's passion.[74] Rādhā accuses Kṛṣṇa of being "a master in blaming others for what [he has] done,"[75] and at this moment the voice of Madhamaṅgala is heard from the background. His misleading use of the word *jaṭilā* in describing the *saptaparṇa* trees[76] causes sudden consternation, and Rādhā, fearing detection by her mother-in-law, flees with her two friends. When he hears the second half of Madhumaṅgala's verse and realizes their mistake, Kṛṣṇa, disappointed, goes to join his companions.

Act VII. The Impersonation of Gaurī

Vṛndā enters, describing the beauty of the forest in the monsoon season. Seeing Abhimanyu conferring with Paurṇamāsī, she waits until they have finished talking before approaching the venerable old woman. Abhimanyu, distressed at the rumors of his wife's affair with Kṛṣṇa, has come to request Paurṇamāsī's permission to take Rādhā to Mathurā. Paurṇamāsī immediately expresses the fear that moving to the royal city would be tantamount to placing Rādhā in the hands of the wicked King Kaṁsa, and manages to persuade Abhimanyu to wait until he has firsthand evidence bearing on the matter of Rādhā's infidelity. Abhimanyu's parting request, that Rādhā be initiated into the worship of Caṇḍī,[77] is deftly answered by Paurṇamāsī with an ambiguous promise: Rādhā will soon worship the one who is auspicious toward all.[78]

After sharing with Paurṇamāsī her utter delight at beholding the sweet love of Rādhā and Kṛṣṇa, Vṛndā expresses her apprehensiveness because Rādhā is late for her rendezvous with Kṛṣṇa, who has requested the pleasure of her company on *Saubhāgyapūrṇimā*.[79] She is especially concerned because of the recent bragging of Padmā, who has deliberately misconstrued Kṛṣṇa's request, making it seem to refer to Candrāvalī. Just then Lalitā arrives and tearfully reports that she has seen Padmā wearing the very garland that Rādhā had lovingly presented to Kṛṣṇa. Vṛndā, however, has meanwhile learned from the old monkey woman that Padmā stole the garland while Kṛṣṇa was bathing. Lalitā is relieved, but the three women still worry that the scheming Padmā may have taken Candrāvalī to Gaurītīrtha, where Kṛṣṇa is awaiting Rādhā. However, Viśākhā appears at that moment with the happy news that Candrāvalī's grandmother Karālā has ordered Candrāvalī to join her husband Govardhana for this festival day. Trusting that their path is thus clear, the women arrange to bring Rādhā to Kṛṣṇa. Seeing Candrāvalī's friends in the vicinity of Gaurītīrtha, however, Lalitā and Vṛndā decide to wait for Paurṇamāsī before getting Kṛṣṇa.

Padmā is attempting to console Śaivyā, who is dejected on account of Karālā's command. As they hear it again from backstage, Padmā suddenly hits upon a solution: by taking Candrāvalī to Gaurītīrtha, which is next to Mount Govardhana, they will be obeying the letter if not the spirit of Karālā's order.[80] As they hasten there, Padmā informs Śaivyā that she has given Madhumaṅgala the offering for Gaurī. Padmā's verse anticipating the sight of Candrāvalī and Kṛṣṇa together is parroted by the old monkey, who departs with a threat, and Kṛṣṇa and Candrāvalī enter as Padmā describes their moment of meeting.

Thinking that she is his beloved Rādhā, Kṛṣṇa teasingly blocks Candrāvalī's way and enumerates the signs of her eagerness. When Padmā and Śaivyā appear and take her part, Kṛṣṇa is startled to discover that it is Candrāvalī instead of Rādhā, but he soon becomes reconciled to the situation and resolves to please her. Ascertaining from the behavior of his pet deer that Rādhā has come to Gaurītīrtha, he delays for a time so that they will not encounter her. As he exchanges puns with Padmā and Candrāvalī, Lalitā and Vṛndā join them in order to size up the situation. Under the guise of a lighthearted exchange about the love affair of the two pet deer, Lalitā manages to learn from Kṛṣṇa of his abiding love for Rādhā. Padmā and Śaivyā proceed to argue with Lalitā and Vṛndā, each asserting through obscure riddles and intricate puns the superiority of her heroine's love for Kṛṣṇa and of his corresponding favors. When the deflated Padmā finally reminds Candrāvalī of their intention to worship Gaurī, Karālā appears in a rage and chastises the wayward couple for their violation of *dharma*. Impelled by Lalitā, she then turns upon Padmā, who alleges that she was simply following Karālā's orders. Vṛndā explains Padmā's "confusion" of Mount Govardhana with Candrāvalī's husband, and Karālā, somewhat mollified, leaves with Candrāvalī and Śaivyā. Padmā, vowing to get even with Lalitā, meanwhile departs in search of Jaṭilā.

Accepting from Vṛndā the *campaka* blossoms sent by Rādhā, the delighted Kṛṣṇa promises to meet his beloved soon. As the two women proceed toward Gaurītīrtha, Vṛndā expresses to Lalitā her envy of the *kadamba* tree, whose blossoms adorn Kṛṣṇa continually, and then suddenly exclaims at the sight of Rādhā, whom she perceives as the very embodiment of beauty and love. As if resonating to Vṛndā's sentiment, Paurṇamāsī, speaking from backstage, similarly describes Kṛṣṇa as the embodiment of Yaśodā's motherly affection, and Lalitā and Vṛndā observe in utter rapture as the lovers meet, their playful gestures becoming increasingly impassioned. After Rādhā and Kṛṣṇa have disappeared into the grove, and subsequently left it again, Lalitā and Vṛndā, who cannot get enough of the wondrous vision of their love, view there the signs of their enjoyment, and Vṛndā reflects in amazement upon the triumph of this mere girl over the Lord of the entire universe. They then come upon the pair as Rādhā is instructing Kṛṣṇa to adorn her, and Vṛndā exclaims at the magnificence of his disheveled form: his every feature bears witness to their rapturous union.

At Vṛndā's description, Kṛṣṇa emerges into view, praising Rādhā's natural beauty. After placing in her hair the blossoms proffered by Lalitā and Vṛndā, he resolves to play a joke on her. While Lalitā is gathering more flowers, he asks Vṛndā to enlist the old monkey's aid, and promptly feigns a slip of the tongue, pretending to address Rādhā as Candrāvalī. Rādhā's immediate distress is heightened by the monkey's confirmation of her initial fears. Kṛṣṇa delights in her angry expressions and seems wholly unconcerned when his half-hearted attempts to appease her have no efficacy. When Rādhā leaves in anger, he proposes to Vṛndā that he win her back by disguising himself as a woman of fair complexion, and Madhumaṅgala arrives just in time to inform Kṛṣṇa that the offering for Gaurī presented by Padmā contains everything that he will need. After instructing Vṛndā to address him as her sister, he goes to wait in the sanctuary of the temple of Gaurī for their arrival.

Vṛndā finds Rādhā telling Lalitā and Viśākhā what has just happened. Her friends, having reassured her that Kṛṣṇa could not possibly utter the name of another woman in her presence, express their apprehension that their rivals will now get the better of them. When Vṛndā approaches, they immediately enlist her help. After pretending to chastise Rādhā for her jealousy, Vṛndā informs them that Kṛṣṇa is in the temple of Gaurī, talking with "Nikuñjavidyā." In response to the girls' puzzlement, she punningly identifies Nikuñjavidyā as her sister[81] and proposes that they secure her assistance in winning Kṛṣṇa. When they reach the temple, Vṛndā, looking in and seeing Kṛṣṇa in his disguise, informs them that "the deity of Bhāṇḍīra" is alone, and Rādhā suggests that they go inside and ask her where Kṛṣṇa is.

At this moment, Jaṭilā enters, recounting in soliloquy the news brought to her by Padmā, who alleged that she had just seen Rādhā worshipping Gaurī at Gaurītīrtha. Intent upon blessing her daughter-in-law, she is delighted to see Rādhā's pet deer in the temple courtyard. Suddenly spying Kṛṣṇa's peacock there too, however, she leaves in consternation to get her son Abhimanyu, without disturbing the scene in the temple.

Rādhā is overwhelmed by the unusual beauty of the "fair one"[82] in the temple sanctuary and expresses surprise at the great attraction that she feels for this unknown woman. In response to Rādhā's question about Kṛṣṇa's whereabouts, the voice from the interior of the temple asks enigmatically whether anyone knows him. Further queries are met with teasing verses, and Rādhā, pleased, disappears into the sanctuary, from where her voice is heard as she again entreats Nikuñjavidyā to help them win Kṛṣṇa's favor. Nikuñjavidyā, however, proves to be more aggressively affectionate than Rādhā had anticipated, and Rādhā soon emerges, blaming Vṛndā for deceiving her. Lalitā and Viśākhā, too, have recognized Kṛṣṇa from his amorous overtones toward Rādhā.

With Abhimanyu in tow, the indignant Jaṭilā returns at that very moment to the temple courtyard, pointing out to her son the presence of Tāṇḍavika and Raṅginī, as well as the distinctive fragrance that fills the air. Abhimanyu repeats his intention to take Rādhā to Mathurā, and the two of them station themselves at the door of the temple to observe what transpires.

Emerging into view from the inner sanctuary, Kṛṣṇa, in the role of Gaurī, teasingly instructs Rādhā not to ask him for something so difficult. Smiling mischievously and calling him *Devī*, "Goddess," Rādhā implores him for mercy. When Abhimanyu thereupon bursts into the temple, announcing that he has caught

Rādhā red-handed, she falls on her face in utter terror. Jaṭilā, seeing Kṛṣṇa in his disguise, questions her son about the identity of this woman who is illumining the entire temple with her unearthly[83] beauty. The simple Abhimanyu assumes that it must be the Goddess, who has appeared in response to Rādhā's falling prostrate before her image. When Lalitā and Viśākhā confirm this interpretation, Abhimanyu asks what Rādhā was just requesting of Gaurī, and Vṛndā tells him that a terrible fate is in store for him: he is soon to be sacrificed to Bhairava[84] by King Kaṁsa. In great consternation, Jaṭilā joins Rādhā in begging the Goddess for mercy, and Kṛṣṇa as Gaurī again tells Rādhā that what she is asking is all but impossible. Exploiting to full advantage the situation of marvellous ambiguity that he has created, Rūpa has Rādhā address Kṛṣṇa as *ballavīkuladevatā*, "deity of the *gopīs*," and express her heartfelt petition that she never be separated from her lord.[85] Likewise employing ambiguous language, Kṛṣṇa praises Rādhā for her ever-new devotion, by which he has been captivated, and promises to grant her request if she will always remain in Gokula and worship him. Abhimanyu hastens to pledge that he will never take Rādhā to Mathurā, and he blames Subala for causing false scandal by dressing up as Rādhā. After offering obeisance, he departs with his mother to stop the servant that he had earlier ordered to take his belongings to Mathurā.

Paurṇamāsī, whose initial appearance opened the drama, now enters in this final scene, expressing her joy at seeing Kṛṣṇa in his disguise and her gratitude at being spared the pain of separation from Rādhā. At Kṛṣṇa's invitation, she makes two final petitions: that he may ever engage in the rapturous play of love with Rādhā in Vṛndāvana, and that whoever hears of this marvellous *līlā* may realize the sweetness of supreme love for the Lord. Kṛṣṇa's words assuring her that her requests will be granted and expressing his intention to return to the village to delight his foster parents bring the drama to a close.

CHAPTER IV

AN ANNOTATED TRANSLATION OF THE SEVENTH ACT OF THE *VIDAGDHAMĀDHAVA*

The final act of the *Vidagdhamādhava* represents the drama well in several respects. It is the longest and most complex of the seven acts, and it brings the conflicts in the drama to at least a provisional resolution. Furthermore, although it is not precisely a microcosm of the whole, it picks up certain important threads from the preceding six acts and combines them in new ways. For instance, the story returns in succession to the two chief threats to the clandestine love affair of Rādhā and Kṛṣṇa, Abhimanyu's jealousy and the consequent danger of his taking Rādhā to Mathurā, and the rivalry between Rādhā's faction and that of Candrāvalī. Furthermore, Rādhā's *māna*, portrayed extensively in Acts IV and V, is here recapitulated in brief compass, in response to Kṛṣṇa's deliberate slip of the tongue. Although not typical of the play in every respect--for much of this act is more intense and more "dramatic"--it may serve to illustrate the movement and general character of the drama, as well as the beauty and devotional quality of many of its finest verses.

A Note to the Reader

Like nearly all classical Indian plays, the *Vidagdhamādhava* is written in a combination of Sanskrit and literary Prakrit. Sanskrit is spoken by Kṛṣṇa, his foster father Nanda, and his elder brother Balarāma, as well as by Paurṇamāsī and Vṛndā, both of whom partake to some degree of divinity. With the exception of the *sūtradhāra* and his assistant, the remaining characters speak in Prakrit, except in verses, for which they almost always use Sanskrit. In each case in which a Prakrit-speaking character employs Sanskrit, the stage directions indicate this fact. I have attempted in my translation to render faithfully everything in the text, including all the stage directions.

The editions of the text on which my translation is based are listed in the Bibliography. I have numbered the verses in accordance with the Kāvyamālā edition (KM) because of its greater accessibility; however, I have often found the readings of the two Bengali script editions, those of Purīdās (P) and Basu (B), to be superior, and in such instances I have taken those readings. In citing both plays I have followed the method proposed by Charles R. Lanman in the Harvard Oriental Series edition of Bhavabhūti's *Uttararāmacarita*.* In brief, this convention involves giving for each reference the act number, the verse number, and, for prose passages, the line number or numbers, counting from the end of the preceding verse.

Many of the verses in the following act, as throughout Rūpa's dramas, employ elaborate puns. In such cases I have rendered both meanings, setting off the second meaning from the first with diagonal lines. In the instances in which the pun is less than a full line, I have also indicated the end of the alternate meaning with a diagonal.

Act VII. The Impersonation of Gaurī[1]

(enter Vṛndā)

Vṛndā (looking around)

1 Its breezes fragrant with pollen
 of flowering *kadamba* trees,
Humming with swarms of bees
 that gather on blossoming jasmine,
Verdant with tender barley grain
 and adorned with peacocks:
Now, at summer's end,
 Vṛndāvana delights my heart.[2]

(glancing toward the wings) How is it that Paurṇamāsī is talking with Abhimanyu in the garden outside her leaf hut? I'd better wait here a moment.

(enter Paurṇamāsī [and Abhimanyu] as described)

Paurṇamāsī Abhimanyu, my child, why have you come to see me at such an early hour?

Abhimanyu	In order to secure your permission.
Paurṇamāsī	For what?
Abhimanyu	To take Rādhā to Mathurā.
Paurṇamāsī	(sadly) Whatever for?
Abhimanyu	Because of the dalliance of Rādhā and Mādhava.[3]
Paurṇamāsī	O hero, who told you such a thing?
Abhimanyu	My close friend Govardhana.
Paurṇamāsī	Abhimanyu, my child, though you think yourself clever, you have the understanding of a boor. For you have been deluded by the crooked plot of Kaṁsa.
Abhimanyu	This conduct of theirs is common knowledge; everyone is talking about it.
Paurṇamāsī	Son, surely you have been robbed of your good sense by the insidious gossip of rogues. So listen carefully.
Abhimanyu	Give your command.
Paurṇamāsī	Child, the tiger Kaṁsa, attracted by a mere whiff of the fragrance of her beauty, is searching for the doe Rādhā. Is it wise to deliver her into the clutches of that cruel Kaṁsa-tiger?
Abhimanyu	Madam, there is no danger of that, thanks to my best friend Govardhana--may he prosper--for that king of Mathurā has been captivated by his learning.[4]
Paurṇamāsī	(reflecting a moment, sadly) O most fortunate one,[5] why is it that although you are the cousin of Govinda's[6] mother, you allow yourself to sink to the level of those wicked people[7] who are inimical to Gokula? So today I would like to place some restrictions on you.
Abhimanyu	Deign to give your command.
Paurṇamāsī	Son, if you do not realize that this rumor, started in jealousy, is false, you should at least examine the matter with your own eyes before carrying out your resolve.
Abhimanyu	(respectfully) Madam, I will do as you say.[8]
Paurṇamāsī	(with delight) O moon-faced one,[9] may you be blessed with abundant cows.

Abhimanyu — Madam, my mother tells me again and again: "Son, Govardhana has become true to his name[10] because of Candrāvalī's worship of Caṇḍī.[11] Therefore my daughter-in-law should also be initiated into that practice."

Paurṇamāsī — Well-meaning one, you can be confident that Rādhā will soon be initiated into the worship of the one who is universally auspicious.[12]

Abhimanyu — Madam, you are gracious to me. (leaves)

Vṛndā — (walking around) Respectful greetings to you, madam.

Paurṇamāsī — (looking and welcoming her with blessings) Child, surely your heart's desire has just been fulfilled. So describe the sweet love-play of Rādhā and Mādhava in the grove.

Vṛndā —

2 What supreme enjoyment[13] arises
   when Kṛṣṇa and Rādhā are united!
Who could cease to tell of that
   quintessence of erotic mood[14]
Save one speechless utterly
   with ecstasy?[15]

Paurṇamāsī — (with delight) Daughter Vṛndā,

3 Had Hari not become incarnate[16]
   along with Rādhā, lovely one,
   in Mathurā,
Then this entire world's creation--
   especially Kāma[17]--
   had been in vain.

So I am surprised that you have come into the cowherd village today.

Vṛndā — Madam, I have an urgent matter to attend to, so I am waiting here for Lalitā.

Paurṇamāsī — What is that?

Vṛndā — Yesterday Govinda entreated me in the following words:

4 Clothe Gaurītīrtha[18] in the beauty of spring,[19]
For I wish to enjoy love there with my darling

Who will be decked with a chaplet of lotus
blossoms
And hold a lotus in her hand.[20]

Paurṇamāsī The request is appropriate: today is *Saubhāgya-pūrṇimā*.[21] For it is said,

5 When a woman is adorned with wondrous flowers
By her lover on Śrāvaṇ's full-moon day,
Her widely renowned good fortune[21] increases.

What happened then?

Vṛndā A minah bird repeated the verse in front of the assembled *sakhīs*,[22] and Padmā, even though she realized that the verse referred to Rādhā, said suddenly, with a sidelong glance at Lalitā,

6 The bright luster of the moon,[23]
Encircled by its halo of moonlight,[24]
Makes the day lotuses close.[25]
/The luck in love of Candrāvalī,
Radiant in the presence of Kṛṣṇa,
Makes the faces of the arrogant *gopīs*
grow pale.[26]

Paurṇamāsī (laughing) Then what?

Vṛndā Then Lalitā, giving that foolish Padmā a look of contempt, came with me to tell Rādhā that she should set out to meet Kṛṣṇa early this morning. But look, it's long past sunrise and she's not yet come.

(entering)

Lalitā Friend Vṛndā, Padmā's arrogance was justified. Now I know the story. How could we possibly go there now?[27]

Paurṇamāsī Child, what do you mean?

Lalitā Madam, what is the use of revealing to you the sharp barb of our misfortune?[28]

Paurṇamāsī Child, I want to hear it. Tell me.

Lalitā (in tears) Madam, our dear friend gave Kṛṣṇa a marvellous garland strung with white silk thread.

We saw that garland in Padmā's hair-knot on the very same day.[29]

Paurṇamāsī Your dismay is understandable: that was most improper on Govinda's part.

Vṛndā The problem is solved!

Paurṇamāsī Vṛndā, tell us how.

Vṛndā Kakkhaṭikā,[30] using human speech, told me what happened: Kṛṣṇa hung the garland on the branch of a *kadamba* tree and plunged into the Yamunā. When the wind was filled with *ketakī* pollen, Padmā stole the garland and blamed the wind.

Lalītā You liar, stop making up stories.

Vṛndā I swear by the clusters of blossoms.

Lalitā (believing her) It's true! Padmā displays the garland in front of us, proclaiming her luck in love, but in front of Kṛṣṇa's friends she hides it.

Paurṇamāsī Daughter Lalitā, clearly Padmā, using her skill in deception, has taken Candrāvalī to Gaurītīrtha on this full-moon day in order to foil your plans.

Vṛndā The lady is right. So it seems unwise to take Rādhā to Gaurītīrtha today.

(entering)

Viśākhā Vṛndā, say rather, "It seems wise."

Vṛndā Why is that?[31]

Viśākhā Karālā, having heard about *Saubhāgyapūrṇimā* today from Yaśodā, is sending Candrāvalī to her wrestler-husband's side.

Lalitā (delighted) Viśākhā, may your chosen deity, the lord of lotuses,[32] bless you. So hurry.

Paurṇamāsī Daughter Vṛndā, after I inform Rādhā of Abhimanyu's present cruel intention, I should stay in Gaurītīrtha to allay her anxiety.

Vṛndā Madam, you should go with Rādhā and Viśākhā to the bower of clove trees[33] to the east of Gaurītīrtha. In the meantime, the two of us will bring Mādhava.

(Paurṇamāsī leaves with Viśākhā)

Lalitā (walking about with Vṛndā) Look, friend, way over there to the south is Padmā conversing with Śaivyā.

Vṛndā — Friend, Viśākhā wouldn't tell a lie.[34] (going ahead, reflectively) Friend, in our excitement and great eagerness[35] we've gone a long way without learning whether Rādhā has been persuaded to come. So let's wait a while for Paurṇamāsī here on the bank of the Yamunā.[36]

(they leave)

(enter Padmā and Śaivyā)

Padmā — Friend Śaivyā, don't be discouraged.

Śaivyā — Padmā, my heart is not easily consoled, for we failed to fulfill our great hope.

(from backstage)

Padmā, take Candrāvalī to Govardhana's side immediately, so that my child may be beautifully adorned with flowers.

Śaivyā — Padmā, you hear how the lady Karālā is spewing forth the same old poison.

Padmā — Oho! This is really nectar,[37] for I have regained my strength by drinking it.

Śaivyā — How is that?

Padmā — Fool, Gaurītīrtha is right by the side of Mount Govardhana.

Śaivyā — (with delight) You are a pundit[38] in ferreting out every possible meaning. So come on, let's take Candrāvalī there.

Padmā — I have already sent Candrāvalī. Let's follow quickly.

(they walk around)

Śaivyā — Padmā, where is the offering prepared for Gaurī?

Padmā — I've given it to Madhumaṅgala.

Śaivyā — When I think of how our rivals have been preferred over us, I lose heart.

Padmā — Don't worry, I have destroyed their initiative by displaying this garland.

(Śaivyā embraces Padmā with delight)

Padmā 7 Look at Candrāvalī playing happily with
Hari on *Saubhāgyapūrṇimā*
In Gaurītīrtha, newly filled with blossoms
by Spring.

(the verse is heard again from backstage)

Śaivyā (looking in amazement) Oh! We are being ridiculed by Kakkhaṭikā, who is cocking her head and reciting in a hideous voice.

Padmā (smiling) Pesky monkey, I'll burn your mouth.

(from backstage)

Padmā, you just wait! I'll go into your house while you're gone and eat all the butter.

Śaivyā Look, she means business! She started running even before she finished talking.

Padmā Don't worry, the lady Karālā is at home. (walking around) (in Sanskrit[39]) Look!

8 His figure leaning easily on the
sturdy shepherd's staff,
Arm on hand atop its unbending length,
Subala rests here under a tree,
Pasturing the cows as he sings a carefree song.

Śaivyā (walking around) See, there to the east of Saṅkarṣaṇakuṇḍa is Candrāvalī.

Padmā (with delight) (in Sanskrit)

9 Here in front of us, with smiling lotus-face,
Putting the elephant to shame by his sportive
gait,
Robbing all eyes of sleep by the radiance of
his body,
The Kṛṣṇa-moon[40] finds Candrāvalī.

(enter Kṛṣṇa and Candrāvalī)

Kṛṣṇa (blocking the path) Dear, your beauty has graciously assumed the form of a pitcher of honey for the bees that are my eyes.

Candrāvalī Get out of my way! I'm going to Gaurītīrtha to worship Kātyāyanī.[41]

Kṛṣṇa (smiling)

10 Slender one,
Seeing me within your reach, your hair has risen up as if to greet me,
Your eyes have lovingly offered the *pādya*[42] of their profuse tears,
Your breast, its cloth slipping down in your agitation, has revealed a wondrous[43] seat:
Even though you seem hostile, your retinue has shown me hospitality today.[44]

Padmā and Śaivyā (approaching) Friend, there are many paths. We won't be stopped just because one is blocked.

Candrāvalī (turning her head and looking) Oh, thank goodness you have come.

Kṛṣṇa (to himself) How is it that Candrāvalī has come to meet me when I was eager to see Rādhā?

Padmā (only to Kṛṣṇa) Moon-faced one,[45] having heard your wish, expressed in the phrase "the one who holds Padmā's hand," I have secretly brought Candrāvalī.

Kṛṣṇa (to himself) Oh, I see. By expressing my desire for a lotus-ornament, I provided you with an opportunity. Is that your fault? (aloud) Friend, Padmā's[46] partiality to Padmanābha[47] is well known.

Padmā Quickly take Candrāvalī to Gaurītīrtha.

Kṛṣṇa (to himself) Candrāvalī's arrival is in itself enough to discourage Rādhā from coming. So let me amuse myself for a while by delighting this one, whose love is sincere. (aloud)

11 Friend Candrāvalī /row of moons/, you are wonderful:
You are fulfilled at the side of Kṛṣṇa
/You are full even in the dark lunar fortnight,
You give constant delight to Padmā /the day lotuses,[48]

You appear always without faults
/You shine perpetually instead of rising at night.

(walking ahead) Doe-eyed one, look at the beauty of the forest.

Padmā — Oh, here in front of us is Kṛṣṇa's deer Suraṅga. He has taken Rādhā's deer Raṅgiṇī to wife.

Kṛṣṇa — (apprehensively listening in the direction of the wings, to himself) Surely Rādhā has come, for the soft sound of Raṅgiṇī is coming this way.

Padmā — How is this? Suraṅga is running towards the south.

Kṛṣṇa — (to himself again) This deer has surely gone to Gaurītīrtha, enticed by the sound of Raṅgiṇī. So I'll wait in the row of trees on the edge of Saṅkarṣaṇatīrtha[49] and figure out what to do next.

Padmā — 12 Decked with an expanse of freshly blooming lotuses
/Thronged with hosts of beautiful young women,
Capped with high waves of water that can wash away sins[50]
/Surging with the ecstasy of Kṛṣṇa's *rasa*:[51]
Look! The broad lake in front of us shines like Gokula.[52]

Kṛṣṇa — Dear, look!

13 Bearing a wealth of wondrous love for the sun
/your friend,[53]
Satisfying the bees by its production of nectar
/enhancing the delight of your friends by the upsurge of *rasa*,
Radiant with its beautiful pericarp
/your beautiful earrings:
This lotus, like you, displays her beauty throughout the world.

Śaivyā — Why does the moon make this delightful lotus fade?[54]
/Why does Kṛṣṇa make this lovely woman grow sad?

Padmā — (pointing to the moon, meaningfully)

14 This lotus, emitting fragrance,
bears love in her heart for the sun.
/This lovely woman, giving delight,
has love in her heart for the hero.[55]
O moon, you are crimson only for a moment;
don't cast your ray on her.
/O lord of Rādhā, you are loving only for
a moment; don't lay your hand on her.

Kṛṣṇa — Padmā, it is not the moon that is at fault here, for this lady lotus /lovely woman/ grows pale because she is abandoned by the fickle Lakṣmī[56] /her inconstant friend Padmā/ in the evening.

Candrāvalī — (smiling and looking ahead) (in Sanskrit)

15 It seems that the row of creepers,
Seeing the excessive greed of the intoxicated
bees,
Is laughing with the beauty of its flowers;
But this one tender golden jasmine
Lovingly sheds tears of nectar.[57]

Kṛṣṇa — (smiling) Dear, look--

16 This king of *kadamba*s with head held high
is resplendent,
His glory sung by swarms of buzzing bees,[58]
His body fanned by the myriad fly-whisk
tails of the herd of cows.[59]

Candrāvalī — Ah, how charming is the beauty of Vṛndāvana![60]

(enter Lalitā and Vṛndā)

Lalitā — (looking ahead, sadly) This is a real impasse.

Vṛndā — Karālā's commands may not be disobeyed. So how has Candrāvalī been brought here today by Padmā?

Lalitā — You are expert in all forms of occult science. So lure Kṛṣṇa away from here.

Vṛndā — 17 Candrāvalī is the best vessel of the heavy
jewels of his love,
So how can she be abandoned /removed/ by Hari?[61]

Lalitā	(in Sanskrit)

18 I bow down to that fierce warrior love,[62]
Who has attracted the *nāgara*;[63]
For at the slightest hint of that awesome presence,
The last trace of respect, like a thief,
Is quickly put to rout.[64]

Vṛndā: Friend, what you say is true. But Kṛṣṇa is acting courteous toward Candrāvalī, so I wager that it will be difficult to lure him away.

Lalitā: Vṛndā, you are right. So what is the way out of this dilemma?

Vṛndā: First let us join the group and find out what the situation is.

(they walk around)

Śaivyā: (looking up, only to Padmā) Oh Padmā, alas, surely Rādhā has been brought to Gaurītīrtha. See, Lalitā is coming from there.

Padmā: How can that affect us? Hari cannot leave our dear friend.

Lalitā: (approaching) O Candrāvalī, we should not leave Raṅgiṇī in the dwelling place of that stag, who is a serpent toward the whole herd of does, heedless of the love of his beloved for him. I have come in order to make you a witness to the fact that the young black female antelope has not been remembered by him for a month.

(Candrāvalī smiles)

Kṛṣṇa: (to himself) Alas, Lalitā has come for me! (looking at Candrāvalī and resorting to duplicity, aloud) Lalitā, you are blaming Suraṅga unfairly, failing to realize the intention in his heart. So you should convey this message to her:[65]

19 O beloved of the deer /Kṛṣṇa,
You are always desired by the deer /Hari;
You whose eyes penetrate the heart,
Be assured that his heart is in your power.

Padmā (to Kṛṣṇa only) Kṛṣṇa, you have attained your dear one. You should therefore leave us, who are not fit for union.

Kṛṣṇa 20 O maiden of celestial beauty, my friend,
I swear that I harbor no trace of love
For those perverse *gopī*s, puffed up with pride,
Who bear the scent of Rādhā.

Hidden meaning:

I swear that I bear love for the intoxicated *gopī*s who have the mere scent of Rādhā,[66] but not for those who are hostile toward them.[67]

Padmā (with an insolent smile) Friend Lalitā, what a surprise! How is it that you, who are called Anurādhā, are here today without Rādhā?[68]

Lalitā (in Sanskrit)

21 Greedily the swarming bees
Kiss the elephant's cheek,
But that thirsty elephant prince
Goes to the lake, not she to him.[69]

Padmā[70] 22 My wise friend Śaivyā, let me ask you a riddle:
What woman is always found painted on the canvas of Mādhava's mind?

Śaivyā Friend, Candrāvalī.

Vṛndā (smiling) Well discerned! They[71] call the shield of Viṣṇu[72] *Śatacandra*,[73] for it is adorned with a whole row of moon-discs.

Kṛṣṇa (to himself) Here is a good woman!

(Candrāvalī shyly walks toward the left)

Lalitā 23 Vṛndā, well versed in fine riddles, try mine:
Dear friend, how is Mādhava known in the world?

Vṛndā Friend, as Rādhā.[74]

Kṛṣṇa — Correct, Mādhava and Rādhā are synonyms of Vaiśākha.[75]

Padmā — Śaivyā, enough of this indulgence in riddles! Delight yourself with the *rasa*s of the lotus-eyed one.[76]

Śaivyā — (looking at the lotus pond)

24 The pond of water-lilies /Rādhā
Blossoming /rejoicing/ at dusk
Gives delight to the bee /Kṛṣṇa
Only so long as he does not see
This cluster of lotuses /friend of Padmā.[77]

Padmā — Friend, you are right. For similarly,

25 The constellation Viśākhā /Rādhā
Along with the other stars /her friends
Appears brilliant in the sky as dark as a
tamāla tree /Seems radiant to Kṛṣṇa
Only so long as the moon does not rise
/Only so long as Candrāvalī does not appear.

Lalitā — (laughing) (in Sanskrit)

26 Friend, when appears the lustrous Rādhā
/the radiance of the sun in Taurus,
Even hundreds of Candrāvalīs /moons/
are bereft of their luster.

Kṛṣṇa — (smiling) What good is all this boasting? You should enjoy the fragrance of the newly arrived spring season.[78]

Vṛndā — (smiling)

27 At the advent of spring /Kṛṣṇa[79]
is there a creeper that does not erupt
in an exuberance of blossoms?
/is there a woman[80] who does not feel
her body surge with joy?
But I pay special homage to the Mādhavī creeper
/Rādhā,[81] who bears his name.

Padmā (walking about in a dejected manner, loudly) Say, Candrāvalī, now that you have had your fun with these rascals, why are you so slow in going to worship the Goddess?[82]

Kṛṣṇa (with disapproval)

28 O Padmā, you are forcibly impeding
Candrāvalī, who is clinging to me,
Just as the noxious *karālā*[83] creeper in
front of us
Blocks the jasmine vine proceeding toward
the *tamāla* tree.

(entering)

Karālā Hold it! By good fortune I have caught you all!

(all turn around, flustered)

Śaivyā (preventing Karālā from hearing) Padmā, alas, alas! How did this old woman discover us here?

Karālā Aha! So the old monkey who is greedy for butter was telling the truth!

(Padmā looks at Śaivyā sadly)

Lalitā (to herself) Old monkey Kakkhaṭikā, I will give you butter mixed with sugar.

Kṛṣṇa (preventing Karālā from hearing) Dear, I don't even see a place where you can hide. For

29 To the left is Mount Govardhana,
whose lofty peaks are insurmountable;
Your husband, alas, is herding cows to the
right;
Behind us the land is bare of shrubbery;
In front of us is this cruel old woman:
Where is there a place to flee?

Candrāvalī (to herself) Alas! It is just my luck that the cruelty of this harsh *Caṇḍāla* woman should suddenly manifest itself![84]

Karālā (in a rage) Look, will you, at the lustfulness[85] of this fickle one, black like a mass of flower-oil lampblack, the corners of whose eyes are as dreadful as a black serpent, for he has brought to naught the virtue of all the respectable family women of Gokula. (opening her eyes wide and shaking her head ferociously) O dark one,[86] do you know whose wife this is? Take heed: she belongs to that great wrestler who is Kaṁsa's right-hand man.

Kṛṣṇa Karālikā,[87] so what?

Karālā (furiously) Oh, of course! You think you are a second king in the forest. But when the leader of the cowherd village[88] is brought before the king's court, he will strike his forehead in desperation.[89]

Kṛṣṇa Karālā, I swear to you:
Seeing Candrāvalī, I become frightened and begin to tremble. /Looking at Candrāvalī, I am unhappy that I did not unite with her.[90]

Karālā (looking at Candrāvalī, angrily) O you who spend sleepless nights in the groves, whose cleverness in stealing out to meet Kṛṣṇa was learned when you were a mere girl, whose vow of fidelity has been destroyed by your thirst for the *bimba*-like lips that are the leftovers[91] from thousands of passionate *gopī*s--you wait here! Why are you suddenly afraid?

Lalitā Madam, is the western direction,[92] who is true to Varuṇa, at fault? Or is Sūrya, who eradicates the darkness of night, to be blamed? The fault lies rather with the bawd twilight, who, making them both red /loving/, unites the two.

> [Implied meaning[93]] Is Candrāvalī, who is obedient to her husband,[94] at fault? Is the hero who destroys sins /steals (women) at night/ (i.e., Kṛṣṇa) to be blamed? The fault lies rather with the go-between Padmā, who kindles their love and then brings them together.

Karālā — Daughter, you are right. (with a grand flourish) Servant Padmā, you queen of unchaste women, you who, greedy for the opportunity to serve as a go-between, break up other peoples' homes, how will you elude my grasp? (brandishes her staff)

Padmā — (drawing back) Madam, I don't understand why you are so upset. We are simply following your orders.

Vṛndā — (to herself) So now this wily Padmā is resorting to lies. (aloud) Madam, this simple girl has been confused by the fact that the wrestler and the mountain have the same name.[95] So forgive her this time.

(Karālā lets go of her staff)

Padmā — Lalitā, you just wait. I am going to Jaṭilā to get even with you. (leaves)

Karālā — (looking at Candrāvalī) Come on, you neglectful housewife,[96] let's go. (takes Candrāvalī and leaves along with Śaivyā)

Kṛṣṇa — (with a sigh of relief) Vṛndā, your purpose has been accomplished.

Vṛndā — Mādhava, the graceful beauty of spring /that graceful beauty of yours/[97] is playing at Gaurītīrtha. With her whole heart she offers you this pair of newly opened *campaka* blossoms.

Kṛṣṇa — (accepting them with delight) Vṛndā, while I tell my friends to look after the cows, you two go ahead, and I shall follow you there. (leaves)

Vṛndā — (walking about) Lalitā, behold this king of *kadamba*s in front of us. (approaching) Oh, my!

30 O king of *kadamba*s
Resplendent in Vṛndāvana,
Brahmā himself cannot express
Your extreme good fortune;[98]
For your audacious blossoms
Scorn even the brilliant *kaustubha* gem--
Lakṣmī's illustrious brother[99]--
To adorn the chest of Kṛṣṇa.

Lalitā (looking ahead) Vṛndā, here is Paurṇamāsī hidden in the mango grove with Viśākhā.

Vṛndā (seeing Rādhā near the clove plant) Lalitā, look!

31 Is this beauty incarnate?
Or the splendor of myriad virtues?
Or is this Rādhikā the very embodiment of love?[100]

(looking again)

32 Her ears adorned with lotuses,
A lotus swinging at the end of her braid,
Holding a lotus in her lotus-hand,
She puts even Lakṣmī to shame.[101]

(from backstage)

33 A pair of tender *campaka* blossoms[102] swinging from his ears,
Adorned with a *kadamba* garland,
His flute in his hand,[103]
The moon[104] crowning his hair,
A red *tilaka* mark on his lustrous forehead--
Behold: this embodied essence[105]
Of Yaśodā's lavish maternal affection
Is playing in the distance.

Lalitā Surely Paurṇamāsī has seen Kṛṣṇa from afar, for she is describing him.

Vṛndā Lalitā, Kṛṣṇa must be nearby. For

34 Spreading out his tail in a circle,
This peacock called Tāṇḍavika is dancing here;
Not even for a moment can he bear to live,
My bewitching-eyed friend,
Without seeing the dark clouds /Kṛṣṇa.[106]

Lalitā Look toward the *punnāga* grove to the south, in the *mādhavī* bower.

Vṛndā (looking, with delight)

35 The honeyed sounds of his flute
Captivate the circle of cows:

What use then is his shepherd's staff?
That splendid ornament[107]
Imparts to Madhusūdana[108]
A cowherd king's dignity.

Lalitā The two have still not seen one another. Drawn merely by the sight of Raṅginī, Kṛṣṇa is entering the clove bower.

Vṛndā Look!

36 Sensing the enticing fragrance[109]
issuing from Kṛṣṇa's body,[110] friend,
This artful one has playfully hidden
her vine-like form in the *mādhavī* bower.

(looking again, with eager delight)

37 Following the path of footprints
clearly etched in the dusty earth,
Hari, approaching from behind,
covers Rādhā's eyes with his trembling hands.

Lalitā Oh! This lovely woman,[111] her whole body shivering with excitement, is hitting that lotus-eyed one with her play lotus.[112]

Vṛndā Look, look!

38 Words of protest filled with passion,
Gestures of resistance lacking force,
Frowns transmuted into smiles,
Crying dry of tears--friend,
Though Rādhā seeks to hide her feelings,
Each attempt betrays her heart's
Deep love for demon Mura's slayer.[113]

Lalitā (in Sanskrit)

39 Bold employ of teeth and nails
By one experienced[114] in love sports:
Rādhā's show of opposition
Gives Hari immeasurable delight.

Vṛndā (laughing)

40 Your eyes, flowing with tears of joy,
have attained transcendent purity
/have lost their collyrium;[115]
Your breasts, their unguent washed away by sweat,
have become devoid of passion
/have lost their redness;[116]
Seeing the advent of lustful persons
/Perceiving your swelling breasts[117]
your trembling bosom has become eager
for *yoga* /union;[118]
O Rādhā, it seems that your waist-knot,
its three *guṇa*s become feeble
/its string become slack,
has conceived a desire for *mokṣa*
/becoming untied.[119]

Lalitā How has this clever[120] couple managed to disappear from our sight into the *mādhavī* grove?

Vṛndā 41 Could ever a person become sated
Whose eyes, like avid bees,
Feast on the pure[121] sweet nectar
Of the love-play of Rādhā and Mādhava?[122]

Lalitā Say, why are these bees suddenly heading toward the east, abandoning the cluster of *mādhavī* flowers even though they are dripping with nectar?

Vṛndā Friend, the two supreme *nāgara*s[123] have left the *mādhavī* bower,[124] and the bees are following their fragrance. So come, let us delight our eyes by looking at the enclosure[125] of creepers. (walking about) Lalitā, look!

42 Scattered gems from Rādhā's necklace
glittering like stars,[126]
Strewn bits of gold ornaments, withered
garlands,
A bed fashioned from a heap of flowers:
Everywhere this grove gives witness
To the heights of Kṛṣṇa's[127] rapture.

Lalitā (looking closely) (in Sanskrit)

43 Smeared with saffron from Kṛṣṇa's limbs,
Edged with crimson lac from Rādhā's feet,
Sprinkled with perspiration mingled with vermillion powder,[128]
This wasted bed of flower petals delights my eyes.[129]

Vṛndā (in amazement)

44 Just yesterday[130] she was playing in the dust, her ears newly pierced,
Her hair, barely as long as a cow's ear, tied with a colored thread;
Oh, where[131] has this Rādhā learned such proficiency in the ways of love[132]
That she has conquered the unconquerable?[133]

Lalitā (looking toward the east) Vṛndā, look, Rādhā and Mādhava are not very far away.

Vṛndā Let's listen to what she is saying.

(from backstage)

Rādhā (in Sanskrit)

45 O faultless one,[134] deck my ears with water lilies,
Plait my hair with sturdy clove vines,
Lay a jasmine garland on my bosom,
Tie a string of *kadamba* flowers on my thigh:
O Hari, let my friends not see me unadorned![135]

Vṛndā (smiling)

46 Bearing nail marks more brilliant than bright red threads,
His peacock feather fallen in the turbulent play of love,
Glistening all over with pearly drops of sweat,
This magnificent figure[136] of Madhu's slayer makes me wild with joy.[137]

(enter Kṛṣṇa with Rādhā, whose body is adorned)

Kṛṣṇa

47 Your curls make redundant
your forehead's musk markings;
Your eyes render pointless your dark lily
earrings;[138]
Your radiant smile robs your necklace of
purpose:
O Rādhā, resplendent in every feature,
What use is your ornamentation?

Vṛndā and Lalitā

(approaching) Beautiful one, here is an exquisite ornament of spring flowers.

Kṛṣṇa

(accepting the two clusters of flowers, with delight)

48 O thou of lovely hips,
Repeatedly desired by me,
Who am the object of *mukta*s' meditation,
It is meet that you should be decked
With this bouquet of *atimukta* blossoms.
/It is fitting that you should be served
By the host of the fully liberated.[139]

(He adorns Rādhā with them)

(from backstage)

49 Though the third quarter[140] of the day
is not yet over,
Today, as the rainy season displays
its youthful splendor,[141]
The herd of cows, satisfied by the
abundant tender grass,
Is moving toward Gokula.

Lalitā

Rādhā, let me gather rare spring flowers to adorn you tonight. (leaves)

Kṛṣṇa

(smiling; preventing Rādhā from hearing) Vṛndā, I wish to have some fun.[142] So you see to it that Kakkhaṭī, who has climbed the tree in front of us, the confidante of my darling, takes up my cause.

Vṛndā

All right, I shall try.

Kṛṣṇa (approaching Rādhā) My dear Candrā--[143] (breaks off and feigns confusion)

Rādhā (hurt) Oh, alas! Why haven't my ears burst upon hearing this?

Vṛndā (to herself) Bewitching Kakkhaṭikā by waving my wand of peacock feathers, I shall induce her to say what Hari desires.

(she does that surreptitiously)

(aloud) Friend, don't be hostile on this happy occasion.

Kṛṣṇa My moon-faced darling,[144] why are you suddenly upset?

(from backstage)

Mistress, Lalitā will die at your simplicity!

Rādhā (looking up, to herself) Kakkhaṭikā has dispelled my doubts. (aloud) How can the dreadful roar of thunder be covered up by the sound of a small drum? (turns her face away)

Kṛṣṇa (preventing Rādhā from hearing)[145]

50 Her brows more beautiful than the bow of
Kāma fierce in battle,
Her lotus-eyes tremulous with agitation:
Though contorted in great anger
The face of Rādhā delights my heart.

(drawing back the edge of Rādhā's sari) O beautiful one, this festival of delightful[146] amusement should end with something sweet.[147]

(again from backstage)[148]

Alas, alas! O wicked crane,[149] you mimic of Padmā, even you look askance at me. So why should I go on living?

Rādhā (hearing and moving away angrily) Vṛndā, how much more can I be ridiculed? Therefore quickly stop the stage manager[150] of this drama[151] filled with deceit, who makes bold to instruct the flute to slay creatures in the world /to carry out the work of Kāmadeva in the world[152]/, and who has become a mere dancing monkey for the granddaughter of Karālā.[153]

Kṛṣṇa (with a smile of delight) Friend Vṛndā, appease Rādhā.

Vṛndā Friend Rādhā, you are foremost among experienced[154] women. So don't suddenly drive away the beloved black antelope /Kṛṣṇa, your beloved and very essence/[155] with the hard staff of *māna*.

Rādhā (showing great contempt) It is not proper for me to stay here. (leaves)

Kṛṣṇa Vṛndā, when the fire of anger has grown great, the wine of pacifying words serves only to make it blaze up more violently. So there is no point in following her.

Vṛndā What should we do now?

Kṛṣṇa Vṛndā, I want to win Rādhā by dressing up as a fair woman. So you should agree to help.

(Vṛndā smiles in assent)

Kṛṣṇa Friend, how can I procure a woman's costume and some golden rouge?

(entering)

Madhumaṅgala Dear friend, everything necessary for disguising yourself in that way is in the temple of Gaurī; all those things were given to me by Padmā.[156]

Kṛṣṇa (delighted) Vṛndā, I shall wait in the innermost recess of the temple of Gaurī. You should greet me there as your sister. (he leaves with Madhumaṅgala)

Vṛndā (walking around, then looking off into the distance)

51 While her two friends gather blossoms
of *campaka*, *lavaṅga* and *bakula*,
Rādhā is clearly telling them shyly
what has just happened.

(enter Rādhā as described)

Rādhā — Friend, then I came here after seeing that he wished to appease me.

Lalitā — Rādhā, not even in his sleep is Kṛṣṇa capable of uttering the name of another woman[157] in your presence. Therefore you who put your trust in the prattle of animals, who are by nature unreliable, have been deceived.

Viśākhā — Alas, alas! Lalitā, see, on this *Saubhāgyapūrṇimā* day our powerful rivals have mounted their campaign. So fate has played a trick on us.

Lalitā — Viśākhā, you are right. If our rivals see our discomfiture on this great festival day, they will cast scornful glances and sarcastic words our way.

Rādhā — (to herself) My friends' apprehensions are well founded. So what recourse is there?

Vṛndā — (approaching) Lalitā, at the request of Rāma's younger brother,[158] I am going to bring Rāma.

Lalitā — Why?

Vṛndā — To show him this vernal beauty.[159]

Viśākhā — Friend Vṛndā, stop for a moment and join us /bring reconciliation.

Vṛndā — I tell you truly, it is difficult for me to bring about a reconciliation now.

Viśākhā — Why is that?

Vṛndā — Ask your friend, who has displeased the lotus-eyed one today with harsh words.

Rādhā — (sighing sadly) Oh Vṛndā, you are my only hope.

Vṛndā — (feigning anger)

52 O cruel one, jealousy--that outcaste woman[160]--
Has found a place in your heart.
Sound advice did not penetrate even the
fringe of your hearing.
Served by hosts of bewitching-eyed beauties,
Mukunda has lost all interest in you.[161]
My friend, be unperturbed[161]: why do you sigh
in vain?

Lalitā — Where is that enchanter?[162]

Vṛndā — In the temple of Gaurī.

Lalitā — What is he doing?

Vṛndā — He is talking with Nikuñjavidyā.[163]

All three[164] — Friend, who, pray, is Nikuñjavidyā?

Vṛndā — (laughing aloud) How ignorant these young girls are, that they don't even know the famous Nikuñjavidyā!

All three — (embarrassed) Friend, tell us. We really don't know.

Vṛndā — Oh my, you virtuous ones, what young cowherd girl in Gokula does not know the deity of Bhāṇḍīra,[165] my sister /my very essence?[166]

Lalitā — Vṛndā, give us advice[167] that will save us from this sorry plight.

Vṛndā — Friend, Nikuñjavidyā is the repository[168] of Kṛṣṇa's most intimate secrets. So let us have recourse to her. (all walk around)

Rādhā — Vṛndā, here is the temple of Gaurī. So go in and signal Nikuñjavidyā to come over here.

Vṛndā — (craning her neck to look, to herself) Oh! I see Hari disguised as a fair maiden. (aloud) Friends, the deity of Bhāṇḍīra is here alone, making an ornament of peacock feathers.

All three — O liar, stop trying to fool us: Kṛṣṇa's peacock Tāṇḍavika is in the courtyard.

Vṛndā — O you contentious ones, come see for yourselves. Why rely on guesswork?

Lalitā — Oh, I suppose the peacock was asleep and didn't notice when Kṛṣṇa left.

Rādhā — Come on, let's go into the temple and ask Nikuñjavidyā. (all enact entering)

(entering)

Jaṭilā — Padmā affectionately brought me this news: "Noble Jaṭilā, you are very fortunate. Like Govardhana, your son will soon own vast numbers of cows, for today I saw Rādhā worshipping Gaurī at Gaurītīrtha."

So I'll go there and shower my daughter-in-law with blessings. (walking around and seeing Raṅginī in the courtyard, with joy) Good, Padmā, good, you're no liar. (looking again, with distress) Oh, alas! How is it that Tāṇḍavika is here, perched on the head of Gaurī's lion?[169] I'm going back to get my son! (leaves running)

Rādhā — (only to her friends) Friends, look at the extraordinary[170] beauty of Gaurī.

Lalitā and Viśākhā — Oh, it's true! It's fitting that she has been blessed with the love and confidence of Kṛṣṇa.

Rādhā — I'm very eager to talk with this woman that I've never seen before. (acts bashful)

(from backstage)

Sister[171] Vṛndā, I suppose Rādhā doesn't know me. Yet I've seen her a thousand times.

Vṛndā — (to herself) Amazing![172] This is truly the voice of a woman!

Rādhā — Vṛndā, I don't know why I'm drawn to Nikuñjavidyā by such strong love.

Vṛndā — Friend, I know the reason. It's not surprising, for she has loved you for a long time.

Rādhā — (approaching with joy) O Nikuñjavidyā, where is your Nikuñjanāgara?[173]

(from backstage)

Friend, who is there who knows him?[174]

Lalitā — Friend Nikuñjavidyā, stop teasing us. We're on your side.

(from backstage)

53 Lovely one with eyes like the autumn lotus,
Unless you grasp firmly the truth of things,
How can you obtain the mercury
That has been heated by fire?[175]

Vṛndā — (only to Rādhā)

54 The smile on the cheek of Nikuñjavidyā
Indicates that she will be our messenger.

So soften her /make her amenable, Rādhā,
Lavishing fine oil /love/ upon her.

Rādhā O Nikuñjavidyā, why don't you love me as Vṛndā does?

(from backstage)

55 Making your feet lotus blossoms,
Your thighs young plantain trees,
Your arms lotus fibers,
Your face the moon;
Then realizing that soft things cannot endure
Without something hard to support them,
Brahmā made your heart of adamant.[176]

Rādhā Vṛndā, see, Nikuñjavidyā is teasing me with loving smiles. So I shall go and meet her. (leaves [to go into the inner recess of the temple])

Vṛndā 56 O Nikuñjavidyā,
dear to the women of Gokula /whose mistresses are the women of Gokula,[177]
You have a hard heart,
For even though our friend is drawn to you,
You do not grant her the delight of your embrace.

Viśākhā Rādhā is talking with loving confidence and extending her vine-like arms to embrace Nikuñjavidyā.

(from backstage)[178]

O deity of Bhāṇḍīra, see, the time for returning to Gokula is approaching. Therefore you should quickly procure the favor[179] of Kṛṣṇa so that he will give us the pleasure of his *līlā*.[180]

Lalitā Vṛndā, this sister of yours is embracing Rādhā and kissing her.

Viśākhā (apprehensively) Your Nikuñjavidyā is shamelessly greedy for masculine ways, for she is making nail marks on Rādhā's breasts.

Vṛndā (smiling) Friend, don't be distressed. This is an expression of her great love.

(entering, trembling)

Rādhā	(frowning) Vṛndā, this is a fine piece of deception on your part!
Vṛndā	(laughing) Friend, I don't know what you mean.
Lalitā and Viśākhā	(smiling) Vṛndā, we have recognized your Nikuñjavidyā as Mohinī.[181]

(enter Jaṭilā with her son)

Jaṭilā	Abhimanyu, my child, look, the peacock Tāṇḍavika and Raṅginī are both in the courtyard.
Abhimanyu	Mother, you're right, for I saw Rāma entering Gokula alone[182] with the cows and the other cowherds.
Jaṭilā	My child, this spreading fragrance is enough to betray the presence of the audacious couple.
Abhimanyu	Mother, I'm finished with following Paurṇamāsī's orders. I'm taking Rādhā to Mathurā immediately.
Jaṭilā	Son, luckily there is only one entrance to this temple. So let's stay glued to the door and listen to what they are saying.

(they stand in that way)

(entering)

Kṛṣṇa	(smiling) Rādhā, don't ask me for something so difficult.
Rādhā	(with a mischievous smile) Have mercy, O Goddess, have mercy!
Abhimanyu	(entering the temple) So, audacious one, I have caught you red-handed!
Kṛṣṇa	(to himself) Alas, recognizing Abhimanyu from his voice, my frightened darling has fallen to the ground like a staff!
Jaṭilā	(pointing in astonishment) My child, who is this fair woman[183] who is illuminating the temple with her extraordinary[184] beauty?
Abhimanyu	(reflecting) Mother, Rādhā fell prostrate,[185] saying, "Have mercy, O Goddess, have mercy." So clearly this divinely beautiful consort of Śiva has appeared.

Kṛṣṇa (delighted, to himself) My disguise as a fair woman[186] has served me well.

Lalitā and Viśākhā (with joy) O best of cowherds, Gaurī, whom we were worshipping at your repeated behest, has emerged from the image.

Abhimanyu Viśākhā, what difficult petition was Rādhā making just now at the feet of the Goddess?

Kṛṣṇa Valiant Abhimanyu, a terrible calamity awaits you. She is asking that it be averted.

Abhimanyu (apprehensively) O Goddess, what sort of calamity?

Kṛṣṇa Vṛndā, I shudder to speak of it, so you tell him.

Vṛndā Proud[187] Abhimanyu, two evenings from now Kaṁsa intends to offer you as a sacrifice to Bhairava.[188]

Jaṭilā (with alarm) Have mercy, Goddess, have mercy! Let my son live!

Rādhā (getting up, with relief[189]) Have mercy, Goddess, have mercy.

Kṛṣṇa (smiling) Rādhā, I have already explained to you that this will be difficult to avert now.

Rādhā (making obeisance with profuse lamentations) O deity of the *gopīs*,[190] nothing is impossible for you. So be gracious to me and grant my request that I may never be separated from my lord.[191]

Kṛṣṇa (smiling)

57 O Rādhā, with the bonds of your ever-new devotion,[192]
Hard to forge for even the mightiest sages,[193]
You have captivated me today:
I shall grant your request if you will remain
Forever in Gokula, worshipping me.[194]

Abhimanyu (with a sigh) O you who are affectionate to your devotees,[195] I shall never take Rādhā to Mathurā. Let her remain here and worship you.

Jaṭilā (embracing Rādhā) O delight of Gokula,[196] I am saved!

Vṛndā (looking at Abhimanyu)

58 A virtuous woman, when reviled,
Destroys the lives of men;
Let Gaurī, deity supreme,
Who fathoms all intentions,
Give us her view.

Kṛṣṇa Blessed Abhimanyu, Rādhā is the source of your good fortune: never lose faith in her.

Abhimanyu O Goddess, my mother is made a laughing-stock by Subala, who dresses up as Rādhā. Seeing that, jealous and ignorant folk create false scandal.

Lalitā Abhimanyu, fortunately you yourself have confidence in her.

Abhimanyu Mother, come, let us stop the servant that I ordered to take my household goods to Mathurā. (with his mother he bows to Hari[197] and leaves)

Lalitā and Viśākhā (embracing Rādhā with tears) Ah, dear friend, why were these vile persons set upon taking you to Mathurā?

(entering)

Paurṇamāsī (with a smile of joy)

59 This fair[198] deity of the groves[199]
Whose color[200] steals the radiance of gold
Is giving me delight.

Kṛṣṇa (walking around) Blessed one, I pay you homage.

Paurṇamāsī A hundred blessings upon you! O son of Yaśodā,[201] I am fortunate in being favored by you today, for I have been spared the pain of separation from Rādhā.

Kṛṣṇa

60 Today is Rādhā rescued from great danger;
Relieved of anxiety's needle,
You shall henceforth meet no obstacles;
Likewise freed from apprehension,
Rādhā's friends all share your joy:
O blessed one, what favor may I do for you?

Paurṇamāsī (with tears of joy) O friend of Gokula, my birth has assuredly been rendered fruitful.[202] Even so, I ask for something:

61 Displaying the sweetness of your myriad good qualities,
May you ever enact with Rādhā
The auspicious play of love's rapture[203]
Deep in the groves of Vṛndāvana.

and further:

62 O thou who art ever springtime
For the *mādhavī* creeper that is Rādhā,
May the supreme wave of love for your lotus feet--
Love that bears one to the acme of sweetness[204]--
Arise in him who opens his ears,
His heart filled with reverence,
And partakes of even the drops of spray
From that ocean of pure nectar, your sports in Gokula.[205]

Kṛṣṇa (smiling) Blessed one, so be it. Now come, let us return to Gokula without delay and bring joy to my parents, who must be worried at not seeing me now that the cows have been milked. (leaves)

(all leave)

CHAPTER V

BEAUTY AND PARADOX IN THE FIGURE OF KṚṢṆA

In certain of the classical Sanskrit texts on dramaturgy, it is stated explicitly that the hero of a drama cannot be divine. Abhinavagupta, who articulates this position, points out that a divine hero would be able to accomplish his aims by his own supernatural power;[1] no effort would be required, there would be no real opposition, and there could thus be no true drama. Rūpa's response is unequivocal: Kṛṣṇa is not only a fit subject of a drama, but indeed a most worthy hero (NC 8-9). Rūpa's practical solution to the apparent dilemma lies in emphasizing the humanness of Kṛṣṇa: his omnipotence is not merely veiled by *māyā*, as it is in the *Bhāgavata*, but all overt display of his *aiśvarya*, his lordly majesty, is replaced by subtle allusion.

The unique manner in which "divinity" and "humanness" intersect in the figure of Kṛṣṇa in the *Vidagdhamādhava* is important not merely as a theoretical issue. Our understanding of the relation of drama and devotion for Rūpa, and of the form of *bhakti* that is expressed and nourished by his drama, begins with the way in which Rūpa presents his hero in himself, but also with the responses of the other characters to him. These characters, especially Rādhā, and the drama's structure and recurrent motifs, will in turn serve as points of departure for our exploration of the devotional significance of the *Vidagdhamādhava*.

Kṛṣṇa's Aesthetic Qualities

Even before his first appearance on the stage, we learn of Kṛṣṇa's radiance from the verse of Paurṇamāsī that introduces him: his eyes are more beautiful than the loveliest of water lilies; his yellow garments are more resplendent than fresh saffron; his forest ornaments surpass even divine apparel;[2] and his body has the mind-captivating luster of a brilliant emerald.[3] Subsequent verses enumerate his forest ornaments: his crest of peacock feathers,[4] his garland of wild flowers,[5] the *campaka* blossoms that adorn his ears (VII.33), and his necklace of *guñjā* berries.[6] To these may be added his bejeweled flute (III.1) and his herder's staff (V.5; VII.35), which likewise serve to adorn his graceful form. So well known are some components of his attire that they serve as the basis for certain of his numerous epithets: he is referred to as *barhamauli* (V.8) or *candrakamauli* (VII.52.25), "the one wearing a crest made from a peacock's tail"; as *vanamālin*, "the one garlanded with forest flowers" (V.33.1); and as *pītāmbara*, "the one clothed in yellow" (VI.18).

Even more than his ornamentation, however, it is Kṛṣṇa's own luster that is the subject of repeated comment. In Act VII, for example, his body is described as so brilliant that it "robs all eyes of sleep."[7] The paradox of his being simultaneously dark and luminous occasions wonder; his complexion is the color of a black *tamāla* tree (VI.8.40, 26.4-6; VII.25, 28) or a dark raincloud (I.2.8; II.9) and he is called Śyāma[8] or Śyāmala, "the dark one" (VII.29.6-7), yet his face is like the moon,[9] his eyes are like lotuses[10] (both common Sanskrit conventions), and his whole body has a distinctive luster.[11] Certain images used in the play embrace both halves of the paradox: in Act VI, Rādhā, pretending not to recognize the hiding Kṛṣṇa, remarks on the refulgence[12] of the "blue sapphire pillar" before her, and earlier in the play she employs a still more striking metaphor, referring to him as "dark moonlight."[13]

Kṛṣṇa's attractiveness--expressed in such specific ways as these, as well as by the more general epithet *sundara*, "beautiful one," which frequently appears as a vocative[14]--is not simply static, for he is characterized by grace of movement as well as beauty of form. Commonly enumerated are the playful movements of his eyes[15] and brows (II.3; III.38) and his easy gait, which is likened to that of a young, unruly elephant.[16] (He is, in fact, several times called an elephant.[17]) His charm is enhanced by every aspect of his *līlā*, but especially by his love-making with Rādhā, which creates new ornaments (red nail marks and pearls of perspiration) to replace those that are effaced or dislodged in his passion (VII.46). Indeed, his *līlā* in its entirety, and not simply its individual aspects, is repeatedly characterized as sweet or beautiful (I.1; VII.62).

In his dramas, Rūpa presents Kṛṣṇa's extraordinary beauty, not as an isolable quality of his, but rather in its effects upon those who see him and feel his inexplicable attraction. It is invariably another character who remarks on his charming appearance, often concluding with an expression of wonder, such as that of Vṛndā upon seeing the disheveled Kṛṣṇa in the final act (VII.46), or the closely parallel exclamation of Rādhā herself after she steals a glance at Kṛṣṇa in Act VI: "The sweet beauty of Mādhava makes me wild with joy!"[18] Even when other characters in the drama simply describe him, without commenting explicitly on the effects of his beauty, they give witness to the fascination that his graceful form exerts upon all who behold him.

By far the most common response to Krsna's appearance is one of utter delight. Vṛndā's designation of him as *nayanānandana*, "one who gives pleasure to the eyes,"[19] expresses the feeling of many secondary characters in the drama and most especially of Rādhā and Candrāvalī. In addition to such explicit statements as the exclamation of Rādhā quoted in the preceding paragraph, there are numerous instances of stage directions, such as *sānandam* or *saharṣam*, "with joy" or "with delight,"[20] that indicate the emotional state of those who have the good fortune to see Kṛṣṇa. Finally, evidence for the joy that his presence brings is provided by one of his more common epithets, *gokulānanda*, "joy of Gokula,"[21] and a variant, *gokulamaṅgala*, "welfare of Gokula."[22]

The complex of emotions inspired by Kṛṣṇa's beauty is not exhausted in the simple word "joy," for the inhabitants of Gokula do not experience their unreasoning fascination with him as something unequivocally positive. Their ambivalence is reflected in the epithet *mohana*,[23] which, like *sundara*, is frequently used as a vocative: *mohana* means "fascinating, enrapturing, enchanting," but also "perplexing, deluding, infatuating, stupefying." The last of these meanings, which bears a close relation to another of Kṛṣṇa's epithets, *bhujaṅga*, "snake" (II.52.6), emphasizes the irresistible nature of Kṛṣṇa's attraction, which is as inescapable and incapacitating as the intoxicating effect of a snake's bite. This overpowering quality is likewise attested by the many references to Kṛṣṇa as a thief who steals the hearts of the cowherd women.[24] So intense, in fact, is their response to him that it is characterized--most notably in Rādhā's case--as a form of madness.[25]

Although the largest number of passages evincing Kṛṣṇa's alluring power center upon other characters' responses to *seeing* him, his inexplicable attraction is also conveyed in non-visual ways. Most important of the other senses in this regard is that of hearing: both the nectar-filled syllables of Kṛṣṇa's name and the enchanting melodies of his flute utterly captivate anyone who hears them. An elaborate illustration of the effects of these sounds is furnished by Rādhā's *pūrvarāga*, the first dawning of her love, which occurs even before she first sees Kṛṣṇa. Toward the end of Act I, we find Rādhā in a situation such as the one that Nāndīmukhī has earlier described to Paurṇamāsī (I.14.30-31): in response to Lalitā's seemingly casual mention of Kṛṣṇa, Rādhā eagerly exclaims to herself, "Oh, how sweet (*madhura*) these two syllables are!" (I.32.11). When Lalitā repeats them, at Rādhā's request, Rādhā again muses, "If the mere name of this one so infatuates (*mohayati*) the heart of a woman, what must the person bearing the name be like?" (I.32.14-15). Her response to Kṛṣṇa's flute, which she hears shortly afterward, is even more intense: after expressing wonder at the enchanting power (*mohanatva*) of the sound, she loses all control, subsequently regaining her composure only with difficulty. In the next two verses (I.34-35), she expresses her feelings to Lalitā, saying first that she does not know what sort of sound[26] this is that has reduced her to a state worthy of censure by virtuous women, and then, in response to Lalitā's answer--that this is the sound of a flute (*muralīrava*)--she protests,

> Not cold, yet it makes you tremble
> Not a weapon, yet it pierces you,
> Not hot, yet it burns and torments--
> How can this be the sound of a flute?

"I know a flute when I hear one," she continues, "so stop trying to fool me. This is clearly an enchanting (*mohana*) *mantra* recited by some great *nāgara*.[27] Rūpa's use of *mantra* here, a term with religious overtones, seems deliberate.

The flute is in many respects an extension of Kṛṣṇa: it proclaims his presence, luring the *gopīs* from their homes to sport with him in the fields and groves of Vṛndāvana,[28] and, like Kṛṣṇa himself, its melodies are irresistible. The term *mohana*, an epithet of Kṛṣṇa, is several times used of its sound,[29] and the flute is styled by the *gopīs* a thief (*taskarī*[30]) and a villain (*dhūrtā*, IV.35; V.9). Rādhā calls it cruel (*krūrā*, VI.12), for its shafts of sound, more painful than the arrows of Kāmadeva, reduce her to "a terrible state that is neither death nor life."[31] Finally, its effects, like those of Kṛṣṇa, are not confined to human beings: its soft tones enchant the deer (VI.27) and other animals of Vṛndāvana, who stop their customary activities to gaze upon the youthful flute player (I.26; VI.29-30), and its cosmic echoes bring even the gods from their celestial abodes (I.28-30).

Although sight and sound are the two principal avenues through which Kṛṣṇa's beauty becomes manifest, the senses of smell and touch also figure in the joy that his presence brings. Like his flute, Kṛṣṇa's special fragrance, compared by Nanda to that of a lotus (I.21), indicates his whereabouts: Rādhā early in Act VI likens it to a female messenger (*dūtī*) who leads her to her lover.[32] Yet it is more than a mere sign, for it is, like his graceful form, itself a source of delight. In Act III, when Rādhā despairs of meeting Kṛṣṇa, she longs to become a bee on his wildflower garland so that she might enjoy "the fragrance of his face" (III.16); in Act IV, she uses the word *madayati*, "intoxicates, gladdens"--which she and Vṛndā both employ elsewhere in relation to Kṛṣṇa's visual appearance--to describe the exhilarating effect of his fragrance upon her nostrils (IV.23).

With the exception of a few brief references, the joy derived from touching Kṛṣṇa is not explicitly mentioned, though it is clearly presupposed at points throughout the drama. In the exchange about Rādhā's *romāvalī* (III.29-33), it is Kṛṣṇa's reaction as he approaches Rādhā that is the focus of attention, and in the ensuing discussion about the *guñjā* garland, which Kṛṣṇa puts around Rādhā's neck, her pleasure is indicated only in passing (III.46.7-8, 10-14). One of Kṛṣṇa's numerous epithets, *bimbādharakaṇḍūkhaṇḍana*, "the one who relieves the itching of (your) lips" (used by Rādhā in speaking to Lalitā at VI.8.24), is somewhat more suggestive in this regard. Yet it is only in the scene in Act I in which Nanda and Yaśodā appear with their foster son that we find an explicit description of the bliss (*ānanda*) of touching him: Nanda refers to the exhilaration of embracing Kṛṣṇa as a great festival (*mahotsava*) that is more refreshingly cool than sandal paste, blue water lilies, moonlight, or camphor.[33]

Nanda's use of the word *mādhurī*, "sweetness," in speaking of the coolness conveyed by Kṛṣṇa's touch is noteworthy. Although there is no reference to a literal tasting of Kṛṣṇa, the metaphor of sweetness is found in conjunction with at least three of the other senses. We have already noted Rādhā's utterance of delight in VI.16: after stealing a glance at Kṛṣṇa, she uses there the word *mādhurī* in response to the bewitching movements of his eyes and his charming ornamentation of leaves and flowers. Similarly, when she first sees Kṛṣṇa, thinking that she must be dreaming, she exclaims over the sweetness (again *mādhurī*) of the form that she beholds (II.48.1).

Krsna's sweetness is also relished aurally. As we have earlier observed, Rādhā characterizes as sweet (*madhura*) the syllables of his name; Paurṇamāsī in I.15 calls these two syllables *amṛta*, "nectar." Likewise termed nectar (*amṛta*, *pīyūṣa*, *sudhā*) are his words (II.56) and the sweet sounds of his flute (I.26, 29). It is these sounds to which Viśākhā refers when she arrives with the picture of Kṛṣṇa at the end of Act I and surmises from Rādhā's transformed appearance that "the sweetness of Mādhava has reached [her] ears" (I.36). Finally, the whole of Kṛṣṇa's *līlā* in Gokula is referred to in the concluding verse of the drama as an ocean of pure nectar (*sudhā*), and in the opening verse, translated above in Chapter II, it is said to surpass in sweetness even the moon's ambrosia.

Kṛṣṇa is thus seen to be an aesthetic object *par excellence* for the other inhabitants of Vṛndāvana, who are portrayed throughout the *Vidaghamādhava* as relishing his sweet beauty with all their senses. Yet the aesthetic dimensions of Kṛṣṇa's being are not exhausted in these observations. First, as a superb flute player, he is not merely an *object* of beauty, but also an artist who creates it.[34] Further references to his artistry are found in the passages in the drama that mention his artful sidelong glances and other graceful movements that so fascinate Rādhā and the other *gopīs*.[35] In one conversation with him, Padmā playfully calls him *catuḥṣaṣṭikalāśālin*, "one endowed with the sixty-four arts," thus crediting him with expertise in all the arts traditionally ascribed to Sanskrit heroes.[36] Furthermore, he is also a connoisseur of beauty, a *rasika*, having as the primary object of his aesthetic delight the lovely Rādhā. It is Rādhā's embodiment of beauty and love that will concern us after we consider certain other facets of Kṛṣṇa's character.

Endearing and Exalted Qualities: *mādhurya* and *aiśvarya*

Further Manifestations of the Lord's *mādhurya*

Intimately related to his great attractiveness is another central characteristic of Kṛṣṇa as he is portrayed in the *Vidagdhamādhava:* his amorousness. This quality is pervasively evident: in the very first scene in which he appears, his dalliance with the *gopīs* is alluded to by Madhumaṅgala, and the remainder of the drama is concerned with his love for these women, especially Rādhā, as well as their passion for him. Just as we have seen in the case of his beauty, there are numerous epithets expressive of this element in his nature; these appellations may serve as an index to its many facets.

Two closely related epithets, *vidagdha* and *nāgara*, emphasize his cleverness and worldly-wise aspect, especially his proficiency in the ways of love. *Nāgara*, derived from *nagara*, "city or town," meant originally "town-born and -bred," but it came also to signify "clever" and even "wicked," referring as a noun to one who had contracted the vices of a town.[37] Kṛṣṇa may technically be called a *nāgara* in the original sense, for he was born in Mathurā, the residence of King Kaṁsa; however, from his earliest days he grew up among the cowherds, and neither Rūpa nor the authors of the Purāṇas make much of his city origin. Although Rūpa utilizes in his dramas the sophisticated court tradition, he consistently exalts Kṛṣṇa's natural beauty over artificial ornaments and his pastoral existence in Vṛndāvana over the luxurious court life of Dvārakā.[38] Further evidence that he means *nāgara* in a sense other than its strict etymological one is Rādhā's use of the feminine form *nāgarī* to refer to herself and the other cowherd women who were not born in the city (II.14). The fact that Kṛṣṇa is also called *nāgarīguru* (IV.1), the teacher of the *nāgarī*s, suggests, moreover, that the characteristics embraced by the term *nāgara* are capable of being taught.

It is more difficult to specify precisely what Rūpa *does* intend by his use of the term. That it refers to Kṛṣṇa's amorous inclinations seems clear from its various contexts: in virtually every case, the subject being discussed or represented is that of his love for the *gopī*s. In the first two acts, before Rādhā and Kṛṣṇa have met, the terms *nāgaracakravartin* (II.12) and *nāgarendra* (II.14), "king or prince of *nāgara*s," are used of Kṛṣṇa when Nāndīmukhī and Rādhā note the captivating effects of his sidelong glances, and Rādhā uses the term *mahānāgara* "great *nāgara*" (I.35.2), in exclaiming at the enchanting power of Kṛṣṇa's flute. In the later acts, the focus is not so much upon Kṛṣṇa's alluring quality and Rādhā's response as it is upon his amorous exploits and *his* desire for union with *her*. The generally positive valence of the term may be ascertained most clearly from its use by Lalitā in VII.18. Later in Act VII, Vṛndā refers to Rādhā and Kṛṣṇa, after they have been united in the *mādhavī* bower, as *nāgaramaṇḍalottaṁsau*, "the two best *nāgara*s," a compound that might be translated simply as "the two supreme lovers" (VII.41.3).

The term *vidagdha*, the adjectival element in the title of the drama, is still more elusive. It is sometimes found as a vocative in the same conversations as *nāgara* (e.g. at VI.20.34-39); the *Gauḍīya Vaiṣṇava Abhidhān* in fact gives it as a synonym for *nāgara*.[39] Perhaps the best way of specifying its meaning in the drama is by viewing it in relation to its opposite, *mugdha*, "innocent, inexperienced, artless," with which it is at points deliberately contrasted.[40] Rather than signifying clever in general, it would therefore mean experienced in the ways of love. Although it is, like *nāgara*, most often predicated of Kṛṣṇa, in at least two instances toward the end of the drama it is applied to Rādhā as well (VII.40.1, 50.10), and it is occasionally used to designate an entire class of individuals or couples (V.4.3). In spite of its ironic use by Lalitā on more than one occasion (e.g. III.32.8), it is, like *nāgara*, generally a term of approbation, even of adulation. Shortly after referring to Kṛṣṇa as *vidagdhapuṅgava*, "best of *vidagdha*s" (V.2.5), Paurṇamāsī extols the love of Rādhā and Kṛṣṇa as a model for other *vidagdha* couples (V.4.3).

Not all the epithets referring to Kṛṣṇa's amorous proclivities have such positive connotations. His love for *all* the *gopī*s results in his being styled *bahuvallabha*, "the one with many mistresses" (IV.15.3), and it is also responsible for the even less neutral appellation *capala*, "fickle one."[41] It is in part becuase of the grief occasioned by this facet of his personality that he is repeatedly called a villain (*dhūrta*, V.54.7; *śaṭha*, V.8) and reproached by Rādhā and her friends, as well as by the old women, for being so lustful (*lampaṭa*, III.4.3; VI.8.38; *lubdha*, II.5; *kiśorībhujaṅga*, II.52.6).

Kṛṣṇa's leading characteristics are not all reflected in his most common epithets. His delight in practical jokes and humorous banter, clearly evident at various points throughout the drama, is a case in point. Early in the play, when Rādhā has been brought to her first tryst, her two friends, desiring her cooperation in playing a joke on Kṛṣṇa, describe him with utter aptness as *narmaśīla*, "playful by nature" (III.34.7). In the following act, when Rādhā and Lalitā do not find Kṛṣṇa at the place designated for their rendezvous, Rādhā, hoping at first that he is simply hiding from them, characterizes him as *parīhāsākāṅkṣī*, "fond of playing jokes" (IV.23). Although in this instance she is disappointed, such a trick would be wholly in character: later in the play, after enjoying love with Rādhā, Kṛṣṇa hides in order to play a joke on Lalitā and Viśākhā (VI.33.4).

So strong is the element of playfulness in Kṛṣṇa's character that it sometimes leads him to act in ways that appear to the uninitiated as cruel. Two episodes are especially striking in this regard. When he has just spent the night with Candrāvalī, while the hapless Rādhā and Lalitā were waiting in vain for him in the bower, Kṛṣṇa sees Rādhā with her two friends and counters their accusations with protestations of innocence. After a teasing exchange of insults with Lalitā and Viśākhā, he offers the *nāgakesara* flowers to Rādhā, saying that he is perfumed with their fragrance. Rādhā retorts that it is surely Candrāvalī's perfume that comes from his body, and Kṛṣṇa, instead of denying the truth immediately, agrees with her, only to explain, when she reacts with jealous anger, that he was referring in a punning manner to the scent of camphor.[42] Kṛṣṇa again engages in teasing that seems pointlessly cruel in Act VII, when, feigning an inadvertent slip of the tongue, he s starts to call Rādhā "Candrāvalī" (VII.49.7).

What is one to make of such episodes? On one level, Kṛṣṇa's teasing, like that of Rādhā's friends and Paurṇamāsī, serves to make Rādhā's love for him manifest, to him and to the other characters as well as to the audience. In both the above instances, Kṛṣṇa subsequently delights in the signs of the jealous indignation that his words have evoked in Rādhā (IV.33. 17-18; VII.50), and there seems to be the expectation that his delight will be shared by the audience or reader.

In addition to revealing a crucial facet of Rādhā's love, Kṛṣṇa's teasing and its aftermath exemplify a fundamental psychological principle. In the episode from Act VII referred to above, his deliberate *gotraskhalana* precipitates in Rādhā the condition called *māna*, one of the four forms of love in separation (*vipralambha śṛṅgāra*). According to Rūpā, the pain of separation is necessary to the full bliss of union.[43] Thus we may find meaning in Kṛṣṇa's apparently cruel words on a second level: the temporary suffering that they cause may be seen to be justified by the greater joy of the reconciliation that must inevitably follow. If we remember that a basic purpose of the play is to alleviate the suffering of devotees separated from their Lord, we may see in these and similar episodes a consoling lesson that illuminates the meaning of earthly suffering.

On a third level, such teasing is simply part of Kṛṣṇa's *līlā*, one of the many expressions of the unfettered and unpredictable nature of the Divine.[44] The Lord reverses all man's expectations, eludes the grasp of his most painstakingly devised categories. Thus the teasing episodes in the drama make graphic for the devotee a fundamental facet of Ultimate Reality.

The Question of Kṛṣṇa's Divinity

The seemingly human characteristics discussed above, and others like them, pose a fundamental question for the historian of religion: in what sense may the Kṛṣṇa of the *Vidagdhamādhava* be viewed as divine? There are certain characteristic attributes associated with divinity, such as omnipotnece and omniscience, that he does not display, although both these qualities are predicated of him. He does not employ supernatural means to attain his goals, for example, by appearing simultaneously in two locations when Candrāvalī and Rādhā are both brought to meet him on the same evening,[45] thereby saving Rādhā from the agony of spending the night alone and sparing himself the embarrassment of facing her afterwards. Nor does he invariably exhibit perspicacity. Although he is called clever (*vicakṣaṇa*, V.54.7; *vidagdha*), his intense preoccupation with Rādhā renders him blind, so that he several times mistakes others--Candrāvalī, Subala in disguise, even golden flowers--for Rādhā, and once he inadvertently utters her name just as he is declaring his love to Candrāvalī (IV.9). His unrestrained habit of joking is also at times a cause for regret, as in Act II, when, avowing continence, he dismisses Viśākhā and Lalitā, who have come with a love letter from Rādhā. Repentant, he exclaims to Madhumaṅgala, "In a joking mood, I have done something reckless!" (II.39.14) and laments further, "Alas, out of stupidity (*maugdhyāt*) I have uprooted the tender creeper of my heart's desire, just as it was about to bear fruit!" (II.40).

Kṛṣṇa's foolish mistakes and his subsequent helplessness, together with his irrepressible teasing are, like the childhood pranks described so tenderly in the *purāṇa*s and the Āḻvārs' hymns,[46] an essential part of his sweet charm: such "faults" make him more accessible and thus even more lovable to his adoring devotees. In the *Vidagdhamādhava* it is this "sweetness" (*mādhurya*), rather than his majesty or lordliness (*aiśvarya*), that is depicted in one situation after another. Yet in spite of the fact that his majestic qualities are not emphasized, there are hints here and there throughout the play that point to his transcendent nature. Many of these hints come in the form of epithets that are applied to him, often seemingly in passing, with no explicit attention to their transcendent significance.

Indications of Kṛṣṇa's Transcendence: The Lord's *aiśvarya*

Two of Kṛṣṇa's epithets, *yadupati* (IV.4) and *gokulapati* (I.3), "lord of the Yadus" and "lord of Gokula," point most immediately to his (future) kingly status. By Gauḍīya Vaiṣṇavas, even such a view of Kṛṣṇa as a temporal ruler is thought to set him apart from the other cowherds and increase the respect of his associates and devotees for him. Yet the term *pati*, in addition to its earthly senses of master, ruler, husband, lord, may refer to *the* Lord, as it does, for example, in the Śaiva Siddhānta.[47] It would then widen the gap still further, setting Kṛṣṇa off not only from the ordinary herdsmen, but also from his foster father Nanda, the leader of the cowherd village, who is honored in such epithets of Kṛṣṇa as *gokulendranandana*, "the son/delighter of the chief of Gokula."[48]

Several other epithets and titles used to designate Kṛṣṇa likewise point to his excellence as a man, and some of these display a similar ambiguity. In a punning reference by Lalitā, he is called *punnāga*, "elephant among men" (V.26.23), and Rādhā honors him with the closely related epithet *puruṣottama*, literally, "the best of men" (V.17). The transcendent reference of the latter is unmistakable: *puruṣottama* is a common Vaiṣṇava designation for the Supreme Being, Viṣṇu or Kṛṣṇa conceived as the Lord of the universe.[49] The term *svāmī*, like *pati*, may be used of a human lord, such as a teacher or ruler, but as Rādhā uses it, in combination with the name Hari (VI.29), it clearly points beyond mere human greatness. In a similar manner the term *bhagavat*, rather than simply meaning "the revered or illustrious one," refers in its context in the third verse of the drama to *the bhagavat*, Kṛṣṇa, the Lord of all.

Kṛṣṇa's divinity is indicated somewhat less equivocally by a class of epithets that includes *deva* and *devatā*, the latter often in compound. The term *deva*, although more often used to refer to a god, may also designate a king, and in dramas it is a common mode of addressing a ruler ("your majesty"). It is as a vocative that we find it in Act IV of the *Vidagdhamādhava*, used first by Candrāvalī (IV.12.1) and shortly later by Rādhā (IV.40). May we then assume that it is here, too, simply a term of respectful address? I would argue that the devotional context of the *Vidagdhamādhava* is of crucial importance in this regard: although the word *deva* may have no strong connotations of divinity when it is used in a secular drama,[50] its use here to address Kṛṣṇa must surely suggest his transcendence to the devout Vaiṣṇava.

Less ambiguous in its designation of Kṛṣṇa's divine status is the term *devatā*, "deity, god, divinity," which is used early in the drama and again several times in the final act. Toward the end of Act I, Lalitā warns Rādhā as they enter Vṛndāvana that "the deity who frequents the bowers" (*kuñjecarī devatā*, I.33) will lure her to him, and Paurṇamāsī incorporates a nearly synonymous phrase in a compound when she refers to Kṛṣṇa at the end of the drama as *nikuñjakuladevatā* (VII.59). Coming as it does, however, immediately after the climactic scene in the temple of Gaurī in which Kṛṣṇa appears as the Goddess, Paurṇamāsī's use of the word *devatā* has an added significance. *Devatā* is a feminine abstract noun that refers most properly to the quality of divinity (*deva-tā*); it has, however, also come to designate *a* deity, whether male or female. It is thus admirably suited to Vṛndā's purpose when she earlier resorts to a ruse in order to bring Rādhā and her two friends to the temple in which Kṛṣṇa, disguised as a woman, is waiting: she urges them to betake themselves to "Nikuñjavidyā," literally, "the knowledge of the groves," whom she identifies as *bhāṇḍīradevatā*, "the deity of Bhāṇḍīra" (VII.52.10). The fact that *devatā* is feminine in form likewise makes it possible for Rādhā to use it later to address Kṛṣṇa in the presence of Abhimanyu and Jaṭilā, without either deviating from the truth or giving away her sublime secret. *Devatā* in this complex context thus performs a double function: its feminine form and ambiguity of reference aid in concealing Kṛṣṇa's identity from Jaṭilā and Abhimanyu, lending support to his masquerade as the Goddess, but at the same time its use in reference to Kṛṣṇa reveals his divinity anew to those who see through his disguise and are not blind to ultimate truth.[51]

One of the names of Kṛṣṇa that occur most frequently in the *Vidagdhamādhava*, "Hari," joins the epithets discussed above in appearing to convey a sense of his transcendence.[52] Perhaps originally a name of Indra, "Hari" ("tawny") was early applied to Viṣṇu,[53] and for certain Vaiṣṇava schools it has since become the favorite name of their Lord.[54] In the *Vidagdhamādhava*, it is used in several contexts that are explicitly theological or devotional, including the two Nāndī verses at the beginning of the drama,[55] the third verse in the final act, in which Paurṇamāsī refers to Kṛṣṇa's "descent" into this world, and the stage directions toward the end of the play that describe Abhimanyu and Jaṭilā as doing obeisance to Hari, who appears in the guise of the Goddess (VII.58.7). Its use in these and similar contexts may be construed as evidence that the name "Hari" carries strong theological or devotional overtones.[56] It may then serve to remind the audience that Kṛṣṇa is indeed the Lord of the universe in scenes in which his human aspects are most in evidence. An example of such an occurrence is found in the scene in Act III in which Rādhā has been brought to her first tryst with Kṛṣṇa: before her friends leave, Kṛṣṇa implores the shy Rādhā to look at him, and Lalitā asks her why, having given her body (mentally) to Hari, she is so miserly with a mere glance (III.48). The use of the term "Hari" in this context seems to emphasize the transcendent significance of Lalitā's words: they express Rādhā's surrender of her entire being to the Lord.

At scattered points embedded in conversations or growing out of specific incidents throughout the play are brief characterizations of Kṛṣṇa that likewise suggest his divinity. We have earlier noted that Kṛṣṇa's actions in the drama reveal neither omniscience nor omnipotence; he is, however, said by other characters to possess both these attributes. Madhumaṅgala calls him omniscient (*sarvajña*) when Kṛṣṇa completes the fool's disastrous verse, trying in vain to undo the damage caused by Madhumaṅgala's misguided admission that Kṛṣṇa has spent the night with Candrāvalī (IV.38.1), and Rādhā much later asserts that nothing is impossible for him when she implores him never to let her be separated from her lord.[57] His exceptional or transcendent nature is also indicated by the use of the adjective *lokottara*[58] to refer both to him (III.0.3) and to his beauty (VII.52.36, 56.36). Finally, there are certain notable passages, such as VII.44, in which a divine quality is predicated of him as part of a deliberate paradox: in that delightful verse Vṛndā marvels at the fact that the "invincible" (*ajita*) Kṛṣṇa has been conquered by Rādhā.

A second, somewhat less striking example of the deliberate use of paradox introduces another intriguing aspect of the question of Kṛṣṇa's divinity. When he has brought Candrāvalī to Kṛṣṇa, Madhumaṅgala comments that even though Kṛṣṇa is *anantaguṇaśālin*, "possessed of an infinite number of excellent qualities," he has not been able to untie the knot of Candrāvalī's *māna*.[59] What are meant here by Kṛṣṇa's *guṇa*s? Although they are spoken of as infinite (*ananta*), it seems clear from other contexts that Rūpa does not have in mind, at least primarily, abstract qualities such as omnipotence. In the *prastāvanā*, Rūpa, speaking as the *sūtradhāra*, refers to his play as *hariguṇamayī kṛti*, "a composition made of the *guṇa*s of Hari" (I.6). As we have seen, the *Vidagdhamādhava* is filled with descriptions and portrayals of Kṛṣṇa's radiant beauty and graceful gestures. Two verses describing Kṛṣṇa's despondency at Rādhā's *māna* give us further clues regarding the nature of his qualities: in conjunction with the specific statement that Kṛṣṇa is bereft of his host of *guṇa*s in his confusion,[60] the first enumerates several characteristic poses and activities that are abjured by the pining hero, and a subsequent verse (V.14) adds two more. The list includes holding his shepherd's staff and his horn, allowing his mother or his friends to adorn his body with mineral colors, playing on a leaf, engaging in merry talk (*narmagoṣṭhī*) with his comrades, and making a crest of *campaka* blossoms. His *guṇa*s must therefore be such qualities as elegance, wit, charm, and grace, which would be manifest in these carefree activities.[61]

Of particular religious significance are the many passages in the drama that explicitly refer to Kṛṣṇa as an object of meditation or devotion. A good example is the following verse, spoken by Paurṇamāsī to illustrate the incomprehensibility of Rādhā's love (II.17):

> Seeking to meditate for a moment upon Kṛṣṇa,
> The sage wrests his mind from the objects of sense;
> This child draws her mind away from Him
> To fix it on mere worldly things.
> The *yogī* yearns for a tiny flash of Kṛṣṇa in his heart;
> Look--this foolish girl strives to banish Him from hers!

Sages are again described as intent upon Kṛṣṇa in a punning verse that likens the Yamunā River to an assembly of ascetics (V.40); this time, however, their relation to him is characterized not simply as one of meditation, but rather as one of love (*kṛṣṇaruci*). Even the gods are Kṛṣṇa *bhakta*s: a charming verse in Act III represents Siva and the other deities as performing penance (*tapas*) in order to obtain a brief glimpse of Kṛṣṇa (III.17); and the devotion of Brahmā, Śiva, and Indra is even more dramatically demonstrated in Act I by their ecstasy as they come to listen to his marvelous flute playing.[62] Although these verses have a playful quality, such subordination of other gods to Kṛṣṇa is an unmistakable indication of his *aiśvarya*.

Similarly exemplifying an ideal of devotion to Kṛṣṇa are the verses expressing envy of such objects as his flute (IV.7) and his garland (LM II.21), which enjoy his constant and intimate company. With these verses may be classed another, VII.30, which exclaims at the good fortune of the *kadamba* tree that is privileged to serve Kṛṣṇa continually by offering its blossoms for his garlands. This verse suggests the ritual offering of flowers to the deity in *pūjā*, and the link with devotional practice is strengthened by Rūpa's choice of words in two other passages that mention flowers or garlands. Early in Act VI, Padmā, telling Lalitā of her presentation to Kṛṣṇa of a crest of flowers that she has made, uses a form of the word *upahāra*, which connotes an offering to a deity (VI.1.29). In the second act, Viśākhā rejoices when Kṛṣṇa--as if by mistake--takes off his *raṅgaṇa* garland and gives it to her, and she subsequently uses it to revive the unconscious Rādhā, referring to it as *nirmālya*, "the remains of an offering to the deity" (II.42). Together with the precious garland, which she likens to an enchanting potion, she extols in a verse the magical efficacy of Kṛṣṇa's unguents and his name (II.42), which are likewise important components of Vaiṣṇava ritual. In the next chapter we shall see how Rādhā exemplifies devotion in her response to another of these ritual elements, Kṛṣṇa's name.

Like his flute and his garland, the *gopī*s (III.28) and Kṛṣṇa's intimate companion Madhumaṅgala (I.14.23-24) are said to be blessed (*dhanya*, *anugṛhīta*) because they have the privilege of accompanying him and bringing him joy (*ānanda*). The *gopī*s often express their wonder at this privilege, and Rādhā, overcome with astonishment (*camatkṛti*), faints when Kṛṣṇa is brought to her for the first time (III.27.3). The sense of blessedness and wonder at being in Kṛṣṇa's presence accords with more conventional conceptions of divinity, but the notion that mere mortals (here, the *gopī*s) are able to give pleasure to the Lord is a characteristic Vaiṣṇava reversal of a more orthodox understanding of the nature of the Divine.

We have had a number of occasions to observe the powerful effect exerted by Kṛṣṇa, and by anything associated with him or reminiscent of him, upon the inhabitants of Gokula, especially the *gopī*s. Certain ways in which he affects the entire cowherd village are specified at various points in the drama: Viśākhā in Act III comforts the apprehensive Rādhā with the assurance that Kṛṣṇa gives security to the whole of Gokula (III.41.9-10), and Candrāvalī, referring to Kṛṣṇa as *gokulajanajīvanabhūta*, "the life of the people of Gokula," speaks a bit jealously of his habit of bringing happiness to all (IV.12.1-2). A number of other passages extend such generalizations still further, asserting that the enchantment of his flute (V.26) and the delight that his presence brings (V.36; VI.28) are felt not merely in Gokula, but throughout the entire world. In a verse reminiscent of descriptions of Viṣṇu's *avatāra*s and of Mahāyāna portrayals of the Buddha, Kṛṣṇa compares himself to a dark raincloud filled with sweet new *rasa* that removes the earth's suffering,[63] and Rādhā, conceiving his influence as broader still, refers to him as *trailokyamohana*, "the enchanter of the three worlds."[64] Such cosmic interpretations of Kṛṣṇa's power and purpose are unmistakable allusions to his divinity.

Still more explicit are certain passages that read remarkably like extracts from theological treatises. Some of these, occurring in explanatory scenes, are rather lengthy, and will be discussed elsewhere. Others, however, constitute brief philosophical reflections imbedded in fairly typical, even teasing exchanges. Perhaps the most remarkable of these, in part because of its emotional setting, is found early in Act II, when Lalitā and Viśākhā are exploring the nature of Rādhā's feelings. In response to her anguished admission that she is in love with three men, her friends ask rhetorically how the women of Gokula could love anyone but Kṛṣṇa, and proceed to make a statement strongly reminiscent of a well-known Upaniṣadic utterance: "this great *nāgara* Kṛṣṇa is only one."[65] A comparable reflection, indicative not of Kṛṣṇa's uniqueness but of his transcendence of human knowledge, appears in the form of a seemingly lighthearted question. Near the end of Act VI, when Kṛṣṇa has just hidden at the approach of Rādhā's friends after he and Rādhā have been united, Lalitā sees Rādhā and asks where "that *nāgara*" is. Smiling, Rādhā deftly parries her friend's question with another: "Who truly knows him?" (VI.33.5). This brief exchange occurs again, virtually verbatim, in the final act, but this time it is Rādhā who inquires where Kṛṣṇa is, and Kṛṣṇa himself (disguised as the Goddess) who answers.[66]

A final type of passage that points to Kṛṣṇa's transcendence is one in which he is specifically identified with Viṣṇu. In Act III, pretending to dissuade Rādhā from longing to meet Kṛṣṇa, Paurṇamāsī draws a sharp contrast between "the granddaughter of the old woman" (i.e., Rādhā), and "the one whose feet are stroked by Lakṣmī"[67] (i.e., Kṛṣṇa, conceived as identical with Viṣṇu). In the final act, Kṛṣṇa, punning on the name of Padmā,[68] with whom he is speaking, refers to himself as Padmanābha, "the one with a lotus in his navel,"[69] thus clearly demonstrating his consciousness of his identity with Viṣṇu, and in an earlier punning verse he employs another epithet of Viṣṇu, calling himself *dharaṇīdhara*, "the one who bears the earth."[70]

The preceding paragraphs contain a spectrum of references to Kṛṣṇa's divine stature and cosmic significance that range from the barest of hints, represented by certain epithets, to rather explicit theological statements. In spite of their number, however, it is clear from their form and their context that they are not intended to demonstrate Kṛṣṇa's divinity to the spectator or reader. In the first place, many of the epithets discussed above could be designations of a great human hero;[71] they are hardly sufficient to establish Kṛṣṇa's divinity for persons unaware of this fundamental fact. Furthermore, an audience of *bhakta*s, for whom Kṛṣṇa's lordship is a basic assumption, would surely need no such demonstration. The exclusively devotional context described in the *prastāvanā*[72] indicates that Rūpa did not expect anyone wholly ignorant of Kṛṣṇa's nature to read the *Vidagdhamādhava* or to see it enacted. Finally, certain passages in the drama are unintelligible without a knowledge of Kṛṣṇa's divinity and of his identity with Viṣṇu.[73] It is therefore evident that Rūpa presupposes such an understanding of Kṛṣṇa's nature on the part of the reader or spectator.

If their purpose is not to provide the audience or reader with new information, what is the primary role of these references in the drama? I have earlier suggested that the name "Hari" may remind the audience of Kṛṣṇa's divinity, but even this interpretation is in need of qualification. Ardent devotees of Kṛṣṇa would not be likely to forget his transcendent nature, even during a drama that depicts his human *līlā*; they would thus not need a reminder, in the usual sense, any more than they would need to be informed of Kṛṣṇa's divinity in the first place. It is, on the contrary, the fact of his devotees' awareness of his divine nature that lends such references their power. What epithets like *puruṣottama* and references to Kṛṣṇa's cosmic reality do is sharpen and play upon this awareness, bringing Kṛṣṇa's divinity repeatedly and prominently into focus for the spectator or reader. The resulting juxtapositions of Krsna's *aiśvarya* with his *mādhurya*, of his transcendence with his endearing "sweetness," form a series of epiphanies[74] that repeatedly affirm the coexistence of two levels of reality in the figure of Kṛṣṇa.

CHAPTER VI

RĀDHĀ: EMBODIMENT OF SUPREME LOVE

An interpretation of the nature and devotional significance of Rādhā in the *Vidagdhamādhava* involves attention to several interrelated issues. How important is she in the drama, and in what ways? To what extent does she serve as an ideal of loving devotion to Kṛṣṇa, and to what extent is she, like Kṛṣṇa, an object of such devotion? Finally, is she portrayed merely as an extraordinary human heroine, or does she, too, partake of divinity?

From the two opening benedictory verses and the prose that follows, one might well conclude that Kṛṣṇa stands alone as the central figure of the *Vidagdhamādhava*. It is *his līlā* that is spoken of as a cool drink, to which Rādhā's love, like that of the other *gopī*s, is said merely to impart a certain flavor.[1] It is Kṛṣṇa, too, who is said to have become incarnate as Caitanya, and it is his devotees' great love for Kṛṣṇa that draws them to Vṛndāvana. Yet a careful reading of the drama yields a rather different impression: the parallels between Rādhā and Kṛṣṇa are in some ways extremely close, and Rādhā, especially because of her unique love, seems fully as significant for devotion as Kṛṣṇa himself.

Rādhā's Beauty

Although there are numerous references to Rādhā's loveliness in the *Vidagdhamādhava*, we find fewer details of her appearance than we do of Kṛṣṇa's. Her clothes and ornaments are scarcely mentioned,[2] and the rapturous descriptions of her by the love-sick Kṛṣṇa are cast almost exclusively in the conventional imagery of classical Sanskrit poetry. Like Kṛṣṇa, she is termed radiant,[3] and her face, like his, is repeatedly compared to the moon (often to the moon's decided disadvantage).[4] In Rādhā's case, however, her luster is not part of a paradox, for unlike the dark Kṛṣṇa, she is fair. In addition to her golden complexion, likened by turns to lightning (II.24; IV.22), to gold (VI.26), and to the yellow *campaka* flower (II.2), it is her graceful gestures,[5] especially the bewitching movements of her eyes and brows, that most frequently elicit Kṛṣṇa's adulation. A charming expression of his response is the shy yet unmistakably enthusiastic observation confided by Kṛṣṇa to Madhumaṅgala after he sees her for the first time: "She was, it seemed, instructing the does themselves in sidelong glances" (II.29).

So remarkable is Rādhā's beauty that Paurṇamāsī credits it for Kaṁsa's knowledge of her (I.12.6) and Kṛṣṇa refers to it as uncommon (*asādhāraṇī*) even among the host of lovely *gopī*s (II. 30.3). Yet in spite of its obvious importance, Rādhā's physical loveliness is less significant for devotion than certain of her other characteristics. The very passages to which I have just referred furnish evidence in support of his contention. In Paurṇamāsī's verse expanding upon her assertion that it is Rādhā's great beauty (*saundaryavṛnda*) that has brought her to Kaṁsa's attention, she employs a more inclusive phrase, *lokottarā guṇaśrī*, "the extraordinary wealth of her good qualities" (I.13). Responding to an objection by Madhumaṅgala, Kṛṣṇa, too, qualifies his previous statement that his greater love for Rādhā is due to her sweet beauty (*mādhurī*).[6] When Madhumaṅgala surmises that Kṛṣṇa loved her even before he saw her, and infers that his fascination with her cannot be simply the result of her beauty, Kṛṣṇa agrees, concluding that it must be her "extraordinary greatness" (*mahimonnāha*)[7] that has brought about his intense preoccupation. In the remainder of the drama, it becomes evident that an essential constituent of his "greatness"--indeed, from the standpoint of devotion, its most important component--is her supreme love.[8]

Rādhā's Love and Its Religious Modes of Expression

That Rādhā's passion for Kṛṣṇa is no ordinary love is made explicit at a number of points throughout the drama.[9] Even in its earliest phases, it is remarkably intense:[10] so obsessed does she become with him after merely seeing his picture that Mukharā, upon hearing her words to an imaginary Kṛṣṇa, deems her "mad."[11] It is in part because of the intensity of her emotion that Rādhā, like those who observe her, describes her state as fundamentally incomprehensible.[12] Equally remarkable is the steadfast quality of her love: unlike the fickle Kṛṣṇa, Rādhā is utterly single-minded in her devotion to him. Even when his unfaithfulness becomes obvious, she continues to love him; the anguish of her *māna* only underscores the strength of her passion.

Seeking the cause of the exceptional love for Kṛṣṇa of Rādhā and her close friends, as well as that of Candrāvalī and her companions, Nāndīmukhī hypothesizes that it results from their worship of Sūrya and Caṇḍī. Paurṇamāsī hastens to set her straight on that point: their worship of the deities is only a ruse making it possible for them to go to the woods to meet Kṛṣṇa; on the contrary, is *sahaja*, "natural."[13] It is this spontaneous quality of Rādhā's love, evident throughout the drama, that sets it apart, for example, from that of the meditating hermits and *yogī*s described in II.17:[14] these have to strive to attain even for a moment the one-pointed concentration that simply comes naturally to Rādhā.

Although manifestly unselfconscious, Rādhā's love often expresses itself in religious modes that bear considerable significance for devotion. We have just noted Paurṇamāsī's verse contrasting Rādhā's total preoccupation with Kṛṣṇa with the transitory state attained by the arduous efforts of hermits and *yogī*s. The obverse of Rādhā's single-minded concentration is her utter obliviousness to the world: Lalitā notes with astonishment this sublime condition as she accompanies to a tryst the distracted Rādhā, who has put all her ornaments on wrong.[15] The image of a *yoginī* is similarly evoked by the tender scene toward the end of the second act in which Rādhā's intense desire to see Kṛṣṇa culminates in a supreme effort to make him appear before her eyes by meditating (*praṇidhāna*).[16]

Further indications of the intensity of Rādhā's devotion to Kṛṣṇa are the numerous passages in which she expresses her inability to live without meeting him (e.g., III.12). At the end of Act II, as she contemplates suicide because of Kṛṣṇa's rejection of her, she asks Viśākhā to allow her body to remain in Vṛndāvana with her vine-like arm on the trunk of the *tamāla* tree.[17] Early in the next act, in response to Paurṇamāsī's discouraging words, she expresses a similar aspiration: that she might die and be reborn as a bee on Kṛṣṇa's forest garland, wholly intent upon his redolent face.[18] Classical Sanskrit dramas abound in examples of pining heroines who express the desire to take their own lives; here, however, the motif gains new significance, for Rādhā's utterances are indicative of a profound religious devotion that extends beyond death.

Still more obviously significant for devotion are the passages that depict Rādhā's response to the name "Kṛṣṇa." Even before her first meeting with him, she shows unmistakable emotion whenever her friends mention him by name, as they do deliberately. It is in this connection that Rūpa indicates most clearly the intimate relation between Rādhā's emotion and the experience of ardent Vaiṣṇava devotees. When Nāndīmukhī describes Rādhā's *pūrvarāga* by enumerating the effects of Kṛṣṇa's name on her (I.14.30-31), Paurṇamāsī deems Rādhā's response fitting, and eloquently expresses her own feelings in the following oft-quoted verse (I.15):

> Dancing on the tip of your tongue,
>   they make you long for myriads of mouths,
> Alighting in the hollow of your ear,
>   they make you wish for ears in plenitude,
> And when they reach the doorway to your heart,
>   they still the turbulence of all the senses:
> "Kṛ-ṣṇa"--just two syllables--
>   yet how much nectar do they not contain?

By means of Paurṇamāsī's endorsement, Rādhā's response is explicitly established as an ideal for Vaiṣṇava devotion. That Rādhā also takes a more active role in relation to this name of her beloved is indicated by a punning verse in which Viśākhā describes her as constantly uttering the name "Kṛṣṇa" (II.38). Rūpa thus links Rādhā with Kṛṣṇa *bhakta*s, not only on the level of emotion, but in the realm of ritual as well, for the repeated utterance or singing of Kṛṣṇa's name has been a central element in Vaiṣṇava practice, both individual and communal, at least since the time of Caitanya.[19]

Rādhā as Object of Devotion

Kṛṣṇa's Devotion

The foregoing illustrations of Rādhā's devotion to Kṛṣṇa, in which Rādhā is clearly portrayed as the ideal *bhakta*, represent only part of the picture. In the first place, for virtually every instance that I have cited, one can find a parallel passage attesting to Kṛṣṇa's fervent devotion to her. We have observed above that Rādhā's single-minded concentration on Kṛṣṇa is expressed in terms drawn from descriptions of yogic practice; Kṛṣṇa, too, is on more than one occasion compared to a *yogī*, for he thinks incessantly upon Rādhā, losing sleep and renouncing all other enjoyments so long as he is deprived of her company.[20] Similarly, corresponding to Rādhā's reiterated expression of her utter inability to live without Kṛṣṇa is a passage in which Kṛṣṇa likewise acknowledges that he cannot live even for an instant without Rādhā (III.22), and just as Viśākhā, addressing her, refers to Kṛṣṇa as "the lord of your life" (*te jīvitapati*),[21] so Kṛṣṇa calls Rādhā a life-giving herb,[22] later confessing to her, "You are my life, O Rādhā!"[23] Such parallel expressions of emotion clearly have profound metaphysical implications, to which we shall shortly return.

The intense preoccupation of Rādhā and Kṛṣṇa with one another is indicated by another set of parallel passages with similar metaphysical overtones. So obsessed with Kṛṣṇa does Rādhā become that she sees him everywhere; when she mistakes a black *tamāla* tree for her dark lover, Viśākhā asks her how it is that the three worlds have become Kṛṣṇa for her.[24] Kṛṣṇa poses the corresponding question for himself as he eagerly awaits Rādhā at their point of rendezvous: "Rādhā appears before me on every side; how is it that for me the three worlds have become Rādhā?" (V.18). Rūpa seems to have been especially taken with this mode of indicating Kṛṣṇa's infatuation, for on two additional occasions he has other characters make virtually the same observation about Kṛṣṇa's "delusion" (III.18; VI.23. 20-21). Moreover, it is not only Rādhā in her obsession with Kṛṣṇa who is explicitly termed "mad," but also Kṛṣṇa in his unbridled passion for her. At one point, as Kṛṣṇa is rushing headlong to meet her, Madhumaṅgala, steadying him, asserts that he has been "driven mad (*unmādita*) by an evil spell [uttered] by the wicked *gopīs*" (VI.14.3-4).

Just as Rādhā's devotion to Kṛṣṇa at times assumes worshipful forms,[25] so certain of Kṛṣṇa's words and actions are clearly intended to suggest modes of adoration. In their first full meeting, Kṛṣṇa expresses the desire to be in the nectar of Rādhā's favor (III.43.3), using there the word *prasāda*, "grace," which has strong religious connotations. Lalitā's reply, that he may obtain her favor by serving her (*sevā*), is likewise significant, for *sevā* is the usual Vaiṣṇava term for service to the Lord. Kṛṣṇa is more than willing; his verse in response enumerates the ways in which he proposes to adorn and minister to her (III.44). In the same scene, he voices his desire to serve her as a garland of cooling blue water-lilies (III.41), and subsequently, in a verse closely parallel to those of Candrāvalī and Vṛndā about his flute and the *kadamba* tree, he expresses his envy of the *raṅgaṇa* garland that has the good fortune to reside next to her bosom (III.46). Later in the play, when he tries to appease Rādhā after spending the night with Candrāvalī, he indicates his penitence by making obeisance again and again, his peacock-feather crest touching the dust.[26] Still later, seeing his own worshipful gestures in the world of nature, he describes to Rādhā an expanse of lotuses rippled by the breeze as "doing *ārati* to your smiling face" (V.41).

Even in the case of the most explicitly worshipful element in Rādhā's relation to Kṛṣṇa, her response to his name, there are remarkably close parallels. In Act VI, when Madhumaṅgala promises to bring the hiding Rādhā to Kṛṣṇa, and gives him instead a leaf inscribed with the two syllables of her name, Kṛṣṇa expresses his utter delight at this gift, in a verse (VI.24) that is strongly reminiscent of Paurṇamāsī's rapturous words about *his* name. Moreover, shortly after her verse exclaiming over Kṛṣṇa's name, Paurṇamāsī speaks of Rādhā's with no less enthusiasm as she proposes to entice Kṛṣṇa with its auspicious syllables (I.16.6-7). In the light of Paurṇamāsī's devotion to Rādhā, made explicit, as we shall see below, at numerous points in the drama, this passage may reasonably be construed as signifying that Rādhā's name is sweet not only to

Kṛṣṇa, but also to Paurṇamāsī, and thus to Vaiṣṇava devotees as well.

Devotion Expressed by Others

The view of Rādhā as figuring in the drama solely or even primarily as the ideal embodiment of devotion to Kṛṣṇa is further challenged by a second body of evidence: the attitudes expressed by such secondary characters as Paurṇamāsī and Vṛndā, whose responses to Rādhā as well as to Kṛṣṇa show strong devotional elements. In the introductory scene in Act I, Nāndīmukhī expresses envy of Paurṇamāsī's grandson Madhumaṅgala, who is privileged to enjoy Kṛṣṇa's constant company. Paurṇamāsī's reply indicates that Nāndīmukhī's task, to increase Rādhā's passion for Kṛṣṇa, is no less a privilege, for Rādhā, Paurṇamāsī confesses, means everything to her (I.14.25). In a later conversation with Madhumaṅgala and Vṛndā, Paurṇamāsī reaffirms her deep love for Rādhā, comparing her feeling in its spontaneity and lack of motive with Rādhā's love for Kṛṣṇa (V.2.10-4.4). The devotional significance of Rādhā for Paurṇamāsī, and by extension for the devotee who sees or reads this drama, is likewise evident from Paurṇamāsī's words of gratitude to Kṛṣṇa at the end of the final act. When Abhimanyu is persuaded not to take Rādhā to Mathurā, Paurṇamāsī exclaims with considerable relief that she has been spared the pain of separation from Rādhā (*rādhikāviśleṣavedanā*, VII.59.3). Her expression and the threatened separation that it reflects constitute a reversal of the situation of the *gopī*s depicted in the *Bhāgavata Purāṇa* and the *Lalitamādhava*, in which it is Kṛṣṇa who is taken to Mathurā and the *gopī*s who experience the anguish of separation.

Paurṇamāsī is not the only secondary character in the drama who expresses emotions toward Rādhā that are usually directed toward Kṛṣṇa. The beautiful verse uttered by Vṛndā in the final act (VII.44), in which she juxtaposes Rādhā's youth with her maturity in love, represents *vātsalya* toward Rādhā that is closely parallel to Yaśodā's maternal affection for Kṛṣṇa.[27] Nāndīmukhī, too, comments tenderly on Rādhā's extreme youth, expressing wonder at Kṛṣṇa's great enchanting power (*mohanatva*), which has affected even this innocent child

(II.13, 11). Speaking more generally, Madhumaṅgala refers to the love (*sneha*) that all the older women hold for Rādhā (V.23.8-9), and Jaṭilā's use of the still more inclusive epithet *gokulanandinī*, "delight of Gokula" (VII.57.4), indicates that Rādhā, like Kṛṣṇa, enjoys the affection of the entire village.

Human Emotions and Hints at Divinity

A third consideration arguing against an interpretation of Rādhā as simply a model of *bhakti* is the fact that certain ways in which she is depicted by Rūpa mark her as no ordinary mortal. Like Kṛṣṇa, she embodies elements of divinity as well as qualities that are distinctly human. Her human attributes provide points of accessibility for Vaiṣṇava devotees; references to her cosmic stature, on the other hand, place a measure of distance between her and mere human *bhakta*s. We shall examine each of these categories in turn, and then explore the significance of their coexistence in Rādhā.

In certain respects, Rādhā is even more appealingly human than Kṛṣṇa. She is hesitant at first in expressing her love for him even to her two close friends, and in spite of her eagerness to meet him, she is shy in her early encounters with him.[28] She expresses the characteristically human apprehension that she will be found unworthy of his affection,[29] and she is initially horrified at the audacity of Lalitā's suggestion that she play a joke on him (III.34.7-10). Although she later displays more confidence in her own worth and corresponding boldness in her meetings with Kṛṣṇa, her development in these directions is not wholly consistent, and elements of diffidence persist throughout the drama.

Rādhā is hardly ever certain of anything except her love for Kṛṣṇa; indeed, she is often represented as torn between two conflicting emotions. One such conflict, explored by Rūpa in some detail, is the tension between her growing passion for Kṛṣṇa and her *dharma* as a married woman (I.34; III.18). Another is the anguish of *māna*, in which she is torn between jealous anger and intense desire for reconciliation.[30] Kṛṣṇa's verses musing over her expressions and gestures in such states of inner conflict or distress are among the most poignantly charming in the entire drama. A single illustration--Kṛṣṇa's concluding reflection in the fourth act, after Rādhā and her two friends have been taken away by Mukharā--may serve to convey something of their flavor.

Now assuming a steadfast pose,
  now showing signs of wavering,
One moment uttering scornful sounds,
  the next, words of eagerness,
Now with a look of innocence,
  now with glance bewitching,
Rādhikā is split in two,
  swayed now by anger, now by love.[31]

Rādhā's cosmic significance is suggested largely through brief hints similar to those applying to Kṛṣṇa but occurring less frequently. She is, for example, on more than one occasion addressed by the term *devī*, "goddess."[32] Like *deva*, its masculine counterpart, this term may simply be one of respectful address; in courtly contexts it is applied to a queen or a high-ranking lady. Its use here of a cowherdess,[33] however, is striking, especially in the phrase *pītā pracaṇḍadevī*, "fierce golden goddess," by which Kṛṣṇa addresses Rādhā when he accuses her of stealing his flute (IV.49.11). Likewise occurring in compound as part of a longer phrase is the term *devatā*, which is more commonly used of Kṛṣṇa. Early in the play, Kṛṣṇa refers to Rādhā as *kāntīnām kuladevatā*, "the tutelary deity of radiance" (II.44). In themselves such epithets are inconclusive; taken together with other similar expressions, however, they appear to point to Rādhā's transcendence.

In addition to such explicit epithets, certain adjectives or descriptions of Rādhā may be taken as pointing beyond mere human excellence. Kṛṣṇa calls her *jagadapūrvā*, "unprecedented in the world" (I.31.68), and her beauty, her love, and her *guṇa*s in general are termed *lokottara*, "extraordinary" or "transcendent" (I.13; III.21.19). Her greatness (*mahiman*; *māhātmya*)[34] is referred to at several points; her love in particular is designated great and said to be beyond comprehension.[35] Her cosmic significance is suggested even more strongly by certain passages in the *Lalitamādhava*, notably the benedictory verse of the play-within-a-play, in which her great beauty is said to conquer the three worlds (LM IV.12).

The fact that the word *rādhā* is also the name of a constellation makes it possible for Rūpa to pun on her name in a way that similarly hints at her cosmic stature. The significance of such punning is indicated most clearly in an intriguing parallel. We have already noted Paurṇamāsī's pretense at discouraging Rādhā from desiring Kṛṣṇa: Paurṇamāsī tells Rādhā that one whose feet are stroked by Lakṣmī, that is, Kṛṣṇa conceived as Viṣṇu, is as inaccessible to her as the moon in the sky (III.15). Earlier in the drama, Paurṇamāsī gives similar "advice" to Kṛṣṇa, asking him how a mere mortal could attain "this Rādhā, who roves through the sky" (I.31.58-59). The word that she uses for sky, however, *viṣṇupada*, would allow one to understand her as asking how a mere mortal could attain one who dwells near Viṣṇu's feet. Unlike Rādhā, therefore, who is deeply distressed at Paurṇamāsī's words, Kṛṣṇa is utterly nonchalant, for he perceives through their hidden meaning that Rādhā belongs to him alone. In spite of this difference, however, the uniqueness and relative inaccessibility of the object of love is brought out in both instances by Paurṇamāsī's teasing. In several other passages, Rūpa plays in a similar manner upon the double significance of Rādhā's name; such repetition seems designed to emphasize her transcendent nature (IV.11; V.29; VI.2.29-31).

The metaphysical implications of the devotional parallels that we have noted earlier should by now have become clear. Just as Rādhā's demented state, in which she sees Kṛṣṇa everywhere, perceiving nothing else in the three worlds, is a metaphysically accurate apprehension of reality--for Kṛṣṇa, the Lord, is the reality behind everything in the universe--so his parallel "delusion" may be taken as veridical if Rādhā is considered to be his *śakti*,[36] who, with him, pervades the whole world. The conviction of Rādhā and Kṛṣṇa that each is the life of the other may correspondingly be interpreted as hinting at their metaphysical equality as well as affirming their intimate interdependence. The most explicit indication of equality on one level is the third verse in Act VII, in which Rādhā and Kṛṣṇa are both said to have become incarnate in Mathurā. In the light of the parallels that we have just noted, this verse may be seen as an important corrective to the more exclusive emphasis on Kṛṣṇa represented by the benedictory verses and the opening comments of the *sūtradhāra* in the prologue to the drama.

The strands of evidence that we have just reviewed--the many close parallels between Kṛṣṇa and Rādhā that reveal his devotion to her, the tender affection and reverence for her especially on the part of the older women of the village, and the hints at her divinity--combine to support an interpretation of Rādhā as standing alongside Kṛṣṇa as an object of Vaiṣṇava devotion. Yet the parallels between Rādhā and Kṛṣṇa should not be overemphasized. Although the extraordinary qualities of Rādhā's love are repeatedly remarked upon, the fact of her exclusive love for Kṛṣṇa is generally seen as wholly understandable: early in the play Rādhā's two close friends ask rhetorically how the *gopīs* could love anyone else (II.9.1-2). Rādhā's great power over *him*, on the other hand, is a matter of continual amazement to the others. In addition to Vṛndā's astonished exclamation over the fact that Rādhā has "conquered the unconquerable" (VII.44), there is a closely related verse by Madhumaṅgala praising Rādhā for having gently captivated with her smiles "that willful, capricious elephant among the cowherds" (VI.21). Such verses clearly presuppose an assumption of Kṛṣṇa's superiority: the wonder that they express at Rādhā's feats results precisely from the fact that her victory is the reverse of what is expected. Similarly, when Kṛṣṇa in Act IV acknowledges to Rādhā that he is subservient to her, she retorts that he is independent, that is, subservient to no one (IV.40.1-2; cf. III III.42). The obvious fact of his submission to her in love, in defiance of his *aiśvarya*, is thus wondrous to his devotees precisely because it represents a reversal of what they perceive to be metaphysical reality.

The parallels between Rādhā and Kṛṣṇa are thus not precise in every respect, but they are nevertheless significant. Like Kṛṣṇa's endearing faults and subsequent regret, Rādhā's qualities of shyness and ambivalence contribute to a sense of intimacy with her on the part of her close friends and such characters as Paurṇamāsī, Nāndīmukhī, and Vṛndā. Her uniquely beautiful and extraordinarily intense love, on the other hand, makes her an object of wonder, not only to these women, and thereby to Vaiṣṇava devotees, but also to Kṛṣṇa himself. She thus exemplifies and inspires *bhakti* in others at the same time that she serves with Kṛṣṇa as an object of their loving devotion.

For those Vaiṣṇavas who follow Rūpa and Jīva in regarding Rādhā as the *hlādinī śakti*[37] of the Lord, the parallel between Rādhā and Kṛṣṇa has firm metaphysical grounding. It is these Vaiṣṇavas who would make the most of the hints at Rādhā's cosmic stature that I have discussed above. Just as Kṛṣṇa is represented as both a fallible human hero and the Lord of the universe, so for such devotees Rādhā is simultaneously model *bhakta* and supreme Goddess, earthly beloved and divine consort, shy young girl and eternal *śakti*. Unless they were *sahajiyās*,[38] such devotees would therefore consider it blasphemous to identify with Rādhā in her passion for Kṛṣṇa; although her great love[39] cannot but serve to inspire them, her emotion must surely remain, like Rādhā herself, a distant ideal.[40]

CHAPTER VII

OPPONENTS AND PARTISANS: THE PLAY'S SECONDARY CHARACTERS

A more comprehensive understanding of the place of the *Vidagdhamādhava* in Vaiṣṇava religious life emerges from a closer consideration of the drama's chief secondary characters. The devotional significance of these characters derives almost entirely from their relation to Rādhā and Kṛṣṇa and to the subtly diverse phases of their supreme love. For the most part, the secondary characters fall into two groups, those who facilitate the divine love affair directly, and those who function as temporary impediments to that affair, ultimately contributing nonetheless to its full realization. Among those in the first group, Paurṇamāsī stands out as the one most explicitly engaged in the task of uniting Rādhā and Kṛṣṇa. Aiding her in this endeavor is her granddaughter Nāndīmukhī, and relating to Rādhā and Kṛṣṇa in a comparably helpful fashion is the forest goddess Vṛndā. Although these three often appear separately and participate in somewhat different ways in the dramatic action, they have enough in common that it will be useful to consider them together.

Paurṇamāsī, Nāndīmukhī, and Vṛndā

As her name indicates, Paurṇamāsī is the personification of the full-moon night, a dramatic stimulant (*uddīpana vibhāva*)[1] commonly employed to enhance the *rasa* of erotic love. As an *uddīpana*, she may be compared to Kāmadeva, the intrepid bowman whose flower-arrows are capable of disturbing even Śiva, the greatest of *yogī*s, as he meditates on the slopes of the Himalayas. Paurṇamāsī, however, shares none of Kāmadeva's fiery impetuosity; in Rūpa's dramas she is a wise, gentle, kindly old woman with white hair whose noble work it is to bring about the union of Rādhā and Kṛṣṇa. Her character and its expression in her actions may be seen to represent the gentle yet ineluctable effect of the full moon upon lovers.

It is consonant with her identity as an *uddīpana vibhāva* that Paurṇamāsī functions simultaneously to increase the mutual love of Rādhā and Kṛṣṇa, thereby advancing the dramatic action, and to inspire and stimulate the audience in its realization of *madhura bhaktirasa*.[2] Her role in relation to the audience or reader is likewise dual: she serves as an ideal at the same time that she acts as a commentator. Her untiring efforts to unite Rādhā and Kṛṣṇa, together with her perpetual wonder at the beauty of their love, qualify her as the model *par excellence* of *bhakti* expressed in loving service. At the same time, through her interpretation of the actions and emotions of Rādhā and Kṛṣṇa, she furnishes an intermittent commentary, indicating the devotional meaning of individual episodes and of the drama as a whole.

Corresponding to Paurṇamāsī's role as commentator is that of her granddaughter and assistant, Nāndīmukhī, who serves, especially in the introductory scene, primarily as an interlocutor who elicits the explanations that Rūpa deems necessary background for the events in the story. Among the most important of these explanatory passages is a portion of the introductory scene in which Paurṇamāsī establishes a central theological principle. In reply to Nāndīmukhī's query about the recently celebrated marriage of Rādhā to Abhimanyu, Paurṇamāsī explains that Yogamāyā,[3] in order to deceive Kaṁsa, has created the illusion that Rādhā and the other *gopī*s are married to men of the cowherd village, whereas in reality all these women belong eternally to Kṛṣṇa alone (I.13.8-10). By means of the principle of *yogamāyā*, therefore, Rūpa is able to reconcile the diametrically opposed views of *svakīyā* and *parakīyā*:[4] metaphysically, Rādhā and the others are Kṛṣṇa's eternal consorts, but for the purposes of *līlā* they are married to other cowherds, and their husbands and other relatives serve as the obstacles necessary for suspenseful drama. Nāndīmukhī's innocent comment in Act II likewise functions as an inquiry, inspiring further reflection by Paurṇamāsī on the incomprehensibility of Rādhā's love (II.17.1-II.18).

Largely under the tutelage of Paurṇamāsī, Nāndīmukhī also participates in the dramatic action, encouraging Rādhā's close friends to increase Rādhā's love for Kṛṣṇa, and seeking out Rādhā to ascertain the outcome of their efforts. In her expressions of astonishment at the depth of Rādhā's love and its extreme manifestations, she serves with Paurṇamāsī as an intermediary between the two main characters and the audience or reader, exemplifying and thereby inspiring delight and wonder at their unfolding love. Such intermediaries are necessary not only because of the transcendent nature of both Rādhā and Kṛṣṇa, as we have noted above, but also because of the incomparability especially of Rādhā's love. Because the love of Rādhā for Kṛṣṇa is utterly unique, the deep affection of such figures as Paurṇamāsī and Nāndīmukhī for *both* Rādhā and Kṛṣṇa serves as a more accessible model for Vaiṣṇava emulation.

Like Paurṇamāsī and Nāndīmukhī, Vṛndā, the goddess of the woods that bear her name, shows tender affection for Rādhā; yet her primary relation, unlike theirs, seems to be to Kṛṣṇa. It is at his request that she causes spring flowers to appear at the end of summer, so that he may enjoy love with Rādhā in all its vernal splendor. Moreover, it is she who reports to Paurṇamāsī Kṛṣṇa's dejection at Rādhā's *māna*, and subsequently, when the arranged meeting with Rādhā falls through because of Abhimanyu's summons, it is Vṛndā's suggestion that she and Subala masquerade as Lalitā and Rādhā in order to keep Kṛṣṇa from becoming despondent (V.17.73-74). Her mode of loving service to Kṛṣṇa is indicated most clearly by her expression of grief in the third act of the *Lalitamādhava*, as she contemplates his being taken to Mathurā: "For whose sake shall I make new groves in the forest, prepare beds of flowers, or cause creepers to blossom out of season?"[5]

In addition to their roles as commentators, exemplars, and participants working to advance the cause of Rādhā and Kṛṣṇa, certain of the secondary characters, notably Paurṇamāsī and Rādhā's friends, further Rūpa's purpose in yet another way, by teasing one of the main characters, usually Rādhā, to induce her to manifest her emotion. In Act II, after Mukharā leaves and Paurṇamāsī and Nāndīmukhī reflect briefly upon Rādhā's paradoxical expressions of her new passion, Paurṇamāsī proposes to explore her emotional state (*bhāva*). Addressing Rādhā, she pretends to disapprove of her reckless love for Kṛṣṇa, which, she points out, defies *dharma* and threatens to destroy Rādhā's reputation (II.19). The intensity of Rādhā's feeling is clear from her response: although she has not yet met Kṛṣṇa, she denies her complicity by describing her futile attempts to ward off his supposed advances. In Act III, Paurṇamāsī's seemingly cruel pretense at dissuading Rādhā from hoping to meet Kṛṣṇa, undertaken explicitly to cause her to reveal her love, elicits an even more violent reaction: having expressed the desire to die in order to be with Kṛṣṇa, Rādhā loses consciousness, alarming Paurṇamāsī and Viśākhā (III.14-16.5). Embracing her tenderly, Paurṇamāsī reiterates for Rādhā's sake her purpose in causing her such distress: that her *bhāva* should be revealed. Such manifestation is important both within the world of the drama--for the other characters relish every nuance of Rādhā's emotion--and in relation to the audience or reader, who joins these characters in their wonder at Rādhā's great love. It is significant that none of the characters in the drama, including Rādhā, raises the slightest protest at such treatment of her, so clearly valuable to all, in Rūpa's view, is the expression of every aspect of her emotion.

Nevertheless, although the savoring of Rādhā's love for Kṛṣṇa is of special significance to Paurṇamāsī and other secondary characters in the drama, their longing is not simply for Kṛṣṇa, through Rādhā's emotion, nor solely for Rādhā, but for the privilege of witnessing the entire *līlā* of their mutual love. Paurṇamāsī's penultimate request to Kṛṣṇa at the conclusion of the drama, that he "ever enact with Rādhā the auspicious play of love's rapture deep in the groves of Vṛndāvana" (VII.61), is representative of the attitudes of all the secondary characters who cherish their divine love,[6] and it succinctly expresses the prayer of the devout Vaiṣṇava, which is also that of Rūpa himself.

Lalitā and Viśākhā

Like Paurṇamāsī, Rādhā's two intimate friends, Lalitā and Viśākhā, are utterly devoted to Rādhā, and throughout the drama they serve her in numerous ways. On the most obvious level, they function as messengers, bearing Rādhā's love letter to Kṛṣṇa and arranging for their trysts. Especially in the early acts, they stimulate Rādhā's growing passion for Kṛṣṇa by mentioning his name in her presence, bringing her to the groves of Vṛndāvana, where she hears the sound of his flute, and showing her a picture of him that Viśākhā has painted. Together with Paurṇamāsī, too, they serve to make Rādhā's love manifest, frequently urging her not to conceal her emotions from them (II.2; VI.10). In spite of her innate shyness even with these close friends, her conversations with them provide occasions for her to express her innermost feelings (e.g., at III.12). Testimony to their appreciation of anything that elicits an expression of Rādhā's emotion is Lalitā's statement in Act VI praising Kṛṣṇa's flute for causing Rādhā to reveal her "secret" (VI.9.3-4).

It is not only Rādhā's emotions that her *sakhīs* make manifest, but Kṛṣṇa's as well. The joke that Viśākhā plays on him in Act III, when she comes to bring him to a tryst with Rādhā, is an example: her false intimation that Rādhā has been taken to Mathurā induces Kṛṣṇa to express his total incapacity to live without Rādhā (III.22; cf. III.36). His distress at the thought of her absence is likewise evident from his frantic search and succession of mistakes in Act VI, when Rādhā hides from him and Lalitā tells him that she has gone home. After following a false signal from Lalitā and learning that he has been tricked, Kṛṣṇa refers to "the creeper of [Lalitā's] villainy" (VI.23.31).

On a more subtle level, Lalitā and Viśākhā embody opposite tendencies in Rādhā, thus portraying externally aspects of her inner struggle. In Rādhā's meeting with Kṛṣṇa in Act III, Lalitā represents Rādhā's devotion to *dharma*, requesting Kṛṣṇa to leave, whereas Viśākhā urges Rādhā to fulfill Kṛṣṇa's desire. In the following act, after the episode of Kṛṣṇa's unfaithfulness, Lalitā encourages Rādhā in her *māna*, urging her to be unyielding and to give up her love for this hard-hearted, fickle villain (IV.29; cf. V.7). Viśākhā, on the other hand, reminds Rādhā that a moment becomes an eternity without him, and asks her why she responds with such obstinacy to his entreaties (IV.45). In such moments of inner conflict, her two friends thus externalize Rādhā's opposing feelings, Lalitā almost invariably advocating boldness and opposition, especially in the form of *māna*, and Viśākhā generally counseling acceptance and reconciliation, in accordance with Rādhā's passionate yet restrained impulses.

Kṛṣṇa's Companions

Although Kṛṣṇa has other friends--for example, Śrīdāman, who appears briefly in the first act along with Kṛṣṇa's elder brother Balarāma--only two of his companions, Subala and Madhumaṅgala, figure at all prominently in the drama. Subala's importance is confined to the fourth and fifth acts; in Act IV he reminds Kṛṣṇa of Rādhā after Kṛṣṇa's disastrous slip of the tongue has alienated Candrāvalī, and on more than one occasion he acts as a messenger, helping to arrange meetings between the two lovers. His devotion to Kṛṣṇa is less marked than that of Radha's friends or Paurṇamāsī for her; its most obvious manifestation, in Act V, is his concern that Kṛṣṇa will be disconsolate because Rādhā is unable to meet him, and his consequent participation in Vṛndā's scheme to distract Kṛṣṇa by adopting a disguise. Although his friendship with Kṛṣṇa is less intimate than that of Lalitā and Viśākhā with Rādhā, he may be seen as exemplifying *sakhya bhāva*, one of the five chief modes of relating to Kṛṣṇa that are enumerated in Rūpa's theory.

The figure of Madhumaṅgala is considerably more complex. Like Lalitā and Viśākhā in relation to Rādhā, he serves as Kṛṣṇa's close companion and confidant, discerning at an early stage Kṛṣṇa's enchantment with Rādhā and eliciting expressions of his intense longing. Madhumaṅgala's humorous proclivities are manifest already in the first act, when he pretends to disclose to Yaśodā and Nanda Kṛṣṇa's secret dalliance with the *gopīs*, and throughout the drama he takes Kṛṣṇa's part in lighthearted, witty verbal contests with Rādhā and her two friends. A notable example of his humor that is of special significance for devotion is his description in Act VI of the "worship" (*upāsana*) that he and Kṛṣṇa do as they wait in the forest with unwavering concentration for the arrival of Rādhā (VI.20.53-55).

In his role as humorous companion to Kṛṣṇa, and especially in his untiring labors to advance Kṛṣṇa's love affairs, Madhumaṅgala manifests several characteristics of the *vidūṣaka* or buffoon, a stock figure in classical Sanskrit drama.[7] His simplicity, a typical feature of the *vidūṣaka*, first becomes evident in a harmless situation in Act I: seeing the gods, who come to Vṛndāvana in order to hear the sweet sounds of Kṛṣṇa's flute, he becomes alarmed, thinking them demons. Growing brave, he threatens them with his stick, only to pretend, in his embarrassment when Kṛṣṇa points out his mistake, that he was merely joking. Madhumaṅgala's lack of perspicacity, however, has more serious repercussions in Act IV: his mistaken though well-intentioned "assistance" in bringing Candrāvalī rather than Rādhā to Kṛṣṇa causes considerable awkwardness, and his acknowledgment later in the act that Kṛṣṇa spent the night with Candrāvalī, inspired by his misunderstanding of Rādhā's verse, brings on Rādhā's jealous anger (*māna*).

A second characteristic trait of the *vidūṣaka* evinced by Madhumaṅgala from the very first act is gluttony. In response to Kṛṣṇa's verse describing the beauty of Vṛndāvana as a delight to all the senses (I.31), Madhumaṅgala expresses the desire to return to Gokula, where they could enjoy the food prepared by Yaśodā. Here, however, the stereotype of the *vidūṣaka* is employed in a new way: Kṛṣṇa's response, that the fool should venerate Vṛndāvana, where even the old creepers can fulfill a person's every wish, hints at a spiritual desire that contrasts tellingly with Madhumaṅgala's physical greed. One is reminded of the intense yearning of the devotees described by the stage manager in the prologue, expressed in their eagerness to roll in the dust touched long before by the feet of Kṛṣṇa. Here as elsewhere in Rūpa's dramas, standard dramatic elements are given a new, devotional significance.

Two further ways in which Madhumaṅgala fits the type of the *vidūṣaka* may be briefly mentioned. First, he is a brahman, though apparently one neither ugly nor deformed, as the buffoon is supposed to be according to the classical treatises on dramaturgy.[8] Second, he is querulous and abusive, frequently provoking arguments with Lalitā and Viśākhā and even hurling insults with seeming impunity at Jaṭilā and Mukharā. Madhumaṅgala's flagrant disrespect for such embodiments of conventional morality as the elderly mother-in-law and grandmother of Rādhā does more than inject a note of humor: it underscores Kṛṣṇa's own disregard--manifest in his actions as well as his words--for earthly conventions and their jealous guardians.

As Kṛṣṇa's close companion and helper, ever ready to serve his beloved friend, Madhumaṅgala exemplifies both *sakhya* and *dāsya bhāva*s. In striking contrast to Rādhā, however, he never becomes an object of veneration for the other characters, in spite of his intimate relation to Kṛṣṇa. Although his good fortune to be in Kṛṣṇa's frequent presence occasions an expression of envy by Nāndīmukhī, this envy simply puts Madhumaṅgala in a category with such material objects as Kṛṣṇa's flute, which similarly arouses the *gopī*s' jealousy. In addition to his important role in the humor that is such a prominent feature of this drama, his chief devotional significance seems to be that of hearing, reporting, and even inducing Kṛṣṇa's ardent expressions of his love for Rādhā. The manifestation of Kṛṣṇa's intense emotion, as well as that of Rādhā, is clearly of paramount importance for nourishing the devotion of the *bhakta* who reads or sees this drama.

Candrāvalī

Chief among the impediments to the union of Rādhā and Kṛṣṇa are Rādhā's rival Candrāvalī and her two close friends, Padmā and Śaivyā. These three constitute the southern faction in Vraja, which vies constantly with Rādhā and her own two companions for Kṛṣṇa's attention. In addition to providing dramatic interest, this rivalry serves as the occasion for Rādhā's *māna* and her subsequent reconciliation with Kṛṣṇa, thereby facilitating the full development of her love through all the phases of union and separation enumerated in the textbooks on *śṛṅgāra* and poetics. Without this stage of jealous anger, Rādhā's love would not reach its full intensity.

Candrāvalī's involvement with Kṛṣṇa, which develops before Kṛṣṇa meets Rādhā, is alluded to by Paurṇamāsī and Nāndīmukhī in the drama's first act. Candrāvalī seems to be older than

Rādhā, and her relation to Kṛṣṇa's new beloved parallels that of the older queen to the beautiful young arrival in the classical *nāṭikā*.[9] In the *Lalitamādhava*, which is in certain respects modeled on the *nāṭikā*, Candrāvalī appears in Dvārakā as Rukmiṇī, who marries Kṛṣṇa first, before his marriage to Satyabhāmā-Rādhā.

Candrāvalī's importance in the *Vidagdhamādhava*, however, pales beside that of Rādhā. Indeed, her significance seems largely to be limited to a twofold relation to her more successful rival: she contributes, as we have seen, to the full realization of Rādhā's love, and her affair with Kṛṣṇa serves as a foil for that of Rādhā. Certain of her qualities contrast with Rādhā's, and in general she is presented as far less interesting. Her emotions toward Kṛṣṇa are portrayed but briefly, and whole phases in the development of her love, such as her *pūrvarāga*, are passed over with scarcely a word. Rādhā's *pūrvarāga*, by contrast, is tenderly and elaborately depicted.

In Rūpa's view, what is most distinctive in Candrāvalī's love for Kṛṣṇa is her respect (*ādara*).[10] Her deferential attitude is indicated by her use of the term *deva*, "lord," in speaking to him (IV.12.1); she is, however, also capable of addressing him sarcastically with one of his more common epithets, *gokulānanda*, "joy of Gokula" (IV.12.7), as well as with one of her own choosing, *dānaśauṇḍa*, "one who is intoxicated with giving," "man of great generosity" (IV.9.7). Moreover, her deference does not prevent her from calling him fickle. Yet in spite of being deeply hurt by Kṛṣṇa's neglect and more than a little jealous of Rādhā, she manifests her resentment verbally only through such sarcasm and mild reproach. Her show of politeness, beneath which she conceals her true feelings, finally becomes so intolerable to Kṛṣṇa that he expresses his preference for "the sweet wine of [her] angry words" over "this poison of respect."[11] Although she is capable of leaving Kṛṣṇa out of anger, she does so under a pretense, and her submissiveness is evident from the ease with which she is again reconciled with him. Padmā characterizes her well when she tells Madhumaṅgala, as they set out to find her and bring her to Kṛṣṇa, that Candrāvalī is always quick to get over her anger (IV.16.1-2).

It is in this dimension that the contrast between Candrāvalī and Rādhā is most marked. Unlike Candrāvalī, who is easily appeased, Rādhā persists in her *māna*. It is true that, left alone, she regrets not having accepted Kṛṣṇa's apology; moreover, so great is her fear of rejection that she believes a false message, which describes him as having found diversion elsewhere, and she is elated to learn that he has to the contrary been pining for her. Yet she is not immediately appeased when he subsequently entreats her in person; echoing Lalitā's words of censure, she tearfully accuses him of crookedness. Her willingness thus to express her emotions openly contrasts with Candrāvalī's ironic apology to Kṛṣṇa for the offense of speaking to him audaciously (*pragalbham*, IV.12.8). In the light of Candrāvalī's greater docility, we may discern a measure of truth in Lalitā's teasing verse in Act VII, in which she compares Kṛṣṇa to a male elephant, followed by Candrāvalī but pursuing Rādhā (VII.21). Kṛṣṇa himself underscores the contrast between them: when Candrāvalī is brought to him not long after her peevish departure, he says that she is attained quickly (*añjasā*, IV.19), whereas he describes Rādhā, as he awaits her, with the words *bhṛśam abhisarantī sarabhasam*, "coming with intensity and passion to the tryst" (V.19).

The foregoing incidents exemplify an important theoretical distinction elaborated by Rūpa in his *Ujjvalanīlamaṇi*. In the context of enumerating the increasingly intense stages in the development of the *sthāyibhāva* or permanent emotion of *madhura bhaktirasa*, Rūpa establishes certain categories in terms of which he contrasts Candrāvalī's love for Kṛṣṇa with that of Rādhā. After a general discussion of its basic form, which he terms *prema*, he classifies *sneha*, the second stage of this erotic emotion (*madhurā rati*), into two types, *ghṛtasneha* (love that is like clarified butter) and *madhusneha* (love that is like honey). *Ghṛtasneha* is *ātyantikādaramaya*, made of excessive respect (*ādara*); Rūpa explains that it is so named because it is not relishable alone, but only in combination with another emotion, as clarified butter is enjoyed only when it is mixed with other foods. Carrying the analogy further, he asserts that just as clarified butter hardens when it cools, so this type of *sneha* becomes solidified through mutual respect, which, according to Rūpa, is an extremely cool emotion.[12]

Madhusneha, by contrast, consists of an abundance of *madīyatva* (a sense of possessing the beloved). The commentators[13] explain that in this form of love the conception "he is mine" predominates, and from Rūpa's use of the term *madīyatva* here they infer that *ghṛtasneha* must be characterized by a predominance of *tadīyatva*, that is, by the contrary apprehension "I am his." *Madīyatva* clearly reveals a higher degree of confidence than *tadīyatva*, which expresses greater subservience. The name *madhu*, Rūpa explains, is given to this form of *sneha* because like honey it is in itself sweet, needing nothing else to make it so, and it unites many *rasas*, as honey unites the essences of various flowers.[14]

Corresponding to the distinction between *ghṛtasneha* and *madhusneha* are further differentiations in the three succeeding stages of the erotic emotion. In the last of these, *rāga*, the gradations are rather subtle; we shall here concern ourselves only with the distinctions that pertain directly to the contrast between Rādhā and Candrāvalī. *Māna*, defined by Rūpa as a state in which *sneha* takes on a new sweetness and shows a certain willfulness (*adākṣiṇya*),[15] may be either *udātta* (dignified) or *lalita* (playful). The *udātta* form of *māna*, a development of *ghṛtasneha*, is distinguished from *lalita māna* by its extreme courtesy; although it shows traces of stubbornness now and then, the full extent of its opposition remains hidden. This is the form of *māna* ascribed to Candrāvalī, and certain of its characteristics, notably politeness and the concealing of inward emotion, are also said by Rūpa to be manifest in the next two stages of her love, *praṇaya* and *rāga*. Rādhā's *māna*, by contrast, is marked by independence, humor, and "crookedness." Her bold and independent spirit is likewise evident in the quality of her *praṇaya*, and Rūpa's characterization of her *rāga*, to which he gives the name *māñjiṣṭha*, "bright red," hints at its greater degree of outward manifestation.[16]

From these theoretical distinctions we can discern certain of Rūpa's preferences. Although he holds both Rādhā and Candrāvalī in high esteem, classifying each of them as a *yūtheśvarī* (a "queen" presiding over a group of *gopīs*), he clearly values Rādhā's boldly expressive, willful mode of loving Kṛṣṇa above Candrāvalī's more reticent, docile manner. Indeed, he attributes this strong preference to Kṛṣṇa himself.[17] His partiality for Rādhā's more spontaneous love, with its relative lack of restraint and its sportive humor, is an extension of Rūpa's more general preference for *mādhurya* over *aiśvarya*, and for intimate relational modes in which the awareness of Kṛṣṇa's lordship is largely or wholly subordinate to that of his sweet charm.

As we have seen, the demeanor of Rādhā and Candrāvalī in the *Vidagdhamādhava* accords rather well with the differences between them that Rūpa details in his *Ujjvalanīlamaṇi*. Rūpa maintains further that there is a correspondence between the quality of Kṛṣṇa's love for each *gopī* and that of her love for him:[18] Kṛṣṇa is thus free to be more spontaneous and expressive with Rādhā, whereas he is constrained in his love for Candrāvalī by their deep mutual respect. Kṛṣṇa's actions in the *Vidagdhamādhava* are in conformity with this statement in Rūpa's theory: the stage directions specify that he should approach Candrāvalī with respect (*ādara*) (IV.7.2), and in his conversations with her he is considerably more subdued than when talking with Rādhā and her friends.

The question of the devotional significance of these distinctions, and of the figure of Candrāvalī, is a difficult but important one. How does Rūpa expect individual Vaiṣṇava devotees to relate to Candrāvalī and to her love for Kṛṣṇa? If, apart from her role as jealous rival, she serves chiefly as a foil for Rādhā, are they to view her love primarily as a negative example? Does it serve merely to highlight the uniqueness of Rādhā's love? Or may devotees of a certain temperament, to whom such respect is congenial, find in her mode of loving Kṛṣṇa a direct inspiration for their own devotion?

Arguing against the view of Candrāvalī's love as solely a negative example is the fact that Rūpa regards her as one of the foremost *gopīs*, and he considers the *gopīs* as a group to embody the highest form of love for Kṛṣṇa, contrasting them, for example, with Kṛṣṇa's queens in Dvārakā. Yet both in his dramas and in the *Ujjvalanīlamaṇi* he singles out Rādhā's love for special attention. Devotees are clearly meant to take inspiration from its marvelous qualities, to share the wonder of such characters as Paurṇamāsī and Nāndīmukhī at its depth and its unexpected reversals. Because the drama's characters do not express corresponding wonder at Candrāvalī's love, it seems clear that her love for Kṛṣṇa, however exalted, does not inspire comparable admiration. Unlike Rādhā, she has not become an object of Vaiṣṇava devotion. It is noteworthy that the eighteenth-century commentator Viśvanātha Cakravartī uses the honorific prefix *śrī* in referring to Rādhā, as he does for Kṛṣṇa, whereas he does not use it to refer to Candrāvalī.[19]

In spite of her inferiority to Rādhā and her rivalry with her, however, Candrāvalī is hardly a villain. Her earlier union with Kṛṣṇa is openly favored by Paurṇamāsī, who refers in the first act to her own wholly unnecessary efforts to bring it about (I.14.13-14). Kṛṣṇa himself refers to her noblemindedness (IV.12.17) and speaks with evident approval of her sincere devotion (VII.10.14). In addition to its more specific relation to Rādhā's love, Candrāvalī's involvement with Kṛṣṇa is the most dramatic representation of the fact of Kṛṣṇa's fickleness, which, to the devotee, is ultimately expressive of his universal love. It is noteworthy that Rādhā and Candrāvalī are depicted in the *Lalitamādhava* as affectionate sisters, whose rivalry vanishes as they console one another in their common bereavement at Kṛṣṇa's departure for Mathurā. Finally, although it would not be her primary role and although her importance in this respect would inevitably be vastly inferior to Rādhā's, Candrāvalī could also inspire Vaiṣṇava devotion directly, precisely by representing a more accessible ideal. Yet it is not evident that she has functioned in this way. She is nevertheless clearly a complex character having at least potential religious significance on a number of different levels.

Abhimanyu, Jaṭilā, and Mukharā

Less ambiguous than Candrāvalī in their role in the drama are Rādhā's husband Abhimanyu and his mother Jaṭilā. Abhimanyu, who is explicitly called wicked (*duṣṭa*, I.13.14), constitutes the greatest single obstacle to the love affair of Rādhā and Kṛṣṇa: the fact that he might at any moment decide to take his new bride to Mathurā, the city of King Kaṁsa, is revealed by the anxious Paurṇamāsī in Act I and reiterated periodically during the course of the play. However, although he represents a perpetual threat, Abhimanyu is a weak character who remains behind the scenes throughout most of the drama. His interests are guarded largely by his irascible mother, Jaṭilā.

Although Jaṭilā shares Paurṇamāsī's venerable age, she has none of the latter's dignity. Indeed, the two women are in certain respects polar opposites: the white-haired Paurṇamāsī represents the bright full-moon night, whereas Jaṭilā, grey with age, is compared to the clouds that obscure the moon (II.51.3; II.52). Correspondingly, at the same time that Paurṇamāsī endeavors to effect the union of Rādhā and Kṛṣṇa, Jaṭilā does everything in her power to obstruct that union. As Rādhā's mother-in-law, perpetually vigilant lest Rādhā fall prey to the wiles of the villainous Kṛṣṇa, Jaṭilā is the very embodiment of earthly *dharma*. Rādhā's fear of her is expressed at intervals throughout the drama, from her very first words in Act I to her concluding lines in Act VI, in which she voices her alarm at what she thinks is the arrival of "the fierce old woman" (*bhayaṅkarī vṛddhā*, VI.35.5-6).

Jaṭilā's concern for village standards of conduct is also manifest in her preoccupation with her daughter-in-law's performance of *pūjā* to Sūrya and Caṇḍī. At the same time that she embodies worldly morality, she thus represents the unenlightened worship of what to the Vaiṣṇavas are divinities of a distinctly lesser order. Her lack of perspicacity in relation to metaphysical truth has its parallel in the ease with which she is deceived by specious excuses and surface appearances. In addition to rendering her ineffectual, such lack of discernment makes her a laughing-stock when she takes it upon herself to enforce *dharma*. The episode in which she drags Subala and Vṛndā in their disguises before the women elders ends in her complete humiliation: the women burst into laughter as "Rādhā" turns out to be none other than Kṛṣṇa's friend Subala. It is the contrasts revealed in such episodes--between her assiduous efforts and their utter failure, and between her venerable position as the elderly mother-in-law of Rādhā and the low esteem in which she is held by young and old alike--that make her a comic figure in the drama. Madhumaṅgala is brazen enough to insult her to her face, calling her "hard as the bones of Dadhīci" (II.52.3), and even the elderly Mukharā refers to her as "crooked."[20]

Although Jaṭilā may hardly be said to represent a positive ideal for Vaiṣṇava emulation,[21] she is nevertheless vital to the drama. In addition to her important contribution to its humor, she is crucial to its suspense, and her precipitous appearances, whether actual or only feared, bring three of the play's seven acts to a close. An indication that she is regarded by Rūpa as an integral part of the *līlā* is provided by an intriguing verse in the *Lalitamādhava:* when Kṛṣṇa is taken off to Mathurā, Rādhā asks, among other things, what the elders will henceforth have to gossip about (III.33). Not only is Kṛṣṇa thus asserted to be necessary to them--his amorous exploits providing substance for one of their favorite pastimes--but the verse, by placing this gossip alongside such elements as the nectar of Kṛṣṇa's flute and his beguiling ways, seems to indicate that it is every bit as essential as these to the full panoply of Kṛṣṇa's *līlā* in Vṛndāvana.

A somewhat more sympathetic figure than Jaṭilā is Rādhā's grandmother Mukharā. When we encounter her for the first time, at the beginning of Act II, she is weeping because of Rādhā's unfortunate condition, which she takes to be a form of madness. Although she too appears at awkward moments, when Rādhā and Kṛṣṇa are talking with their friends, and even threatens at the end of Act IV to bring Rādhā before Kaṁsa, she is less vehemently opposed to Rādhā's union with Kṛṣṇa than Jaṭilā, and, half-blind with age, she is even more easily fooled. The scene toward the end of Act III in which Mukharā, having ordered Kṛṣṇa to leave, is credulous enough to believe Lalitā's allegation that the dark figure pulling Rādhā's sari is only the *tamāla* tree with its branches swaying in the breeze, is one of the most humorous in the entire drama.

In her reiterated concern for her young granddaughter, Mukharā, like Vṛndā, exemplifies *vātsalya bhāva* toward Rādhā.

Although she calls Kṛṣṇa a rascal and twice orders him to leave, the verse that she utters when she comes upon him as he is talking with Rādhā and their friends in Act IV reveals a degree of empathy for Radha's feelings that bespeaks her own experience of Kṛṣṇa's irresistible attraction (IV.47).

> He draws your heart from your home
>   and secures it in the forest,
> Obscuring even the memory
>   of strong bonds of family affection;
> He manifests countless traits
>   of all the meanest villains:
> Ah, my innocent child,
>   Even you have fallen into his clutches!

Her sympathy for Rādhā in her love for Kṛṣṇa is revealed even more clearly in the *Lalitamādhava*, in which she expresses the secret wish that Rādhā were married to Kṛṣṇa (LM II.25.24-25). In that drama, too, she is a more playful figure who chases after Kṛṣṇa and searches for him when he hides from her in the groves.

In the *Vidagdhamādhava*, Jaṭilā and Mukharā, together with Jaṭilā's son Abhimanyu, perform two interrelated functions. Most centrally, they introduce the essential element of conflict into the fundamentally idyllic world of Vraja. It is usually the elders who bring about the intermittent separation that is necessary to the full development of the love of Rādhā and Kṛṣṇa. Like Candrāvalī, their role is thus one of ultimately enhancing the very love to which they serve as temporary impediments. Secondly, their bungling attempts to keep Rādhā from Kṛṣṇa render them comic figures who contribute significantly to the drama's playful humor. The conflict that they create, important though it be, is therefore mitigated by their ineptness at enforcing the worldly *dharma* that they represent.

Yaśodā and Nanda

Although they appear but briefly and neither promote nor impede the love affair of Rādhā and Kṛṣṇa, Yaśodā and Nanda, Kṛṣṇa's foster parents, must be included in a discussion of devotionally significant persons in the drama. As we have already observed, they are not the only characters who express *vātsalya bhāva*, tender parental affection, toward Kṛṣṇa; yet the scene near the outset of the drama in which they appear with him constitutes the fullest portrayal of this mode of loving devotion. Yaśodā's first words express her motherly concern: she asks Kṛṣṇa why he stays away so long each day that the sweets she prepares with such great affection (*paramādara*) invariably get cold. Characteristically regarding her son as a mere child, Yaśodā replies to Nanda's query--whether there be a young girl suitable to be married to Kṛṣṇa--that her darling boy is barely weaned! Nanda, too, exemplifies *vātsalya bhāva* after describing the manifestations of Yaśodā's deep emotion as she gazes upon the lovely countenance of her son, Nanda embraces him and expresses his own incomparable delight at Kṛṣṇa's touch (I.19.2-I.22).

Unlike Jaṭilā and Mukharā, Kṛṣṇa's foster parents are never overtly ridiculed. Yet they do not escape altogether the disrespect shown toward these women: Yaśodā and Nanda too are made to appear somewhat foolish when barely veiled references to Kṛṣṇa's dalliance with the *gopīs* can be made in front of them without arousing their suspicion. They are obviously unaware of Kṛṣṇa's amorous sports, and by viewing Kṛṣṇa primarily in one mode they miss not only such delightful juxtapositions of *mādhurya* and *vātsalya* as the one represented by Madhumaṅgala's teasing verse, but also the entire drama of the love of Rādhā and Kṛṣṇa that is about to unfold. Many of the secondary characters, from Paurṇamāsī and Vṛndā to Rādhā's close friends and Madhumaṅgala, together with the entire audience and each of the drama's readers, are therefore privileged to relish central aspects of Kṛṣṇa's *līlā* that are as inaccessible to Kṛṣṇa's foster parents as they are to Abhimanyu and Jaṭilā.[22]

The scene in which Kṛṣṇa appears with Yasodā and Nanda, however, also has a more positive significance. In addition to portraying *vātsalya bhāva*, Kṛṣṇa's foster parents help to establish a mood of harmony and innocence that prevails throughout the drama. In the modern-day *līlā*s of Brindavan, such an atmosphere is created and maintained in part through the use of young boys in a number of the roles, especially those of Rādhā and Kṛṣṇa. It would seem wholly in keeping with the lighthearted spirit of the *Vidagdhamādhava* if children took the parts of all its youthful characters. The tender affection shown by Yaśodā and Nanda in the first act reminds the audience or reader of Kṛṣṇa's extreme youth, thereby helping to surround his dalliance with the *gopīs* with an aura of playful innocence.

We have seen that each of the drama's main secondary characters contributes directly or indirectly to the *līlā* of Rādhā and Kṛṣṇa. The recognition of Rādhā's dual status as supreme *bhakta* but at the same time eternal consort leads us to look elsewhere in the drama for the devotee's chief models. Candrāvalī would seem to represent a more accessible ideal, but she does not in fact appear to have served as a model for Vaiṣṇava emulation. It is rather the champions of the love of Rādhā and Kṛṣṇa, notably Paurṇamāsī, Nāndīmukhī, and Vṛndā, who are the clearest exemplars of Vaiṣṇava *bhakti*. Their delight and wonder at the sublime love of Rādhā and Kṛṣṇa, together with their devoted service, may inspire comparable emotions in Vaiṣṇavas who read or see this drama. The example of these secondary characters thus reinforces the hints at Rādhā's own divinity in directing the devotee's attention not simply to Kṛṣṇa, but to the entire *līlā* of the mutual passion of the eternal pair.

CHAPTER VIII

STRUCTURE AND SIGNIFICANCE: THE *VIDAGDHAMĀDHAVA* AND ITS MAJOR ANTECEDENTS

Our discussion of the characters in the *Vidagdhamādhava* and their mutual interrelations has yielded important insights into the nature of the devotion exemplified and nourished by the drama. An examination of certain of the play's structural characteristics, in the light of Rūpa's theory of *bhaktirasa*, may help us to discern more clearly the place of this drama in the devotional life of members of the Gauḍīya Vaiṣṇava community. We shall explore the structure of the drama on three interrelated levels, looking first at the plot in its broadest outlines as a sequence of stages in the developing love of Rādhā and Kṛṣṇa; moving next to an intermediate level on which characteristic situations within the larger divisions are repeated with slight variations; and turning finally to individual verses in which recurrent themes and patterns are manifest.

The Drama in Its Largest Divisions

Viewed in broad outline, the *Vidagdhamādhava* is structured around the successive stages in the developing love of Rādhā and Kṛṣṇa, beginning with the strong passion that arises even before their first meeting. Rūpa discusses these fundamental stages in the section on *śṛṅgārabhedaḥ*, the divisions of the erotic *rasa*, in his *Ujjvalanīlamaṇi*. In his analysis, he follows most earlier treatises on dramaturgy[1] in distinguishing two complementary phases of *ujjvala* or *śṛṅgāra rasa*: *vipralambha*, "love-in-separation," and *sambhoga*, "love-in-union." His definition of *vipralambha* reveals his conception of the significance of separation in relation to union, a conception that is fundamental to our understanding of the interplay of these two phases in his dramas.

> *Vipralambha* is that mutual emotion (*bhāva*) of two young people, whether separated or united, which increases when they do not receive the embraces and so forth that they desire, and which enhances the pleasure of union (*sambhoga*).[2]

In support of his last point, Rūpa quotes an earlier source, which states explicitly that separation is necessary to the full realization of union (3). Even though it involves great anguish, *vipralambha* is therefore not something fundamentally negative. Such an understanding of separation has obvious implications for the devotee suffering in the toils of *saṁsāra*.

Vipralambha: Love-in-Separation

Having made this basic distinction, Rūpa proceeds to enumerate four varieties of *vipralambha: pūrvarāga*, *māna*, *premavaicittya*, and *pravāsa*. He then discusses these four forms of love-in-separation in some detail, illustrating their various aspects with verses drawn primarily from his own dramas and poetic works. After giving Rūpa's definition for each of these types, I shall consider its scope and significance in the *Vidagdhamādhava*.

Pūrvarāga Rūpa defines as "love (*rati*) that is awakened in both persons before union, for example, from seeing or hearing about one another."[3] From the verses of the *Vidagdhamādhava* that he uses to illustrate five of the ten states of fully developed *pūrvarāga*,[4] it is clear that he considers this stage to extend, not merely to the first brief meeting of Rādhā and Kṛṣṇa at the end of Act II, but to their first full union, which takes place in Act III. The order in which these verses occur in the drama--the one that exemplifies the first state coming last--also indicates that Rūpa did not regard them as stages that must succeed one another in a fixed order. The second (*udvega*, anxiety) and the eighth (*unmāda*, madness) are illustrated by two consecutive verses from the scene near the beginning of Act II in which Rādhā is unable to conceal her intense emotion from her two friends (II.2, 3); the sixth (*vaiyagrya*, defined by Rūpa as the inability to tolerate the disturbance caused by the depth of one's emotion), by the verse later in the act in which Paurṇamāsī reflects upon Rādhā's futile attempts to forget Kṛṣṇa;[5] the tenth (*mṛtyu*, the desire to die[6]), by the poignant verse at the end of the act, overheard by Kṛṣṇa, in which Rādhā expresses her intention to die because he has rejected her, and asks that her body might remain in Vṛndāvana with her vine-like arm upon the trunk of the *tamāla* tree (II.47); and the first (*lālasa*, ardent desire), by Viśākhā's verse in Act III describing to Kṛṣṇa the signs of Rādhā's intense longing (III.23). It is noteworthy that all these examples are of Rādhā's *pūrvarāga*, although the drama depicts Kṛṣṇa's *pūrvarāga* as well, if less elaborately. Rūpa's partiality to Rādhā's emotion and that of the other *gopī*s may also be seen from his statement in the *Ujjvalanīlamaṇi* that even though Kṛṣṇa's love may develop earlier, the *gopī*s' love for him should be related first because it is more charming (*cārutādhikā*) (15).[7]

To a modern Western reader, love of such intensity before union is almost inconceivable, but Indian theorists from the time of the *Nāṭyaśāstra* or even earlier have enumerated similar conditions of those in whom love has newly dawned, and extant Sanskrit poetry and dramas are filled with examples of heroes and heroines languishing in such states.[8] If anything, however, the next two types of *vipralambha*, *māna* and *premavaicittya*, are even more difficult to comprehend for one unfamiliar with classical Sanskrit drama or its Vaiṣṇava adaptation. In the case of *māna*, moreover, the definition given by Rūpa is manifestly inadequate to convey the subtle nuances that this term suggests to an Indian steeped in the Sanskrit literary tradition. We shall, however, use Rūpa's words as a starting point.

"*Māna* is an emotion (*bhāva*) that impedes two fond lovers, even though they are together, from sharing the embraces and glances that they desire."[9] In his discussion of the types of *māna*, Rūpa indicates that *īrṣyā*, "jealousy," is a prominent feature of this condition.[10] Simply to equate *māna* with jealousy, however, is to miss many of its essential qualities. The term designates an emotional complex that is wholly untranslatable, paradoxically embracing both righteous anger and deep affection, simultaneous repulsion of endearment and intense longing.[11] Indeed, it is precisely such juxtaposition of apparently incompatible elements that lends to this state its enduring fascination for Vaiṣṇava poets and devotees from Jayadeva in the twelfth century to the present. A charming verse from the *Vidagdhamādhava* in which Kṛṣṇa observes Rādhā in precisely such an emotional state of anger mixed with love is translated above as an illustration of Rādhā's frequent moments of inner conflict.[12]

Judging from the proportion of the play devoted to each form of separation, *māna* is second only to *pūrvarāga* in its importance in the *Vidagdhamādhava*. We have seen that the episode with Candrāvalī at the beginning of Act IV serves largely as the occasion for Rādhā's *māna*. Rūpa's elaborate portrayal of *māna* in its effects on both Rādhā and Kṛṣṇa includes two scenes in which they are together while yet estranged from one another by Rādhā's feelings of hurt and anger, as well as an intervening period of physical separation and mutual longing. Like the other forms of *vipralambha*, especially *pūrvarāga* and *pravāsa*, *māna* may thus be seen to increase the longing of both lovers, thereby enhancing the joy of their subsequent union. In his discussion of this emotion in the *Ujjvalanīlamaṇi*, Rūpa indicates another central function of *māna*, that of making manifest the love of each for the other. The verse that he quotes from an earlier theorist draws this important inference from the fact that there can be no jealousy (*īrṣyā*) without deep affection (*praṇaya*) (72).

Premavaicittya, the third form of *vipralambha* discussed in the *Ujjvalanīlamaṇi*, is defined by Rūpa as "pain arising from a [paradoxical] feeling of separation in the presence of the beloved, an experience attributable to the nature of supreme love."[13] The verse from the *Vidagdhamādhava* that Rūpa quotes to illustrate this state, in which the bewildered Rādhā asks why Kṛṣṇa has abandoned her, makes it clear that such anguish is not merely her painful awareness of imminent separation in the future,[14] but her false apprehension of the absence of her beloved in the present, a mistaken perception that arises from the intensity of her emotion. Like *māna*, this form of separation paradoxically occurs when Rādhā and Kṛṣṇa are together, and it likewise serves to manifest the depth of Rādhā's love. Unlike both *pūrvarāga* and *māna*, however, *premavaicittya* has only a small place in one act of the drama (V.46-49.2). Although its scope is thus more limited, its function of revealing the intensity of Rādhā's emotion is no less significant.

Unlike the first three forms of *vipralambha*, which figure more or less prominently in the *Vidagdhamādhava*, the fourth type, *pravāsa*, is wholly absent from this drama. Easily the most straightforward of the four varieties, *pravāsa* is defined as "the separation of two lovers who have previously been united, brought about by such circumstances as a journey to another region."[15] Whereas Rūpa illustrates the first three kinds of love-in-separation with verses from the *Vidagdhamādhava*, as well as from other works, he draws his examples of *pravāsa* largely from the third act of the *Lalitamādhava*, in which he has represented at length the extreme anguish of the inhabitants of Vraja at Kṛṣṇa's departure for Mathurā. The fact that this form of separation occurs in Rūpa's dramas only after Rādhā and Kṛṣṇa have experienced each of the other three, leads one to expect that it would involve the greatest intensity of emotion. Yet Rūpa's plays as well as his theory indicate otherwise. We have already noted the remarkable strength of Radha's emotion in the early acts of the *Vidagdhamādhava*, even before she meets Kṛṣṇa. Furthermore, the ten states of *pravāsa* enumerated in the *Ujjvalanīlamaṇi* are no more extreme than those attributed by Rūpa to fully mature *pūrvarāga*, and seven of the ten states in the two lists are identical.[16]

The development of Rādhā's love in the course of the two dramas is therefore not a growth in the intensity of her emotion; what change we see is rather the gradual attainment of greater self-confidence, manifest most clearly in her increasing boldness in teasing Kṛṣṇa as the drama proceeds. One has only to contrast her reluctance to play a joke on him when her friends urge her to participate in their scheme to deceive him in Act III (III.34.6-10) with her own initiative in proposing that she hide from him in Act VI (VI.23.3-5). Like the classical Sanskrit dramatists, however, Rūpa did not consider development of character to be essential to a drama. We shall have occasion to return to the question of relative intensity of emotion in the next section.

Sambhoga: Love-in-Union

In Rūpa's writings and in Vaiṣṇava literature in general, separation is never final; it is, on the contrary, inevitably followed by union. More significant for our purposes than the rather general definition of *sambhoga* given by Rūpa or the four degrees of intensity into which he classifies it are the specific actions that he enumerates as comprising this broad category, for it is only at this point that he quotes from the *Vidagdhamādhava*. Like the scenes of union in his dramas, from which he draws many of his illustrations, this list includes a number of the situations of playful rivalry that are so familiar to *bhakta*s steeped in the traditions of Kṛṣṇa's childhood and youth. Among these are the episodes of Kṛṣṇa as the ferryman and Kṛṣṇa as the toll collector, the stealing of Kṛṣṇa's flute and the *gopī*s' garments, verbal deception, blocking the path, and hiding in the groves. To illustrate the last two of these, Rūpa quotes verses spoken by Kṛṣṇa in the sixth act of the *Vidagdhamādhava:* the first as he playfully blocks Rādhā's way when she pretends that she is leaving him in order to worship Sūrya (VI.19), and the second when he has finally discovered the grove of trees in which she is hiding (VI.25). In addition to such humorous pastimes, Rūpa lists more explicitly erotic actions, such as touching, kissing, and embracing, which culminate in sexual union.[17]

The Interplay of Separation and Union in the Drama

Illuminated by the most basic categories in Rūpa's *Ujjvalanīlamaṇi*, the *Vidagdhamādhava* may thus be seen as an alternation between the fundamental phases of separation and union. The duration of each of these phases may be briefly summarized. Rādhā's *pūrvarāga* is first described by Nāndīmukhī early in Act I, and depicted, along with Kṛṣṇa's, later in the act; the portrayal of this stage of mutual longing extends through Act II and much of Act III. A jocular scene toward the end of the third act, involving Kṛṣṇa, Rādhā, and their intimate friends, culminates in a moment of tenderness in which Kṛṣṇa, having won over the shy Rādhā, leads her into the love bower. The episode with Candrāvalī at the beginning of Act IV in turn sets the stage for Rādhā's *māna*, which is portrayed in varied settings for the remainder of that act and the greater part of Act V. A brief representation of *premavaicittya*, in which Rādhā mistakenly thinks that her beloved has left her, is found toward the end of the fifth act, in the scene of Rādhā's reconciliation with Kṛṣṇa. In the first five acts, Rūpa has thus represented all the forms of love-in-separation except *pravāsa*--which does not occur until the third act of the *Lalitamādhava*, the *Vidagdhamādhava*'s sequel--and he has interspersed his elaborate depiction of these forms with briefer periods of union.

The last two acts are somewhat more difficult to classify according to the above categories. In these acts, Rūpa appears to be picking up central motifs from the preceding five, recapitulating certain themes in brief compass, and developing some of them further. For example, although the major portion of Act VI portrays the two lovers with their friends in a series of teasing pastimes typical of *sambhoga*, a scene early in the act, in which Rādhā is infatuated by the sound of Kṛṣṇa's flute, is strongly reminiscent of her *pūrvarāga*, as represented in the drama's first acts. Act VII likewise presents periods of separation and union that do not accord perfectly with Rūpa's schema. Unlike Kṛṣṇa's union with Candrāvalī in Act IV, the successful efforts of Candrāvalī's friends to take her to Kṛṣṇa in this act do not lead to Rādhā's renewed *māna*, which is brought about only later, by Kṛṣṇa's deliberate slip of the tongue. Thus the delay in Kṛṣṇa's meeting with Rādhā that is caused by Candrāvalī's presence, though it represents a sort of separation, has no precise equivalent among Rūpa's most general theoretical divisions. The final climactic scene in the drama, characteristic though it is of the juxtapositions that occur throughout, likewise fits none of Rūpa's categories exactly.

In our analysis we have noted two general ways in which separation and union are related in the *Vidagdhamādhava*. First, these two phases in their diverse forms succeed one another in an alternating rhythm throughout the entire drama. Secondly, each period of separation enhances the joy of the union that follows it. One final observation regarding their interrelation leads directly into our next section. The scenes of separation in both dramas, especially those of Rādhā's *pūrvarāga* and her agony at Kṛṣṇa's departure, are invariably more intense than those representing union. What is most characteristic of the scenes in which Rādhā, Kṛṣṇa, and their friends are together is the abundance of playful humor, a mode of interaction that is designated by the Sanskrit term *narma* in its broadest sense.[18] Within union, however, there is an internal dialectic, for even *narma*, lighthearted though it is, has its more serious moments. Chief among these are the brief interludes of separation brought about by the hiding of Rādhā or Kṛṣṇa from the other and invariably spent by the other in an eager search. Although their hiding from one another is treated, together with similar forms of teasing, as an element of love-in-union, such forms of *narma*, like the situations that Rūpa classifies as varieties of love-in-separation, increase the suspense and the mutual longing for full union. Kṛṣṇa himself indicates the kinship of *narma* with *vipralambha* in Act VI when he suggests to Rādhā that they desist from their teasing, which only serves to separate them, and retire instead to a nearby grove of trees (VI.31.7-9). The greater intensity of the emotion expressed in separation, whether in its fully developed forms, which are explicitly designated as types of *vipralambha*, or in the more abbreviated forms that are found in scenes of union, has important implications for devotion that we shall consider in what follows.

Recurrent Emotional Situations

Within the larger structural units of the *Vidagdhamādhava* are certain basic emotional situations that form recurrent patterns. It is undoubtedly such virtual repetition, in part, that lies behind S. K. De's criticism of Rūpa's plays as lacking in consistent dramatic development.[19] After looking at representative examples of configurations that appear repeatedly in the drama, we shall consider the religious significance of such repetition.

Longing in Separation

The fundamental emotional situation that is most characteristic of Rūpa's dramas is the longing of Rādhā or Kṛṣṇa for the other in *vipralambha*. Within this broad category may be grouped several more specific forms, each of which recurs with slight variations at a number of different points. The first and most poignant of these is a situation in which the beloved is considered, for any of a variety of reasons, to be unattainable. Three instances of Rādhā's distress at the thought that Kṛṣṇa is beyond her reach are found in the second and third acts, the first when she fears that she is in love with three men and curses her depravity (II.7-9), the second when Kṛṣṇa makes a pretense of refusing to meet her (II.41-47), and the third when Paurṇamāsī teases her about Kṛṣṇa's inaccessibility in order to induce her to reveal her emotion (III.12-16). In each instance, Rādhā's extreme anguish culminates in the desire to end her life. Although the specific circumstances and particular words in which the emotion is expressed differ, the underlying pattern in each is much the same. The second and third show a particularly close relation: in both situations Rādhā fears Kṛṣṇa's rejection of her, and her wish to die takes explicitly devotional forms in both.[20] In addition to these prominent examples from Rādhā's *pūrvarāga*, there is at least one related but somewhat less extreme instance later in the drama, when a misleading letter indicating that Kṛṣṇa has found other diversions because of Rādhā's *māna* causes her once again to express her fear of Kṛṣṇa's rejection (V.12). Kṛṣṇa's response to similar circumstances is usually considerably less intense, but there is one comparable occasion--when he is led to believe for a moment that Rādhā has been taken to Mathurā and thus cannot come to their first tryst--on which he too responds in desperation that he is wholly unable to live without his beloved (III.22).

A second characteristic situation in which the longing of Rādhā or Kṛṣṇa is expressed is that of the overheard conversation or soliloquy. As in the preceding case, the more frequent of these involve the overhearing by one or more characters of Rādhā's expressions of love and longing. Especially memorable is the scene toward the end of Act II in which Kṛṣṇa, hearing Rādhā's words of utter devotion, comments at intervals to Madhumaṅgala on the extraordinary beauty of her love (II.45-48). In the next act, Kṛṣṇa and Viśākhā, coming to the tryst, pause to listen as Rādhā expresses her great eagerness.[21] Early in Act V, it is Paurṇamāsī and Lalitā who listen unobserved as

Rādhā reveals her intense desire for Kṛṣṇa, which causes her to repent of her *māna*; this time Paurṇamāsī provides the running commentary, pointing out the excellence of Rādhā's love (V.7-9.2).

A third type of situation in which the longing of Rādhā or Kṛṣṇa is revealed is one in which the signs of love displayed by one of them are described to the other. In addition to several individual instances, there are two noteworthy pairs of situations of this sort, one in *pūrvarāga* and the other in *māna*. In the opening scene of Act III, Paurṇamāsī and Lalitā reveal Rādhā's longing to Kṛṣṇa as they learn of his love from Madhumaṅgala. Paurṇamāsī's punning verse describing Rādhā's trembling and fainting from excitement whenever she thinks that Kṛṣṇa is nearby (III.10) is typical of such revelatory passages. In the next scene, Paurṇamāsī and Lalitā bear similar good tidings to Rādhā: after teasing her to elicit an expression of her love, Paurṇamāsī consoles her with the news that Kṛṣṇa has grown thin out of intense longing for her, and Lalitā elaborates upon Paurṇamāsī's comforting remark, describing to Rādhā the evidence of Kṛṣṇa's complete obsession with her (III.18).

A more complicated sequence is found in the section depicting Rādhā's *māna*. As Rādhā and Lalitā come upon Kṛṣṇa after his night with Candrāvalī, Lalitā, accusing Kṛṣṇa of falsehood, informs him that Rādhā felt each moment to be an eternity as she waited all night in vain for him in the bower (IV.29). When Rādhā subsequently spurns Kṛṣṇa's attempts at conciliation after it has become obvious that he was at that time in the company of Candrāvalī, Viśākhā, in a futile attempt to persuade Rādhā to accept Kṛṣṇa's heartfelt entreaties, reminds her of the fact that a moment seems endless when she is separated from him (IV.45). Although her words are addressed to Rādhā, they are said in Kṛṣṇa's hearing, and they thus acquaint him with an important manifestation of her deep love. Correspondingly, while Rādhā is repenting of her *māna* and pining for Kṛṣṇa once again, Nāndīmukhī arrives and describes to her the symptoms of Kṛṣṇa's despondency (V.14). Later, when Kṛṣṇa encounters Rādhā, who is still hurt, Vṛndā, in a double revelation, points out Rādhā's anguish and urges her to look compassionately upon Kṛṣṇa, whom she describes as "languishing pitiably before you" (V.30).

Longing is also a prominent element in verses of regret over things left undone when separation is brought about suddenly, usually by the advent of Jaṭilā or Mukharā. Such verses are found in scenes portraying all three of the forms of love-in-separation included in the *Vidagdhamādhava: pūrvarāga* (II. 56; III.2), *māna* (V.6), and *premavaicittya* (V.47).[22]

Illusory Perception

A second broad category of repeated situation is one in which the intensity of love is so great that it leads to a fundamental transformation of vision. In each of the two major forms of separation depicted in the *Vidagdhamādhava*, *pūrvarāga* and *māna*, Rādhā's emotional state is so intense that even though Kṛṣṇa is not physically present, she experiences him as appearing in front of her and forcefully trying to take her hand or embrace her (II.5-6; V.8.3-4). In Chapter VI we noted a number of closely related passages in which the complete obsession of Rādhā and Kṛṣṇa with one another is indicated by their "mistakes" in seeing each other everywhere and in everything.[23] The inverse of such situations in which the beloved, though absent, appears to be present is that of *premavaicittya*, in which Rādhā thinks that Kṛṣṇa has departed when he is in fact standing immediately in front of her (V.46-48). Both types of situation serve to manifest the depth of the passion of Rādhā or Kṛṣṇa for the other.

What is noteworthy about these situations is not only the virtually identical structure of those in each type, but also the close similarity among certain of the terms and images used to express the different states of love and longing. In Chapter VI, we surveyed some of the many parallels between Rādhā and Kṛṣṇa, especially in the ways in which their devotion to one another is depicted. What is important for us to note here is the similarity of situation and form of response from one portion of the drama to another. Several illustrations may be drawn from the instances that we have just reviewed. One obvious example is Rādhā's reiterated expression of her wish to die because she fears that her intense passion must remain forever unfulfilled. A second example, overlapping in one case with the first, is the teasing of Rādhā for the explicit purpose of causing her to manifest her emotion. Often consequent upon Rādhā's response to this teasing is a third recurrent element, the wonder expressed by various characters at the unique beauty of her love. Finally, balancing the emphasis on Rādhā's emotion in the first three is a fourth notable example, the revelation to Rādhā, through terms and imagery drawn from asceticism and *yoga*, of Kṛṣṇa's utter preoccupation with her. Such revelation occurs first in *pūrvarāga*, in Paurṇamāsī's verse suggesting a comparison between Kṛṣṇa's emaciated state and that of the gods who perform austerities (*tapas*) out of eagerness for a glimpse of him; and later in *māna*, when Nāndīmukhī likens Kṛṣṇa to a *yogī* in his abjuring of all other pleasures to meditate upon Rādhā's lovely countenance.

Deception Through Ambiguity

A third variety of situation that recurs throughout the drama is one of deliberate ambiguity. Scenes of this sort typically involve two groups of characters, one that perceives the state of affairs truly and one that is in some fundamental way deluded. Madhumaṅgala's teasing verse in Act I alluding to Kṛṣṇa's dalliance with the *gopī*s, for example, is understood in all its implications by Kṛṣṇa and his companions, but not by Nanda and Yaśodā. Likewise, Rādhā's love-sick condition, recognized immediately by her friends as well as by Paurṇamāsī and Nāndīmukhī, is perceived as demon-induced madness by Mukharā, who gullibly accedes to Paurṇamāsī's proposed cure, exposure to a glance from the enemy of demons (Kṛṣṇa). Jaṭilā's comparable credulity makes possible the extended exchange at the end of Act II, in which Kṛṣṇa, Madhumaṅgala, and Viśākhā are able to talk in front of her about the love of Rādhā and Kṛṣṇa by means of thinly veiled references in such a way that she does not suspect the truth. One of the pairs of allusions to Kṛṣṇa and Rādhā introduced there by Viśākhā, that of buck and doe, is used once again to good advantage by Lalitā early in the final act, in order to learn clandestinely from Kṛṣṇa, in the presence of Candrāvalī and her friends, of his undying love for Rādhā.

By far the most dramatic instance of such ambiguity, however, is the scene toward the end of the seventh act in which Jaṭilā and Abhimanyu come upon Kṛṣṇa with Rādhā and her friends in the temple of Gaurī. Misled by his disguise and by Rādhā's "prostration," Jaṭilā and her son remain unaware of his true identity, whereas Rādhā and her friends, themselves previously deceived for a short while by Vṛndā's hoax, now recognize Kṛṣṇa and are able to turn the situation to their own advantage. This marvelous climactic scene is adumbrated by Paurṇamāsī's ambiguous remark at the beginning of the act, when she promises Abhimanyu that Rādhā will soon worship "the one who is auspicious toward all" (VII.1.36-37).

Although neither the preceding list of characteristic situations nor the group of examples given for each is exhaustive, they demonstrate the considerable extent of such virtual repetition in the *Vidagdhamādhava*. In exploring the religious significance of this prominent structural feature, we shall look first at what these repeated situations have in common, and then consider the devotional purpose of such repetition.

Central to virtually all the examples given above, especially those in the first two major categories, is the manifestation of the emotion of Rādhā or Kṛṣṇa to certain other characters (including in some cases the beloved) and thereby to the audience or reader as well. We have seen that it is more often Rādhā's love that is so revealed. In the extensive portions of the drama representing aspects of her emotion, such as the scenes of longing and those in which she experiences Kṛṣṇa's presence when he is absent (and vice versa), it is the remarkable intensity of her love and the exclusiveness and persistence of her devotion that are most prominent. Intensity, exclusiveness, persistence: a better characterization of Vaiṣṇava devotion at its best would be hard to find.

In the chapter on Rādhā we have reviewed evidence showing that she is for Rūpa no ordinary mortal. First, she is herself an object of Vaiṣṇava devotion. Secondly, although she serves as a model in her supreme love for Kṛṣṇa, her passion is represented as utterly unique. In the *Ujjvalanīlamaṇi*, the highest and most intense levels of the erotic emotion are explicitly said to be achieved by Rādhā alone.[24] The wonder at the depth and beauty of her love expressed at points throughout the drama by Paurṇamāsī and Nāndīmukhī, as well as by Kṛṣṇa himself, likewise emphasizes its extraordinary nature.

However, in spite of its transcendence, which renders its full realization impossible even for Candrāvalī and the other *gopī*s, Rādhā's emotion as it is portrayed in the *Vidagdhamādhava* clearly has great devotional significance. The proportion of the drama devoted to it, and the extent to which other characters elicit from her its expression and comment on its unprecedented quality, testify to its paramount importance. It is nevertheless difficult to specify the precise nature of its significance on the basis of the drama itself. However, Rūpa's theory of *bhaktirasa*, as I have outlined it in Chapter II, provides us at this point with a useful theoretical framework. We have seen thit Rūpa considers *mādhuryabhāva*, the devotional mode of erotic love, to be the highest of the five chief emotions that a devotee can adopt in relation to the Lord. Both in Rūpa's theoretical works and in his dramas Rādhā exemplifies this supreme form of devotion to Kṛṣṇa at its most profound level. Without presuming that they will ever come to experience it fully--for that would put them on a par with Rādhā--*bhakta*s whose mode of devotion is *mādhuryabhāva* may derive profound inspiration from her supreme love.

We are now is a position to answer our final question, that of the devotional significance of the virtual repetition of these fundamental emotional situations, especially those in which intense love and yearning are expressed. In his *Bhaktirasāmṛtasindhu* Rūpa outlines a process through which the devotee's *bhāva* for Kṛṣṇa is deepened and refined until it becomes a *rasa*. The conception is an aesthetic one based on the *rasa* theory of classical Sanskrit poetics; and dramatic representations of the love of Rādhā and Kṛṣṇa, whether enacted, read, or visualized without such aids, serve as primary modes of realization. It is the absorption in the emotional situations being depicted that is crucial for Gauḍīya Vaiṣṇava devotional life, not the learning of theological truths or ethical principles.[25] (Such didactic elements are, as we have seen, not entirely lacking in the *Vidagdhamādhava*, but they are far from its central thrust.[26]) The recurrence of certain basic emotional configurations is thus intimately related to the devotional purpose of the drama: such repetition deepens the devotee's *bhāva* by allowing him or her to experience its most profound moments repeatedly and over a considerable period of time.

These observations provide the basis for a reevaluation of the length and structure of the *Vidagdhamādhava*. From the point of view of a Gauḍīya Vaiṣṇava devotee, especially a *rasika*[27] of the sort described in the prologue, neither the unusual length of the play (in comparison with most classical Sanskrit dramas)[28] nor its repetitive quality would constitute an aesthetic or dramatic fault. On the contrary, both qualities allow the devotee to be steeped in the emotion of love in all its varied aspects. Unlike many Western plays and the well-known classical Sanskrit dramas, the movement of the *Vidagdhamādhava*, especially after Act III, is not toward a single goal; one might rather characterize it as the representation of eternal moments in the unfolding love of Rādhā and Kṛṣṇa. The play is thus somewhat episodic in structure rather than strictly causal: certain portions, such as all or most of Act VI and parts of several other acts, could be omitted without significant loss to the thread of the narrative.

Judged according to Aristotelian canons, therefore, the *Vidagdhamādhava* may indeed be seen to lack coherence and dramatic effect, as De alleges. When one views the drama in terms of its devotional significance, however, it readily becomes apparent that its principle of coherence is not one of action, but rather of emotion or, more strictly, of *rasa*. Likewise, the chief effect sought is not one of suspense, as in much Western drama, but something fundamentally different: the enhancement of devotion, of *mādhuryabhāva*, until it matures into the ultimate spiritual experience, the tasting of *madhurabhaktirasa*.

To this point our discussion of the religious meaning of repeated situations in the drama has centered upon those in the first two groups. Somewhat different in tone and purpose, although likewise of devotional significance, are the scenes of deliberate ambiguity that comprise the third general category. A prominent feature common to these situations is their humor. In every case the audience or reader shares the author's point of view, clearly perceiving the irony of the situation and delighting in the confusion or naïveté of the ignorant party. A closer look at two somewhat different examples of such ambiguity will reveal other levels of religious significance.

In the scene in the first act in which Kṛṣṇa and his friends appear with Nanda and Yaśodā, the ambiguity is created by juxtaposing the two most intimate modes of perceiving and relating to Kṛṣṇa: *vātsalya*, consistently embodied by Kṛṣṇa's foster parents, and *mādhurya*, represented by the absent *gopīs*, to whom Madhumaṅgala's suggestive verse deliberately alludes. Kṛṣṇa the darling toddler whose charming smile and ceaseless pranks endear him to the women of the village and Kṛṣṇa the handsome youth and lover of many of these same women are at one level incompatible, and their superimposition is startling. The religious meaning of such juxtaposition may lie precisely in the element of simultaneity: Kṛṣṇa is at the same time eternal child and eternal lover, and the two corresponding modes of relating to him, *vātsalya* and *mādhurya*, exist as eternal possibilities for devotion. Thus the humor, based upon the simultaneous perception of two apparently incompatible elements, may lead the astute devotee to the perception of religious truth.

Metaphysical truth is likewise conveyed through dramatic juxtaposition in the climactic scene in the final act in which Kṛṣṇa appears as the Goddess. In the chapter on Kṛṣṇa we saw that the feminine form *devatā*, which can refer to either a male or a female deity, is used with deliberate ambiguity by Rādhā to address Kṛṣṇa in front of Jaṭilā and Abhimanyu. However, what is perceived by the other characters and the audience or reader is not simply the fact that it is Kṛṣṇa and not the Goddess to whom Rādhā directs her petition, but the more profound truth that it is he and not Gaurī who is *the devatā*, the Lord and ultimate reality of the universe. Given the fact that the Goddess is the great rival of Kṛṣṇa in Bengal, it seems hardly accidental that Rūpa has chosen to end his play with this scene of Kṛṣṇa disguised as Gaurī.[29] Here once again a humorous situation of ambiguity is the vehicle of profound religious realization.

The Drama's Smallest Units: Characteristic Verses

Intimately related to the recurrent emotional situations that we have just considered are the smallest structural units of the *Vidagdhamādhava*, its individual verses, for it is in these that the emotions and ambiguities are typically expressed. From the fact that Rūpa quotes single verses from his own and other literary works in illustrating his theoretical categories, it is clear that he conceives these verses as fundamental building blocks. The fact that such verses have also been taken out of their contexts and collected in anthologies likewise indicates that they have been viewed by Rūpa and others as capable of being understood and relished separately. Reviewing the form and content of the most common types of verses in the drama, with special attention to their devotional significance, may therefore enhance our understanding of the work as a whole. As in the preceding section, our survey will be selective rather than exhaustive.

Most of the characteristic situations described above are epitomized in single verses, and just as these situations recur with slight variations, so the individual verses expressing them also exhibit recurrent elements. Especially frequent are verses revealing the emotional state of Rādhā or Kṛṣṇa; these are of two major types, those in which the hero or heroine expresses his or her own emotion, and those in which another character describes the signs of emotion revealed by one of them. In discussing instances of the first two broad categories of emotional situation in the preceding section, I have given numerous examples of both types of verse. An especially common form of the second main type is one in which a secondary character, usually Paurṇamāsī or one of Rādhā's friends, enumerates the signs of love displayed by Rādhā or Kṛṣṇa.

Verses of a related sort likewise infer emotions and their expression from signs, but in these instances it is more remote traces, such as footprints or the condition of the love bower, that are revelatory. Although there is one such verse in which the concerned Kṛṣṇa learns of Rādhā's distress from the condition of the grove in which she and Lalitā waited in vain for him (IV.28), most verses of this type express the delight of the speaker at the implications of what is seen. This is clearly the case in the verse in which Viśākhā deduces three different modes of interaction--intimate conversation, joking, and embracing--from the row of Rādhā's and Kṛṣṇa's footprints (VI.32). Vṛndā's words introducing her verse on the love bower in the final act (VII.42) anticipate her joy in seeing it, and Lalitā, in her parallel verse describing the wilted bed of flower petals (VII.43), explicitly echoes Vṛndā's delight. Shortly later, Kṛṣṇa's own disheveled appearance elicits from Vṛndā a yet more enthusiastic response (VII.46).

Such verses serve two important purposes. First, they suggest to the audience or reader the intimate forms of expression of Rādhā's and Kṛṣṇa's love that may not, according to Sanskrit dramatic convention,[30] be explicitly represented on the stage. Secondly, by revealing the rapt wonder of such important devotional figures as Vṛndā and Lalitā, they encourage the audience or reader to share in their joy at the sublime union of Rādhā and Kṛṣṇa. Although there is an important class of verse already familiar to us in which Rādhā or one of the other characters expresses delight at Kṛṣṇa's radiant appearance or wonder at his alluring qualities *per se*, it is more often an aspect of the relation of Rādhā and Kṛṣṇa to one another that elicits such appreciation. Two verses in which Vṛndā declares her endless fascination with the ecstasy of their supreme love (VII.2; VII.41) also represent Rūpa's attitude as he invites the devotee to partake of the wondrous vision of this divine *līlā*.

Turning from verses revealing emotion to those expressing ambiguity, we find two prominent types, those employing puns (*śleṣa*)[31] and those in which incongruous or apparently contradictory elements are deliberately juxtaposed (*viṣama* or *virodhābhāsa*).[32] Punning verses are found in a number of the scenes of ambiguity described earlier; these typically facilitate the communication of essential information to certain characters in front of others who must be kept ignorant of these secrets. Puns are not, however, limited to scenes in which troublesome characters like Jaṭilā appear; they are also found repeatedly in scenes of union, as part of the *narma* or sportive humor of which Kṛṣṇa and the other young people are so fond. Like the alliteration and other forms of word-play that are employed throughout the *Vidagdhamādhava*,[33] *śleṣa* is a classical Sanskrit literary device that gains new meaning in the context of Kṛṣṇa *līlā*: it represents the element of playfulness that is a prominent characteristic not only of Rūpa's dramas but of Kṛṣṇa devotion in general. Moreover, like the two ambiguous situations that we considered in some detail, such punning may have a deeper significance: by representing different levels of reality simultaneously, these verses illustrate the coexistence of such diverse levels, thereby disposing the audience or reader to perceive metaphysical reality beneath surface appearances.

Two closely related figures of speech employed in verses throughout the *Vidagdhamādhava*, *virodhābhāsa* and *viṣama*, both involve the juxtaposition of two seemingly irreconcilable elements. Certain of these verses center upon Kṛṣṇa, who is the very embodiment of paradox: although noble and virtuous, he drives Rādhā mad with his *līlā*s (III.5; cf. VI.20.3-4); though a rogue, he brings welfare to all (V.35).[34] His flute shares his paradoxical nature: likewise of excellent lineage (*vaṁśa* means family as well as bamboo), it stupifies the *gopī*s with a wicked[35] *mantra* (V.17); though it drinks sweet nectar from Kṛṣṇa's lips, it emits a disturbing[35] sound to which the entire world succumbs (V.26); and its further effects, as Rādhā and others observe on numerous occasions, are similarly contradictory.[36] The love of the *gopī*s for Kṛṣṇa is no less paradoxical: Paurṇamāsī describes it as more bitter than deadly poison, yet sweeter than nectar, and asserts that only one who has experienced it "knows its tortuous and sweet steps" (II.18). Some of the most charming verses of this sort involve the paradox of Rādhā's power over Kṛṣṇa: Paurṇamāsī observes that Kṛṣṇa himself has been brought to a condition of rapt meditation by Rādhā (III.4), and in more than one verse his power as an invincible slayer of demons is dramatically juxtaposed with her conquest of him.[37] Such verses, like the juxtapositions in which the author of the *Bhāgavata* takes such obvious delight, are vehicles of joy and wonder as well as of profound religious realization.

Although the figures of speech that we have just surveyed are found in classical Sanskrit literature, their consistent use to express metaphysical truth in veiled forms and to evoke religious awe at the sublime paradox of the supreme Lord who is subject to human passion and submits himself to his devotees in love is only dimly foreshadowed in the earlier courtly poetry and drama. Nor do we find precedent in the classical plays for the repetitive quality of Rūpa's dramatic works. For the sources of these characteristics, which play a central role in the devotion expressed in the *Vidagdhamādhava*, we must therefore look elsewhere.

The *Vidagdhamādhava*'s Main Antecedents

If classical Sanskrit drama and aesthetic theory, even as that theory has been transformed by Rūpa, do not fully account for certain essential features of the *Vidagdhamādhava*, where do we find antecedents of these features? Earlier forms of the Kṛṣṇa narrative, especially the tenth book of the *Bhāgavata Purāṇa*, from which Rūpa draws many of the illustrations for his theoretical works, and the *Gītagovinda*, in which Rādhā figures as the heroine, are obvious sources. In addition to such purāṇic texts and poetry in Sanskrit, there has been a strong tradition of poetry and dramas in the vernacular languages, much of which has unfortunately not survived. We have earlier explored possible relations between vernacular dramas and those of Rūpa; we shall here merely note certain prominent continuities between the two most significant earlier Sanskrit works of Kṛṣṇa devotion, the *Bhāgavata Purāṇa* and the *Gītagovinda*, and Rūpa's plays. It is not my intention to treat fully the question of Rūpa's sources here,[38] but simply to indicate the general nature and scope of such influence.

At first glance, the Kṛṣṇa narrative in the tenth book of the *Bhāgavata* seems to have little in common with Rūpa's dramas.

The many stories of Kṛṣṇa's childhood feats of prowess in slaying demons that fill its early chapters are only alluded to in the *Vidagdhamādhava*,[39] as is the *rāsa* dance that forms the heart of the five chapters on Kṛṣṇa's amorous relations with the *gopīs*. In the *Bhāgavata* account, too, it is Kṛṣṇa's love for *all* the *gopīs*, rather than his special passion for Rādhā, that is represented.[40] Yet when we shift our focus from external events, in which the differences are most marked, and look instead at recurrent patterns of expression and characteristic emotions, we cannot fail to perceive a close kinship between these two texts. Indeed, careful scrutiny reveals many more parallels than we can consider in detail. We shall therefore relegate specific instances to the notes and confine ourselves here to broad areas of similarity, beginning with the deliberate use of paradox that we have earlier seen to be characteristic of Rūpa's dramas.

The fundamental paradox stated and represented repeatedly in the *Bhāgavata* is that of the Lord of the universe who through *māyā*[41] assumed human form: although as the Absolute he is unborn, he took birth in the world (III.1.44-45), and though he is of lordly majesty, he chose to spend his early years among simple cowherds (X.15.19). This basic paradox in its various forms is stated directly, in verses that may well have served as prototypes for Rūpa's, and it is also graphically illustrated in marvelous stories. Among these, two in particular stand out. The first is the striking incident in which Yaśodā, looking in the infant Kṛṣṇa's mouth for the dirt that he has allegedly eaten, sees instead the entire universe (X.8.33-45). A second episode from the *Bhāgavata* has even clearer echoes in the *Vidagdhamādhava*. In it Yaśodā is portrayed as running after Kṛṣṇa, "whom even the minds of *yogīs* cannot catch,"[42] and trying to tie a string around the waist of her haughty child, who is in reality the universe itself (X.9.12-19). It is only after her strenuous efforts to find or assemble a rope long enough to go around him have all failed that Kṛṣṇa, seeing his mother's exhaustion, compassionately allows himself to be bound.

Parallel in both imagery and religious implications are such metaphors in the *Vidagdhamādhava* as that of the wild elephant (Kṛṣṇa) who is bound by Rādhā's smiles (VI.21). Although the emphasis is somewhat different in the two texts, for it is Rādhā's inexplicable power over Kṛṣṇa that occasions comment in the *Vidagdhamādhava*, rather than his deliberate abdication of his own supremacy, as in the *Bhāgavata* story, the similarity in conception as well as expression is unmistakable. In both texts loving devotion to Kṛṣṇa, as epitomized by Yaśodā and the *gopīs* in the *Bhāgavata* and by Rādhā in the *Vidagdhamādhava*, is represented as incomparably superior to the strenuous efforts of ascetics and *yogīs*, and both texts paradoxically attribute to such supreme love the power of captivating the Lord to whom is subject the entire universe (BhP X.9.19; VM VII.57).

It is not only in their deliberate use of paradox and in their preference for *bhakti* over other religious paths that we find close parallels between the *Bhāgavata Purāṇa* and the *Vidagdhamādhava*, but also in the very ways in which their authors conceive and portray devotion. In both texts there is an emphasis on strong emotions that are expressed in the context of intimate personal relationships. In our analysis of the *Vidagdhamādhava* we have seen the unceasing delight and wonder that are evoked in those persons who observe the love of Rādhā and Kṛṣṇa. These two emotions are likewise the most frequent responses of the *gopīs* and others in the *Bhāgavata* who behold Kṛṣṇa's youthful charm or witness his boyish pranks and feats of valor (e.g., X.8.23-24; X.9.17). Again we may discern a difference of emphasis, due largely to Rādhā's preeminence in the *Vidagdhamādhava* and to the role played throughout the drama by the secondary characters, who delight in and comment upon her love. Yet even here the difference is not so marked as it would at first appear. It is true that Kṛṣṇa alone occupies the center of the stage in the *Bhāgavata*, and all the inhabitants of Vraja are depicted as his *bhakta*s: the *gopīs* in particular are described as listening enraptured to stories of his deeds and, deeply moved, singing his praises as they rock their babies to sleep and perform their daily chores (X.44.15). Yet the narrator himself, together with such persons from outside

Vraja as the proud scholar Uddhava and the women gathered in the Mathurā arena in which Kṛṣṇa slays Kaṁsa, praises the *gopī*s' love and exclaims at their extreme good fortune.[43] In short, a theme developed more fully in Rūpa's dramas--the wonder and delight at the unique love of Rādhā for Kṛṣṇa, repeatedly expressed by the secondary characters--is already found in relation to the *gopī*s in the *Bhāgavata Purāṇa*.

In addition to the frequent use of paradox fraught with metaphysical significance and the consistent representation of a highly emotional form of *bhakti* centering upon personal relationships to Kṛṣṇa, the *Bhāgavata* shares with the *Vidagdhamādhava* a prominent structural characteristic in its abundance of repetition. The numerous demon-slaying exploits of Kṛṣṇa's childhood inherited and transformed from earlier accounts are clearly regarded by its author as less significant for their ingenious differences of detail than for the profound wonder that they repeatedly arouse in those who hear them and for the attachment to Kṛṣṇa that they engender and nourish (X.6.44; X.7.1-2). I have suggested that it is the repetition of characteristic emotional situations and expressions in the *Vidagdhamādhava* that deepens and transforms the devotee's *bhāva*; although the author of the *Bhāgavata* may not have conceived the process in terms of an elaborate theory, such as Rūpa's theory of *bhaktirasa*, he seems to have had a comparable sense of the development of devotion through stories in which emotions are expressed and thereby evoked in those who hear them.

More obviously akin to the *Vidagdhamādhava* as a literary portrayal of successive stages in the love of Rādhā and Kṛṣṇa is the *Gītagovinda* of Jayadeva. Frequently styled a dramatic poem, this lyrical, sensuous work has been sung in both North and South Indian musical idioms and represented in various styles of dance throughout India as well as beyond her borders.[44] Far more concise than the *Vidagdhamādhava*, it nevertheless contains in embryo a number of the essential elements of Rūpa's play. Especially prominent among these is its repeated portrayal of the lovers yearning for one another in separation, and in particular, its poignant depiction of Rādhā's *māna* (VIII). In focusing almost exclusively on these stages in their love, it includes no depiction of their *pūrvarāga*, elaborated at considerable length by Rūpa, nor does it contain scenes of humorous repartee like those in the *Vidagdhamādhava*. The result is a poem of great intensity and power; Rūpa's plays, by contrast, are more varied and playful.

In spite of the obvious formal differences between the two works, however, they have certain common structural characteristics. The most obvious is their use of repetition: like the *Vidagdhamādhava*, the *Gītagovinda* portrays Rādhā and Kṛṣṇa in successive emotional situations that overlap to a considerable extent. In the *Gītagovinda*, the prolonged period of separation is punctuated by periodic refrains in which Jayadeva's devotional relation to the sublime love that he is depicting is given explicit expression. Like the interpretive remarks of such secondary characters as Paurṇamāsī and Vṛndā, these comments indicate the devotee's relation to the events being described. As in the *Vidagdhamādhava*, too, the devotee is clearly expected to relate to the entire drama of love, and not to identify simply with any one of the characters in it. Noteworthy in this respect is Jayadeva's assertion that the poem should be enacted mentally (*manasā naṭanīyam*, IV.9): such visualization and concomitant emotional participation is precisely what Rūpa would seem to expect of the devotee.

In our exploration of Rūpa's *Vidagdhamādhava*, we have discerned its kinship with various types of literature: with Sanskrit courtly poetry as well as more popular vernacular dramatic representations; with extended purāṇic accounts as well as more highly concentrated devotional lyrics.[45] Like the *rasa* that it distils, the *Vidagdhamādhava* represents a unique blend of elements from these and other sources, which unite to form a devotional drama of considerable power and beauty.

CHAPTER IX

CONCLUDING REFLECTIONS

We have seen that dramatic forms and conceptions have long been central to Kṛṣṇa devotion, and that drama has been especially pervasive in the highly emotional *bhakti* movement inspired by Caitanya. The study of a single Kṛṣṇa drama by Caitanya's prominent disciple Rūpa Gosvāmī, the *Vidagdhamādhava*, a play that has been virtually ignored by scholars in spite of its manifest importance within the Vaiṣṇava community, is thus a most appropriate avenue into the heart of Gauḍīya Vaiṣṇava devotion. In this drama Rūpa has represented his vision of the love of Kṛṣṇa, the Lord of the universe, in the beguiling form of a cowherd youth, and Rādhā, his eternal *śakti*, manifest as a damsel of surpassing charm. Through its kaleidoscopic succession of situations, in which Rūpa has portrayed the *līlā* of their love in all its delightful variety, the *Vidagdhamādhava* has evoked a similar vision in subsequent generations of Vaiṣṇava devotees and enhanced their emotional participation in the divine drama.

According to Rūpa's theory of *bhaktirasa*, the devotee's emotion toward the Lord may assume any of several relational modes, the highest of which, *madhurā rati*, is the *sthāyibhāva* or fundamental emotion in each of his three dramas. Precisely what Rūpa understands a human *bhakta*'s assumption of this *bhāva* to entail, however, is not clear from his writings. Consequently, the question of the way in which an ordinary devotee is to relate to the characters of the Vraja *līlā*--especially Rādhā and the other *gopīs*, who are the highest embodiments of *mādhurya bhāva*--has been a controversial one. In the course of our inquiry into the devotional significance of Rūpa's drama, we have found it necessary to pursue this issue at some length. Although several questions remain unresolved, certain tentative conclusions may nevertheless be drawn.

What is at stake in the differences of interpretation that we surveyed in Chapter II is a matter fundamental to both theology and practice: that of the accessibility of the Lord.[1] The advocates of *mañjarībhāva*--in which the devotee partaking in the mode of *madhurā rati* imagines himself or herself, not as Rādhā, nor even as one of Rādhā's close friends, but as a humble maidservant of one of these *gopīs*[2]--are, whether consciously or unconsciously, giving greater prominence to Kṛṣṇa's *aiśvarya*, his lordly majesty, and conceiving Rādhā and the other chief *gopīs* as sharing significantly in Kṛṣṇa's exalted nature. A certain distance is thus put between the characters of the Vraja *līlā* and ordinary human *bhaktas*. One well-known Vaiṣṇava scholar in Calcutta with whom I read and discussed the *Lalitamādhava*, Janardan Chakravarty, denied, remarkably, even the possibility that Kṛṣṇa dramas could be enacted by devotees, claiming that the seriousness of purpose of a Vaiṣṇava's religious life would be utterly destroyed if he were to impersonate Kṛṣṇa.[3] The text that he used in support of this position is the frequently quoted statement *jīvo nityakṛṣṇadāsaḥ*, "The individual soul is the eternal servant of Kṛṣṇa."[4] No Vaiṣṇava with whom I spoke would take issue with the fundamental assertion that the purpose of human existence is to serve the Lord. The question, however, is what constitutes appropriate service. On the specific issue of whether the dramatic enactment of Kṛṣṇa's deeds is a proper form of service, we have seen that there have long been views diametrically opposed to that of Professor Chakravarty.

In Chapter I we observed that the *Gītagovinda* was sung and danced as early as the fifteenth century in the Jagannātha temple in Puri. The occasion, specified in the temple inscription, for singing and enacting in dance the love of Rādhā and Kṛṣṇa as portrayed in Jayadeva's dramatic poem, is highly significant: the performance is to take place before Lords Balarāma and Jagannātha between their evening meal and their bedtime meal. From the inscription it thus seems evident that the daily performance, like the repeated offerings of food, is itself a form of worship (*pūjā*) intended to please the Lord. In our survey of popular forms of drama and dance drama in the same chapter, we noted that the *aṅkiyā nāṭs* of Assam and the *kuchipuḍi* dance dramas of Andhra have similarly been conceived as offerings to the Lord.

Although the prologues to Rūpa's two major dramas do not indicate that they were to be performed as religious offerings, in each of these dramas we find a disguise adopted or a play performed expressly for the purpose of consoling Kṛṣṇa. In the fifth act of the *Vidagdhamādhava*, Subala and Vṛndā dress up as Rādhā and Lalitā to keep Kṛṣṇa from becoming despondent when Rādhā is prevented from coming to meet him. The play-within-a-play (*garbhāṅka*) found in the fourth act of the *Lalitamādhava* is even more explicit in this regard, for here it is no mere disguise, but an entire drama, called *Rādhābhisāra*, "The Nocturnal Meeting with Rādhā," that is put on for Kṛṣṇa's pleasure. Kṛṣṇa's response to the *gandharva* actor's portrayal of "Mādhava," Kṛṣṇa as he was in Vṛndāvana, is also highly instructive: he is so strongly attracted by this representation of his former self that he rushes forward in order to embrace that Kṛṣṇa. Here as elsewhere in Rūpa's dramas, as well as in his theory,[5] we have an unambiguous indication of his preference for the Kṛṣṇa of Vraja, distinguished from the Kṛṣṇa of Mathurā, and even more from that of Dvārakā, by the preponderance of his *mādhurya*, his endearing sweetness, over his *aiśvarya*, his lordly majesty.

However, subsequent developments in the Gauḍīya Vaiṣṇava community--at least in its more scholarly circles--have taken the direction of increased awareness of the "otherness," not only of Kṛṣṇa, but of Rādhā as well, and indeed of all the important characters in the Vraja *līlā*. It is difficult not to see in the practice of *mañjarīsādhana* a greater sense of distance between these characters and the ordinary human *bhakta* than Rūpa's *Vidagdhamādhava* and his theory seem to require. Rūpa's view of the superiority of more intimate relations between the devotee and the Lord, as articulated in the *Bhaktirasāmṛtasindhu*, is a radical and daring one, and it is hardly surprising that elements of *aiśvarya*--in a new guise--have reemerged with the passage of time. Parallels for such a reemergence are not wanting in the history of religions.

In the Gauḍīya instance, the intimacy of *madhura bhaktirasa* may have seemed too great for those accustomed to regarding their deities with a certain awe. In Brindavan, iconographic developments, notably that of the *yugalamūrti*s, pairs of images of Rādhā and Kṛṣṇa prevalent in temples from approximately the second half of the sixteenth century,[6] expressed and in turn influenced conceptions of Rādhā as Kṛṣṇa's eternal consort and co-divinity. In Brindavan and in Bengal, Jīva's theological distinction between Kṛṣṇa's *antaraṅgā* or *svarūpa-śakti*, which includes his friends and relatives in Vraja, and his *taṭasthā* or *jīva-śakti*, which is composed of ordinary human *bhakta*s, may, as we noted earlier, likewise have represented and solidified a perception of sharper lines and thus of greater distance between the characters in the Vraja *līlā* and human devotees. Of such a distinction I have found no trace in the works of Rūpa. Finally, in Bengal the stern presence of the British, who fundamentally misjudged the Vraja *līlā* as they misunderstood tantric symbolism, may also have contributed to the evolution of conceptions and practices that kept the devotee several steps removed from the inner circle of Kṛṣṇa's associates. Further historical research would be required to substantiate these conjectures, of course, but the main lines of development seem clear.

All this is not, however, to say that there is no basis whatever in Rūpa's works for the practice of *mañjarīsādhana*. In spite of Rādhā's warm humanness, she is for Rūpa an object of devotion, and not merely a model of love for Kṛṣṇa. Her supreme love is indeed her primary characteristic, but this love is unique and incomprehensible even to others in Vraja. Furthermore, the many close parallels between Rādhā and Kṛṣṇa, together with the fact that such secondary characters as Paurṇamāsī and Vṛndā, although they are not *mañjarī*s, take pleasure in serving *both* of them, indicate that the devotee is expected to relate, not solely to Kṛṣṇa, but to the entire *līlā*. Indeed, it is noteworthy that just as Rādhā and Kṛṣṇa are represented as languishing in separation and giving life to one another in union, so the representation of the drama of their eternal love is said in the prologue of the *Vidagdhamādhava* to be capable of giving life to earthly devotees separated from their Lord. Finally, in his *Saṁkṣiptabhāgavatāmṛta*, Rūpa states explicitly that the worship of Kṛṣṇa's *bhakta* is a practice as indispensable as the worship of Kṛṣṇa himself, adding that the greatest *bhakta* of Kṛṣṇa is his eternal consort Rādhā.[7] Thus we may discern hints of later developments, notably that of *mañjarīsādhana*, in Rūpa's works themselves.

How, more positively, may we characterize Rūpa's own view of the devotional life, as expressed especially in his *Vidagdhamādhava*? His drama presents us with a *darśan*, a direct vision, of love: the sublime love of Kṛṣṇa and Rādhā and the wondering love of all those in Vraja who serve and bear witness to their mutual passion. Through this vision the devotee is able to participate emotionally in the timeless *līlā* of Vṛndāvana. Yet even a phrase like "emotional participation" is too restrained to convey the full measure of what is possible: the ideal is to lose oneself completely in this love, to live one's life wholly absorbed in it and transformed by it. John Hawley's characterization of the purpose of pilgrimage to Brindavan as that of "drowning" in a sea of love[8] is relevant not only to the Brindavan *līlā*s but to Rūpa's dramas as well: the *Vidagdhamādhava*, through its vivid portrayal of emotion, draws the reader or spectator out of the mundane world and into the blessed realm of Vraja, where love is so intense that it knows no bounds.

There are a number of indications that love is itself an absolute for Rūpa. It serves as a final court of appeal in his discussion of the status of subsidiary *bhaktirasa*s: he says that *bhāva*s like anger (*krodha*) may become permanent (*sthāyin*) in persons hostile to Kṛṣṇa, but he adds that they cannot become true *bhaktirasa*s because they are devoid of love (*rati*; BRS II.5.35). In the *Vidagdhamādhava* the importance of manifesting Rādhā's (and less often Kṛṣṇa's) love, both to the other character and to the audience or reader, is so great that it outweighs all other considerations, even the pain that temporary deception may cause them. Finally, expressions used to designate Rādhā's *bhāva*, such as *durūha* or *durvibodha*, "difficult to fathom" or "incomprehensible," are reminiscent of terms earlier applied to *ātman* or *brahman*, the "self" or the absolute sought to be comprehended in portions of the Upaniṣads and throughout much subsequent Indian philosophy. It is significant that the absolute for Rūpa is not a metaphysical principle, but a transcendent emotion; it is with such love, and not with *brahman*, that unity is sought.

It is not only in replacing *brahman* with supreme love that Rūpa's exposition of the religious life departs substantially from classical Indian ideals of spirituality. Two of the three "roots of unwholesomeness" (*akuśalamūlas*) of the early Buddhist tradition, likewise regarded as hindrances in the Upaniṣads and the *Bhagavadgītā*, are wholeheartedly embraced by Rūpa. Instead of the passionlessness and wisdom that are so ardently sought by earlier Hindu and Buddhist sages and those who follow their teachings, Rūpa advocates their direct opposites: *rāga* ("passion") or *lobha* ("greed") for the first, and *moha* ("infatuation, delusion") for the second. Only the third *akuśalamūla*, *dveṣa* ("hatred, aversion"), which the *Bhāgavata* includes among its list of strong emotions toward Kṛṣṇa that can lead to the realization of Truth, is not found in Rūpa's scheme. Furthermore, the still more comprehensive term *tṛṣṇā*, "thirst," "craving," given in the Buddhist formulation of the "Four Noble Truths" as the cause of the arising of *duḥkha*, the quality of pain or unsatisfactoriness that pervades all phenomenal reality, is likewise accorded positive religious significance by Rūpa.

However, it is not attachment, greed, or craving in general that Rūpa values and urges the devotee to cultivate, but attachment to Kṛṣṇa, greed for the emotions toward him of the people of Vraja, and thirst to hear or see his blessed *līlās* with Rādhā. In his valorization of passionate love as the highest form of *bhakti*, as well as in his view of *moha* as a blessed delusion through which Kṛṣṇa's lordly majesty is veiled in his Vraja *līlā*, so that the devotee might be able to relate fully and intimately to him as the embodiment of pure sweetness, Rūpa is following the lead of the *Bhāgavata*, in which it is through *māyā* that Kṛṣṇa draws his devotees to himself.

Just as Rūpa reverses the value of certain emotional states regarded as obstacles to spiritual advance throughout much of the earlier Indian tradition, so he also consistently subordinates other deities to Kṛṣṇa and Rādhā. We have seen the way in which Śiva is typically portrayed as a devotee of Kṛṣṇa, for example, in the prologues to both of Rūpa's *nāṭakas*. The final scene in the *Vidagdhamādhava*, in which Kṛṣṇa appears as Gaurī, may similarly be construed as a deliberate statement that as Lord of the universe he is the power behind even the Goddess. Other deities, such as Brahmā and Indra are, like Śiva, portrayed as fascinated by Kṛṣṇa or otherwise subservient to him (e.g., I.28-30). Rādhā is at several points in the dramas associated with Sūrya, but her worship of him is explained as merely a ruse to enable her to meet Kṛṣṇa, and its efficacy in bringing about her love for Kṛṣṇa is emphatically denied (I.15.1-3; I.16). Sūrya is also punningly subordinated to Kṛṣṇa in the *Lalitamādhava*, in which Kṛṣṇa is described as *parābhūtasūryalakṣa*, one who has conquered hundreds of thousands of suns/Sūryas (II.22.5). Finally, Lakṣmī, consort of Viṣṇu, is represented as inferior to the *gopī*s and especially to Rādhā in both the *Ujjvalanīlamaṇi* and the *Vidagdhamādhava*, as is illustrated by a punning verse in the drama's final act, in which Rādhā's loveliness is said to put even Lakṣmī to shame (VII.32).

Rūpa's relation to other antecedent and contemporary elements in the Indian religious complex is not, however, one of wholesale rejection or invariant reversal. In specifically rejecting the formulations and practices of the school of Śaṅkara, especially its identification of the *jīva* with *brahman* and its corresponding conception of *mokṣa* as a state in which this identity is fully realized, Rūpa draws extensively on the *purāṇa*s, especially the *Bhāgavata*, as well as on much other *bhakti* literature. At the same time, he assimilates a great deal from the Indian aesthetic tradition. Many of its ordinary dramatic and poetic elements are given religious significance in the devotional context of Rūpa's plays. Moreover, the juxtaposition of explicitly religious elements with erotic love, already common in classical Sanskrit verses, here likewise takes on new meaning, for the love with which these elements are juxtaposed is itself a form of devotion.

The first of these adaptations has already been illustrated in the last chapter in our discussion of Rūpa's use of punning, a common device in Sanskrit poetry. Through puns and related figures of speech, two contradictory aspects of Kṛṣṇa, usually his transcendent nature and his human limitations, may be represented simultaneously: the truth may thus be seen to lie neither wholly in the one nor exclusively in the other, but rather in the sublime paradox of their union. An example of the second sort of adaptation is given in the summary of the sixth act, in which Madhamaṅgala humorously describes to Rādhā and her two friends the "worship" (*upāsana*) that he and Kṛṣṇa do as they keep vigil with one-pointed attention in expectation of Rādhā. The use of terms like *upāsana*, *mantra*, and *yoga* to describe the love of Rādhā and Kṛṣṇa is almost certainly deliberate: it serves to emphasize the fact that their love is an all-encompassing religious form that simultaneously embraces and supersedes all others. The elaborate verse in Act VII that juxtaposes Rādhā's abandonment to Kṛṣṇa with final liberation (*mokṣa*) makes the same point (VII.40).

In certain cases, the new devotional context of conventional elements, such as the superlatives applied to the hero, or the desire of the heroine unable to attain the object of her love to take her own life, allow these elements to achieve a level of truth otherwise inaccessible: what is hyperbole in the case of an ordinary human hero is literally true for Kṛṣṇa, and the Lord, not an earthly hero, is an object of devotion for whom it is worth giving up everything, even life itself.

Prominent among the elements from Rūpa's cultural and religious heritage that he incorporates and transforms are devotional and aesthetic forms and conceptions. We are left with the question with which we began this study, that of the relation of aesthetics and devotion in the *Vidagdhamādhava* and in Rūpa's theoretical writings. Even such a formulation of the problem, however, is predicated upon the assumption that there are *two* discrete or at least distinguishable realms to be related. Rūpa appears not to share this assumption. His identification of aesthetics and devotion is indicated in his theoretical works by his use of the compound *bhaktirasa*, the aesthetic "mood" (*rasa*) of devotion (*bhakti*), or perhaps *rasa* which is *bhakti*.

Easier than stating precisely what Rūpa understands to be the relation of aesthetics and devotion is specifying certain alternative understandings that he appears not to intend. First, he seems not to be identifying the two realms totally; we might say that he is interested in the area where the two intersect. Thus he would not identify everything usually considered beautiful as divine or a vehicle of the divine. Indeed, he describes in the *Bhaktirasāmṛtasindhu* (I.1.19) the aversion to worldly enjoyments that comes with the dawn of *rati*, love for Kṛṣṇa. Morespecifically, he is clearly aware of the fact that not all dramas are devotional, or portray the *līlā* of Kṛṣṇa. Conversely, he does not present all devotion as aesthetic; he carefully differentiates *vaidhī bhakti*, devotion that follows the injunctions of scripture, from *rāgānugā*, the more spontaneous form of devotion that is further analyzed in his subsequent discussion of *bhakti* as a *rasa*.

However, these exclusions are not so unambiguous as they at first appear. One could argue that no "aesthetic" object not connected with Kṛṣṇa's *līlā* would for Rūpa be truly beautiful. Worldly enjoyments, including secular drama, are for him clearly no sources of genuine *rasa*. Similarly, it is significant that *vaidhī bhakti* is for him only a preliminary stage designed to lead the aspirant to higher forms of *bhakti*, those described in his discussion of *bhaktirasa*. True or ideal *bhakti*, then, is a *rasa*, just as genuine *rasa* is devotional.

The unity of aesthetics and devotion for Rūpa may be shown in various ways. First, we may note the thoroughgoing manner in which aesthetic elements permeate his manifestly devotional dramas. Throughout the *Vidagdhamādhava*, as we have pointed out earlier, Kṛṣṇa, the Lord and primary object of devotion, is described in aesthetic terms. The loveliness of Rādhā, too, is frequently observed. It is in the figure of Rādhā that the unity of aesthetics and devotion may be perceived most clearly, for it is not merely her physical appearance, but more significantly her great love for Kṛṣṇa, that renders her surpassingly beautiful. Finally, the entire *līlā* of their mutual love, together with its setting, Vṛndāvana, is in the drama a constant source of aesthetic delight.

Two further illustrations of the integral relation of aesthetics and devotion in Rūpa's vision reveal at the same time the close link between the classical Indian aesthetic theory and the Vaiṣṇava view of reality, a degree of rapport that made their marriage at Rūpa's hands an ideal arrangement. The first is the persistence in Rūpa's theory of the universal quality of aesthetic experience. Just as the classical theory of *rasa*, worked out in the context of the drama, provided through the impersonality of its conception of aesthetic experience the basis for the noted philosopher Abhinavagupta to compare it to the bliss of tasting *brahman*,[9] so the relational modes conceived by Rūpa on the model of this theory, through which the Vaiṣṇava experiences the Lord, are archetypal or universal. Yaśodā, as she is represented in the *Bhāgavata*, is less a specific individual than an ideal type, motherhood itself embodied. Likewise, the *gopī*s, although they may be named in some of the later literature, such as Rūpa's plays, remain for the most part members of a class, who blend into one another as they do still more obviously in the *Bhāgavata* and earlier texts, in which they are wholly anonymous. In consonance with the classical theory, Rūpa is not advocating identification with concrete personalities, but participation in ideal modes of love and service.

A second example of the conjunction of aesthetics and devotion in Rūpa's works similarly illustrates the appropriateness of the classical aesthetic theory to Kṛṣṇa devotion. Several of the classical writers isolate *camatkāra*, "surprise, wonder," as a central element in aesthetic experience. In the Vaiṣṇava *purāṇa*s, especially the *Bhāgavata*, *vismaya*, "astonishment, wonder," is likewise a reiterated response of the inhabitants of the Vraja to Kṛṣṇa's marvellous deeds. Rūpa points to the wonder (*vismaya*) that is evoked by Kṛṣṇa's every deed (BRS IV.2. 6-7), and he asserts the close kinship of *adbhuta*, the *rasa* of wonder, with all five primary *bhaktirasa*s (BRS IV.8.9). Elsewhere he describes Kṛṣṇa's pastimes as *sarvādbhutacamatkāra*, altogether wondrous and astonishing (BRS II.1.33). For Rūpa, it is in the *līlā* of Kṛṣṇa, whose very essence is his alluring beauty, and Rādhā, his greatest *bhakta*, whose unparalleled devotion is likewise supremely beautiful, that aesthetics and devotion are most truly represented and most fully one. In the light of this fundamental unity, the formulations of Sylvain Lévi and S. K. De, who assert that Rūpa used drama for the purposes of devotion,[10] are seen to be not only inadequate but also misleading. They imply a conscious subordination of one realm to another, whereas for Rūpa the two form a unique and essential whole.

Aesthetics, and more specifically drama, has been shown to lie at the heart of Gauḍīya Vaiṣṇava devotion, especially as that devotion has been interpreted and in turn shaped by Rūpa. In his works the devotee is represented not only as witnessing the eternal drama of Kṛṣṇa and Rādhā, but also as assuming universalized roles in relation to the Lord. On this basis one might characterize Gauḍīya Vaiṣṇava religious life as essentially play-acting. Such an interpretation may seem condescending, but it is so only if we assume that we know what reality is, and that we are thus in a position to judge everything else to be illusion. This assumption was challenged as early as the third century B.C. by the Chinese philosopher Chuang-tze, who recounts a dream that he was a butterfly and muses over the question of whether he is Chuang-tze who dreamed that he was a butterfly, or a butterfly now dreaming that he is Chuang-tze. In Bengal the nineteenth- and twentieth-century poet Rabindranath Tagore, who drew considerable inspiration especially in his early years from Vaiṣṇava lyrics, expressed similar reflections in a short story entitled "The Hungry Stones."[11]

For Gauḍīya Vaiṣṇavas, the *līlā* of Kṛṣṇa with Rādhā and the others is metaphysically real: what appears to be play-acting from the perspective of the ordinary mundane world is from a different vantage point participation in the eternal drama that is ultimate reality. When a member of the Bengali Vaiṣṇava community dies, the expression generally used to communicate that fact to other Vaiṣṇava devotees is *tini nityalīlāy prabriṣṭo hayechen*, which means, literally, "He has entered the eternal *līlā*."[12] Correspondingly, the Gauḍīya Vaiṣṇava ideal for the religious life is perpetual absorption in the divine *līlā*. As we have seen, the *bhakta*'s consciousness of that *līlā* is enhanced through participation in group practices (*saṅkīrtan*, *pūjā*) and especially through drama, whether enacted physically or envisioned mentally. The *Vidagdhamādhava*, Rūpa's fullest depiction of Kṛṣṇa's *līlā* with Rādhā and his other beloved friends and relatives in Vraja, thus provides the Vaiṣṇava devotee who reads it in Sanskrit or in a vernacular translation, or sees it enacted, with a concrete mode of religious realization.

Rūpa's integral vision represents a challenge to current Western ideas of what religion is. It calls into question the conceptual distinction between the aesthetic and the religious, a distinction sharp enough that there is need of special categories--"sacred music," "religious art," "devotional drama"--to designate those points at which the "two" realms overlap.[13] It causes one to question the usually unspoken assumption that religion and eros are inherently opposed, or at least invariably separate.[14] Finally, its abundance of playful humor, like that of the medieval Christian mystery plays, challenges one to reexamine the often unwritten presupposition that religion is a serious, even somber affair, and that levity is something frivolous and therefore necessarily irreligious.[15] Through a study of the *Vidagdhamādhava* and its significance for Gauḍīya Vaiṣṇava devotion, our understanding not only of devotional drama but of religion itself is thus broadened and deepened.

APPENDIX: DRAMATIS PERSONAE

(including names and epithets of Kṛṣṇa)*

Abhimanyu	Husband of Rādhā (through the illusion created by Yogamāyā)
Aghamathana	"Destroyer of sins/(the demon) Agha," an epithet of Kṛṣṇa
Candrāvalī	Rival of Rādhā; wife of Govardhana, the superintendent of Kaṁsa's herds
Govinda	"Cowherd" (literally, "one who finds the cows"), a name of Kṛṣṇa
Hari	"Tawny," a name of Kṛṣṇa
Jaṭilā	Elderly mother of Abhimanyu; mother-in-law of Rādhā
Kakkhaṭikā	(also Kakkhaṭī) old female monkey
Kaṁsāri	"Enemy of Kaṁsa," an epithet of Kṛṣṇa
Karālā	Maternal grandmother of Candrāvalī
Kṛṣṇa	Supreme Lord of the universe; youthful cowherd; lover of the *gopī*s
Lalitā	Girl friend of Rādhā
Mādhava	"The springtime," a name of Kṛṣṇa
Madhumaṅgala	Brahman friend and confidant of Kṛṣṇa
Madhusūdana	"Slayer of (the demon) Madhu" (also, "bee"), an epithet of Kṛṣṇa
Mukharā	Maternal grandmother of Rādhā; nurse to Yaśodā
Mukunda	"Giver of release," a name of Kṛṣṇa
Murabhid	"Destroyer of (the demon) Mura," an epithet of Kṛṣṇa
Nanda	Head of the cowherd village; foster father of Kṛṣṇa

*I have made no attempt to include in this list all the many epithets of Kṛṣṇa used in the play; I give here only those that figure prominently in Act VII.

Nāndīmukhī	Granddaughter and assistant to Paurṇamāsī
Padmā	Girl friend of Candrāvalī
Pāripārśvika	Assistant to the stage manager
Paurṇamāsī	Saintly go-between; grandmother of Madhumaṅgala
Rādhā	Young bride of Abhimanyu; *gopī* most beloved of Kṛṣṇa
Rāma	Balarāma, elder brother of Kṛṣṇa
Raṅginī	Rādhā's deer
Śaivyā	Girl friend of Candrāvalī
Sāraṅgī	Young niece of Jaṭilā
Śrīdāman	Friend of Kṛṣṇa
Subala	Close friend of Kṛṣṇa
Suraṅga	Kṛṣṇa's deer
Sūtradhāra	Stage manager
Śyāmala	"Dark one," an epithet of Kṛṣṇa
Tāṇḍavika	"Dancer," Kṛṣṇa's peacock
Viśākhā	Girl friend of Rādhā
Vṛndā	Goddess of the forest Vṛndāvana, which she beautifies for Kṛṣṇa
Yaśodā	Foster mother of Kṛṣṇa

NOTES

INTRODUCTION

[1] I use the term "Gauḍīya," literally, "of Gauḍa, i.e., Bengal," rather than "Bengali," its English equivalent, because for the native English speaker Gauḍīya does not have the linguistic or regional associations of the term Bengali. The *gosvāmī*s lived in Vṛndāvana (modern Brindavan), in the Braj region of present-day Uttar Pradesh, and they wrote, not in Bengali, but in Sanskrit. Although the Gauḍīya Sampradāya has been strongest in Greater Bengal, its importance has not been confined to a single geographical area.

[2] The absolute, elsewhere in the Upaniṣads called *brahman* or *tat* (neuter), is here called *saḥ* (masculine), "he." Kṛṣṇa, the Lord (*bhagavat*), is identified by Rūpa and Jīva with the highest *rasa*, that of erotic love, called *śṛṅgāra* by the classical writers on aesthetics, and *ujjvala* or *madhura* by Rūpa. See S. K. De, *Early History of the Vaiṣṇava Faith and Movement in Bengal* (hereinafter VFM), 2nd ed. (Calcutta: K. L. Mukhopadhyay, 1961) 281.

[3] The similarities between *rasāsvāda* and *brahmāsvāda* according to Abhinavagupta's exposition are summarized by J. L. Masson and M. V. Patwardhan in *Śantarasa and Abhinavagupta's Philosophy of Aesthetics* (Poona: Bhandarkar Oriental Research Institute, 1969) 161-62. Abhinavagupta's definition of *rasa*, in which he explicitly states this comparison, is quoted by Mammaṭa in his *Kāvyaprakāśa*, in the prose section following IV.26 (lines 17ff. in the Bhandarkar Oriental Research Institute edition, Poona, 1950 [6th ed.]).

[4] Edwin Gerow, "The Persistence of Classical Esthetic Categories in Contemporary Indian Literature: Three Bengali Novels," in Edward C. Dimock, Jr. et al., *The Literatures of India* (Chicago: University of Chicago, 1974) 215.

[5] The *nāṭaka* is the full-length dramatic form that is regarded as the most basic and highest type of Sanskrit drama. Although written in the form of *nāṭaka*s, Rūpa's two dramas are considerably longer and more elaborate than their classical exemplars. In addition to his two *nāṭaka*s, Rūpa also wrote a shorter play in one act, the *Dānakelikaumudī*, which is classified as a *bhāṇikā*.

[6] On Yadunandanadāsa, see Sukumar Sen, *A History of Brajabuli Literature* (Calcutta: University of Calcutta, 1935) 180-83, 219-30.

[7] The translation of Rāmanārāyaṇa Vidyāratna is included in the Murśidābād edition of the LM, the first edition of which is dated 1288 Sāl (= ca. 1880 A.D.).

[8] Dīnśaraṇ Dās, personal communication. Haridās Dās, in *Gauḍīya Vaiṣṇava Sāhitya*, 2nd ed. (Navadvīp: Haribol Kuṭī, 483 Gaurābda = ca. 1966 A.D.), characterizes the *Vidagdhacintāmaṇi* as a series of Oriya verses describing the various *līlā*s of Kṛṣṇa, and gives Śaka 1679 (= ca. 1757 A.D.) as the year of Abhimanyu Sāmanta Siṅgara's birth (vol. 2, p. 61). He makes no mention of the *Vidagdhamādhava* as the prototype for this work, although the similarity of title suggests such a relation.

[9] For a discussion of the dates of Rūpa's works, see De, VFM, 160-63.

[10] VM: *nandasindhurabāṇendusaṁkhye saṁvatsare gate*
LM: *nandeṣuvedendum ite śakābde śuklasya māsasya tithau caturthyām/ dine dineśasya...*
The commentator glosses *śukla* with *jyeṣṭha* (May-June). The dates 1524 and 1529, arrived at by Sukumar Sen (*Bāṅgālā Sāhityer Itihās*, vol. i, 5th ed. [Calcutta: Eastern Publishers, 1970] 300), are apparently based on a mistaken equivalence of *nanda* with 1 instead of 9. In n. 2, he also gives *sindūra* for *sindhura*.

[11] For a list of Rūpa's works, see De, VFM, 152-56.

[12] The term *gosvāmī*, literally, "owner of cows," is a title of respect applied initially to the six learned teachers of Vṛndāvana whose writings constitute the most authoritative literature of the Gauḍīya Vaiṣṇava school. On the obscurity that surrounds the origin of the term, see De, VFM, 110 n. 1.

[13] CC Antya 1. See especially verses 88-90, which describe the ecstasy of Caitanya and Haridāsa when Caitanya reads VM I.15; Haridāsa in fact begins to dance. The second episode is narrated in verses 105-57 and the Sanskrit "*śloka*s" interspersed among them.

[14] CC Antya 1.139-40. Translation by Edward C. Dimock, Jr., HOS (forthcoming).

[15] Sukumar Sen, personal communication.

[16] For a brief description of *kīrtan*, see my "Images and Roles of Women in Bengali Vaiṣṇava *Kīrtan*," in Ellison B. Findly and Yvonne Haddad, eds., *Women, Religion and Social Change* (Albany, NY: State University of New York, 1985). I am working on a book-length study of this devotional musical form.

[17] BhP X.33.27-32. On the erotic aspects of Vaiṣṇava devotion, see Edward C. Dimock, Jr., *The Place of the Hidden Moon* (Chicago: University of Chicago, 1966) esp. 1-25.

NOTES

CHAPTER I

[1]Those that mention drama only briefly if at all include R. G. Bhandarkar, *Vaiṣṇavism, Śaivism and Minor Religious Systems* (Strassburg: Grundriss der indo-arischen Philologie und Altertumskunde, III, 6, 1913); Shashibhusan Dasgupta, *Obscure Religious Cults*, 3rd ed. (Calcutta: K. L. Mukhopadhyay, 1969); Jan Gonda, *Aspects of Early Viṣṇuism*, 2nd ed. (Delhi: Motilal Banarsidass, 1969); Jan Gonda, *Viṣṇuism and Śivaism: A Comparison* (London: The Athlone Press, 1970); Suvira Jaiswal, *The Origin and Development of Vaiṣṇavism* (Delhi: Munshiram Manoharlal, 1967); Rasik Vihari Joshi, *Le Rituel de la Dévotion Kṛṣṇaïte* (Pondicherry: Institut Français d'Indologie, 1959); Melville T. Kennedy, *The Chaitanya Movement*(Calcutta: Association Press, 1925); and A. K. Majumdar, *Caitanya, His Life and Doctrine: A Study in Vaiṣṇavism* (Bombay: Bharatiya Vidya Bhavan, 1969).

[2]Norvin Hein, *The Miracle Plays of Mathurā* (New Haven: Yale University, 1972) Chapter 9.

[3]I use the modern forms Braj and Brindavan in discussing recent or contemporary practices, but retain the Sanskrit forms Vraja and Vṛndāvana both for events in the life of Kṛṣṇa and for the time of the six *gosvāmīs*, who wrote in Sanskrit. It must, however, be borne in mind that the term Vraja, as it is used, for example, in the *Bhāgavata Purāṇa*, is different from modern-day Braj: the latter term designates an entire region, including the city of Mathurā, whereas the former designates the cowherd village of Nanda, where Kṛṣṇa grows up, and to which Akrūra comes in order to take him to Mathurā.

[4]Hein, *The Miracle Plays*, 259 n. 68, 113-14, 232. On Buddhist dramas, see A. Berriedale Keith, *The Sanskrit Drama* (London: Oxford University, 1924) 42-44. Especially significant for the early history of drama in India are the fragments of dramas by Aśvaghoṣa.

[5]Hein, *The Miracle Plays*, 259.

[6]There are also surprisingly few classical Śiva dramas. Yet the dramatists Śūdraka, Kālidāsa, Harṣa, and Bhavabhūti consistently extol Śiva in their prologues (Keith, *The Sanskrit Drama*, 42).

[7]For Gauḍīya Vaiṣṇavas, Kṛṣṇa is no mere *avatāra* but the Lord himself, the *avatārin*. In support of this conviction, they cite the line *kṛṣṇas tu bhagavān svayam*, BhP I.3.28.

[8]Hein, *The Miracle Plays*, 258-63.

[9]As early as the *Bhagavadgītā* we thus find a deliberate use of paradox that is reminiscent of later texts about Kṛṣṇa, notably the *Bhāgavata Purāṇa* and Rūpa's dramas.

[10]Cf. VP V.20.85-86.

[11]The term *līlā* expresses the view that the Lord is beyond the realm of purposive activity, especially as purpose is conceived by humans. His actions are thus wondrous to his devotees and ultimately incomprehensible. For a succinct discussion of this fundamental term, see Ananda K. Coomaraswamy, "*Līlā*," *JAOS* 61 (1941) 98-101. A systematic study of the term and its significance in the major Sanskrit texts of the Hindu tradition is the dissertation of Bettina Bäumer ("Schöpfung als Spiel: Der Begriff *līlā* im Hinduismus, seine philosophische und theologische Bedeutung" [München, 1969]). This research was first made available to me in India in the form of an unpublished paper by Bettina Bäumer entitled "*Līlā*." The dissertation of David R. Kinsley ("The Divine Player: A Study of Kṛṣṇa-līlā" [Divinity School, University of Chicago, 1970]) likewise focuses on *līlā*, especially but not exclusively in relation to Kṛṣṇa.

[12]HV II.21.26: *kṛṣṇalīlānukāriṇyaḥ*; VP V.13.28: *kṛṣṇalīlānukāriṇī*; BhP X.30.14: *līlā bhagavatas tās tā hy anucakrus tadātmikāḥ*. In the first two passages, the term is in compound and could thus be either singular or plural; in the third, however, it is clearly plural: "the Lord's *līlā*s." As Hein points out, the accounts become increasingly specific.

[13]VP X.13.25, 26; cf. BhP X.30.3.

[14]Hein, *The Miracle Plays*, 232, 259.

[15]Bettina Bäumer suggests that this may be one of the earliest passages in which Viṣṇu's *avatāra*s are likened to actors ("*Līlā*," 9). The idea that the gods and goddesses become incarnate among the Yādavas, through *aṁśa*s or portions of themselves, before the birth of Kṛṣṇa, is set forth in BhP X.1.22-25. Significant for the later tradition is the fact that the goddesses and also the celestial serpent Ananta, who becomes incarnate as Kṛṣṇa's elder brother Balarāma, are instructed to do so expressly for the Lord's pleasure.

[16]*Adbhuta* is one of the eight *rasa*s of the classical theory, enumerated in NŚ VI.15.

[17]The classical writers on aesthetics, beginning with Bharata (NŚ VI.17), give *vismaya* as the *sthāyibhāva* or permanent emotion of *adbhutarasa*.

[18]Cf. BhG 18.76-77, in which Sañjaya twice uses the verb *hṛṣyāmi*, "I thrill with joy." It is noteworthy that *romāñca* ("thrilling," "horripilation") is in dramatic theory one of the eight *sāttvika bhāva*s, involuntary expressions of emotion.

[19]E.g., BhP X.29.38 (*dehi dāsyam*); X.29.39 (*bhavāma dāsyaḥ*); X.29.41; X.31.2. Cf. VP V.13.41-45, in which the *gopīs* are likewise represented as quasi-devotees: they sing songs about him, meditate upon his form, and utter his name again and again.

[20]BhP XI.11.23-24. Hein quotes this passage as evidence for a tradition of enacting events in the life of Kṛṣṇa at the time of the *Bhāgavata* (*The Miracle Plays*, 262-63). For an early account of the joy derived from telling of Kṛṣṇa, see BhG X.9.

[21]Sten Konow (*Das Indische Drama* [Berlin: Walter de Gruyter, 1920] 99-102) gives the fullest and most systematic list. (The English translation by S. N. Ghosal [*The Indian Drama* (Calcutta: General Printers and Publishers, 1969) 160-65] contains serious errors.) A briefer list, together with scattered references, is found in M. Krishnamachariar (*History of Classical Sanskrit Literature*, 3rd ed. [Delhi: Motilal Banarsidass, 1974] 694), and references may also be found in Keith (*The Sanskrit Drama*, 247), and by consulting the indices of Sylvain Lévi (*Le Théatre Indien* [Paris: Collège de France, 1963; orig. ed. 1890]), and other general works on Sanskrit literature.

[22]VFM, 582-89.

[23]Rūpa's *Lalitamādhava* is unusual in combining these two phases of Kṛṣṇa's career. It is also noteworthy that it was the role of Rukmiṇī that Caitanya assumed when he and his associates staged a dramatic performance. See below, n. 51, and Chapter II, p. 40.

[24]Konow, *Das Indische Drama*, 100-101.

[25]Of these, the *Jagannāthavallabhanāṭaka* of Rāmānanda Rāya is a devotional drama on the love of Rādhā and Kṛṣṇa, and the *Kṛṣṇabhakticandrikā* of Anantadeva is from its title also clearly devotional.

[26]The *Kṛṣṇalīlā* of Vaidyanātha and the *Kṛṣṇalīlātaraṅginī* of Nārāyaṇa Tīrtha. Konow says that the second of these makes use of the *Gītagovinda* (*Das Indische Drama*, 100).

[27]Konow mentions three *Vidagdhamādhavas*, an anonymous one listed in *Sanskrit, Jain, and Hindi Manuscripts in the Sanskrit College Benares* (Allahabad, 1902, nos. 795, 778), one attributed to Śaṅkaradeva (*Alphabetical Index of Manuscripts in the Government Oriental MSS. Library Madras* [Madras, 1893]), and finally that of Rūpa. According to Śrīvatsa Goswāmī, who has examined the two manuscripts of the "anonymous" *Vidagdhamādhava* in the library of the Vārāṇaseya Saṁskṛta Viśvavidyālaya in Banaras, "they are definitely the work of Rūpa Goswāmī as the text reveals at the first glance" (personal communication). Although I have not confirmed the fact, I am fairly confident that the Madras manuscript is also of Rūpa's *Vidagdhamādhava*, for the name Śaṅkaradeva is found early in the prologue of that drama

as the one who spoke to Rūpa in a dream and told him to stage a drama representing the *līlā* of Kṛṣṇa. See Chapter III, n. 3.

[28] I intend some day to make a study of these dramas.

[29] Bak Kunbae, *Bhāsa's Bālacarita* (Delhi: Meharchand Lachhmandas, 1968). For a brief discussion of the question of Bhāsa's authorship of the thirteen Trivandrum plays, see J. L. Masson and D. D. Kosambi, *The Avimāraka* (Delhi: Motilal Banarsidass, 1970) 5-7. The *Bālacarita* is not one of the four plays that Masson tentatively assigns to a third-century A.D. playwright called Bhāsa.

[30] In the fifth act of the *Lalitamādhava*, Nārada enters singing a similar hymn of praise to Kṛṣṇa.

[31] M. Winternitz, "Kṛṣṇa-Dramen," *ZDMG* 74/1 (1920) 125.

[32] John Stratton Hawley, *Krishna, The Butter Thief* (Princeton: Princeton University, 1983) 26-28.

[33] Summarized by H. H. Wilson, *Select Specimens of the Theatre of the Hindus*, 3rd ed. (London: Trubner, 1871) II, 400-402.

[34] Summarized and discussed in De, VFM, 577-80.

[35] Ibid., 221.

[36] See the single illustration quoted by De in VFM, 580.

[37] An important difference is its inclusion of the episode of Kṛṣṇa's slaying the demon Ariṣṭa (Act V); however, Rāmānanda's use of this episode closely parallels that of the slaying of Śaṅkhacūḍa in LM II.

[38] De gives the Sanskrit of this verse (VFM, 579).

[39] "Een onbekend Indisch Tooneelstuk (Gopālakelicandrikā). Tekst met Inleiding door W. Caland," *Verhandelingen der Koninklijke Akademie van Wetenschappen te Amsterdam*, Afdeeling Letterkunde, N. R. deel XVII, No. 3 (1917). See also Winternitz, "Kṛṣṇa-Dramen," 137-44. Keith (*The Sanskrit Drama*, 274) cites the play's quoting of the *Bhāgavata Purāṇa* and mentioning of the *Mahānāṭaka*, together with the fact that the name of the author's father is given as Devajī, as evidence for its late date.

[40] Winternitz, "Kṛṣṇa-Dramen," 138.

[41] Ibid., 140; Caland, *Verhandelingen der Koninklijke Akademie*, 49. Cf. LM I.43.3, in which *āratī* is likewise offered to Kṛṣṇa.

[42] Caland, *Verhandelingen der Koninklijke Akademie*, 150. The *rāsa* dance is described in VP V.13.14-61 and BhP X.33.2-36.

[43]*Śakti*, literally "power, ability, energy," is the active power or energy of a (male) deity, often represented as his consort. The Gauḍīya Vaiṣṇavas refer to Rādhā as the *hlādinī śakti* (blissful energy) of Kṛṣṇa. See De, VFM, 279-81.

[44]F. S. Growse, *Mathurā: A District Memoir*, 3rd ed. (Allāhabad: North-Western Provinces Government Press, 1883) 79-80.

[45]Winternitz, "Kṛṣṇa-Dramen," 139. On the *svāng*, see Sir Richard Carnac Temple, *The Legends of the Panjāb* (3 vols.) (Bombay: Education Society's Press, 1884-1901) I, viii, and Nos. 6, 10, 18 and 30.

[46]Winternitz, "Kṛṣṇa-Dramen," 143.

[47]Ibid., 143, 139.

[48]Two fairly recent books surveying these forms are Balwant Gargi (*Folk Theater of India* [Seattle: University of Washington, 1966]) and J. C. Mathur (*Drama in Rural India* [New York: Asia Publishing House, 1964]). For further bibliography, see Hein, *The Miracle Plays*, 1-3 nn. 1-8.

[49]Mathur, *Drama in Rural India*, 8-11.

[50]Lévi, *Le Thêatre Indien*, 372.

[51]Gargi, *Folk Theater of India*, 117-18, 195. Mathur describes a performance of the famous *Rukmiṇī Haraṇ* of Śaṅkaradeva, commenting explicitly upon its devotional setting and religious quality (*Drama in Rural India*, 60-63).

[52]Gargi, *Folk Theater of India*, 190.

[53]K. N. Sitaram, "Dramatic Representations of South India," *JRAS* (1924) 233-34. Sitaram states, though without giving any evidence, that the *kṛṣṇanāṭṭam* goes back some four centuries, and that the only episode that was enacted was Kṛṣṇa's Rāsakrīḍa (p. 233). K. Bharatha Iyer, in *Kathakali: The Sacred Dance-Drama of Malabar* (London: Luzac, 1955), discusses the form in somewhat greater detail, stating that the performance of "*Kriṣṇāṭṭam*," which lasts for eight nights, is always a votive offering, and that the actors fast on performance days. In contrast to Sitaram, he gives a plurality of themes from the legends of Kṛṣṇa, including his birth, and states that *kriṣṇāṭṭam* was first staged about 1650 A.D. (p. 20). Cf. Enakshi Bhavnani (*The Dance in India* [Bombay: D. B. Taraporevala, 1965]), who likewise gives 1650 A.D. as the approximate date of the origin of this dramatic form (p. 43). On *kūṭiyāṭṭam* and *kathakali*, see Iyer (*Kathakali*, 17-19, 23ff.). On *kūṭiyāṭṭam*, see also the articles of K. Rama Pisharoti and Kunjanni Raja cited in Masson and Kosambi (*The Avimāraka*, 21-23 n. 20).

[54]Gargi, *Folk Theater of India*, 127.

[55]Hein, *The Miracle Plays*, 31-54.

[56]Gargi also mentions *rās* dancers of Gujarat and Saurashtra, but gives no further information about them. The *chau* of Seraikella in Bihar is a dance drama that includes Kṛṣṇa episodes in its repertoire (*Folk Theater of India*, 173).

[57]Ibid., 195-96. During my stay in Brindavan in August and September of 1972, I heard several highly moving performances by the outstanding Bengali *kīrtan* troupe of Nanda Kiśor Dās.

[58]S. K. De, in his *Bengali Literature in the Nineteenth Century* (2nd ed. [Calcutta: K. L. Mukhopadhyay, 1962]), says that the earliest *yātrā* of which there is mention was known as *kṛṣṇayātrā* and enacted themes of *kṛṣṇalīlā* (p. 408). Unfortunately, he supplies us with neither approximate dates nor references.

[59]William Ward, in a voluminous work published in 1811, writes that it was the Kṛṣṇa *yātrās* (as opposed to those about Rāma and Durgā) that were the most popular and drew the largest crowds; *Account of the Writings, Religion, and Manners of the Hindoos*, Vol. 2 (Serampur, 1811) section XVIII, as quoted by Ramakanta Chakrabarty in his introduction to the Indian reprint of Niśikanta Chaṭṭopādhyāya, *The Yātrās: Or the Popular Dramas of Bengal* (Calcutta: Granthan, 1976) 11 n. 14.

[60]For statements attesting to the emotional quality of *yātrā* performances, see P. Guha-Thakurta, *The Bengali Drama* (London: Kegan Paul, Trench, Trubner, 1930) 28; B. H. Bon, "Drama," *Indian Philosophy and Culture*, Vrindaban, XI/4 (December, 1966) 6-7; and Gargi, *Folk Theater of India*, 15. Gargi states that the highly emotional theme of Kṛṣṇa's departure for Mathurā has been a favorite of singers and players (p. 14).

[61]De mentions three such themes: the *dān*, *mān*, and *māthur līlās* (*Bengali Literature in the Nineteenth Century*, 408).

[62]These include the following: *Mānabhaṅga*, *Kalaṅkabhañjana Dānakhaṇḍa*, *Naukākhaṇḍa*, *Vastraharaṇa*, *Rāsa*, *Goṣṭhayātrā*, and *Rādhikā Rājā*. *Ṭulīsaṁvada* may also be on this theme.

[63]Śukdeb Siṁha, *Srīrūp O Padāvalīsāhitya* (Calcutta: Bharati Book Stall, 1967).

[64]This excerpt, which portrays Rādhā's mad search through the forest for her departed lover, has been translated by Chaṭṭopādhyāya (*The Yātrās*, 41-47).

[65]Ibid., 13-14. Chaṭṭopādhyāya is not altogether clear on this point; see his comments on Jaṭilā and Kuṭilā (pp. 12-13).

[66]In the folk version, Jaṭilā and Kuṭilā are sisters-in-law of Rādhā, and their brother, not named by Chaṭṭopādhyāya, is a hermaphrodite! Kṛṣṇa is about to be caught with Rādhā in her house, but at the critical moment, aware of the sisters' plot,

he assumes the form of the goddess Kālī, and Rādhā judiciously affects an attitude of worship as the two sisters and her husband burst in to apprehend them.

[67]Hein, *The Miracle Plays*, Part II; John Stratton Hawley, *At Play with Krishna: Pilgrimage Dramas from Brindavan* (Princeton: Princeton University Press, 1981). Both these works consider the *rās līlā*s in a broad context: Hein's book is especially instructive regarding the economic and social circumstances of the performances, whereas Hawley's distinctive strength is in illuminating the plays' religious significance by exploring their contexts of pilgrimage and worship. On the *mākhan corī līlā*s, those representing the thievery of Kṛṣṇa, especially his stealing of butter, see Hawley, *Krishna, The Butter Thief*, Part III.

[68]Hein enumerates the main elements of the *rās* and describes each of them in succession (*The Miracle Plays*, 143-52).

[69]For a description of a dramatic form that approximates still more closely to image worship, see Hein's discussion of *jhāṅkī* (*The Miracle Plays*, 17-30).

[70]An alphabetical list of more than a hundred *līlā*s, a succinct plot summary for each, is given in Hein (*The Miracle Plays*, 165-78).

[71]The contrast and tension between *aiśvarya* and *mādhurya* in the *līlā* of Kṛṣṇa is explored by Jīva Gosvāmī in his *Prītisandarbha*, summarized by De (VFM, 380-412; see esp. 399-400).

[72]Hein, *The Miracle Plays*, 164-65.

[73]Ibid., 153.

[74]Ibid., 156.

[75]Ibid., 178 no. 103. Cf. VM II, in which Rādhā, lovesick for Kṛṣṇa, is presumed to be ill, and Kṛṣṇa is said to be the only one who can cure her. Still closer to Cācā Vṛndāvanadāsa's disguise *līlā*s is the episode in LM II in which Kṛṣṇa comes to Rādhā in the guise of a brahman priest and assists her in worshipping Sūrya. Another disguise episode is found in the *garbhāṅka* (play-within-a-play) in *Lalitamādhava* IV, in which Kṛṣṇa dons the garb of Abhimanyu and thereby deceives Jaṭilā, who allows him to meet Rādhā.

[76]Ibid., 156.

[77]See, for example, the episode of Śiva's adoption of the disguise of a brahman youth in Kālidāsa's *Kumārasambhava*, V.30ff.

[78]I intend to explore this possibility in a subsequent study, assuming that earlier sources than those presently available can be found.

[79]As mentioned above, *kīrtan* is a semi-dramatic musical form representing episodes from the love of Rādhā and Kṛṣṇa. The performances that I attended in 1972 were by an outstanding troupe from Bengal. Its leader, Nanda Kiśor Dās, was able to hold the audience spellbound for hours as he sang of the subtle intricacies of Rādhā's and Kṛṣṇa's unfolding love.

[80]These include the *Nāṭyaśāstra*, the *Daśarūpaka*, the *Sāhityadarpaṇa*, and the *Rasārṇavasudhākara*; see De, VFM, 202, 221.

[81]*Śāstras* are systematic treatises on diverse areas of knowledge, such as philosophy, grammar, medicine, law (understood in an extremely broad sense: *dharma*), and aesthetics (including dramaturgy). Rūpa was especially well read in Sanskrit poetry, drama, and aesthetics, as well as in the *purāṇas*.

[82]For Sanātana and his works, see De, VFM, 146-49, 151-52.

[83]In this connection it is noteworthy that Rūpa's first dramatic work, the one-act *Dānakelikaumudī*, may have been written as early as 1495, long before Rūpa met Caitanya and took up residence in Brindavan; see De, VFM, 161-62 n. 1. In his *Chandidas* (New Delhi: Sahitya Akademi, 1971), Sukumar Sen mentions a village near Rāmakeli (the home of Rūpa, Sanātana, and Jīva), Kānāir Nāṭsāla (literally, play-hall of Kṛṣṇa), which was famous for some form of dramatic representation of the *līlās* of Kṛṣṇa (p. 16). Unfortunately, he gives no references, and the sources on which he is drawing are vague about the sort of performance that took place there. Cf. CC II.1. 213: "Prabhu came to Kānāir Nāṭaśālā, and saw there all the līlā of the acts of Kṛṣṇa" (Dimock, trans.)

[84]Although the *Gītagovinda* is not a drama in the strict sense of the term, its dramatic qualities have long been recognized in descriptions and designations. For a representative sample, see S. C. Mukherji, *A Study of Vaiṣṇavism in Ancient and Medieval Bengal* (Calcutta: Punthi Pustak, 1966) 98-99. Barbara Stoler Miller, in the introduction to her *Love Song of the Dark Lord* (New York: Columbia University, 1977), likewise styles it "a dramatic lyrical poem" (p. 9) and suggests that Rādhā, Kṛṣṇa, and Rādhā's friend function in the poem much as do the characters of a drama (pp. 15-16). She also mentions several devotional contexts in which the poem has been sung and danced. The *Gītagovinda* itself, together with its performance traditions, therefore constitutes additional evidence for the central importance of drama in Kṛṣṇa devotion.

[85]The inscription is given in English by Barbara Miller (*Love Song*, 6). See Monmohan Chakravarti, "Uriya Inscriptions of the 15th and 16th Centuries," *JASB* 62/1 (1894) 88-104.

NOTES

CHAPTER II

[1]A *pada* is a highly concentrated and expressive verse form employed in Bengali and Brajabuli lyrics. For a brief characterization of its form and subject-matter, see Edward C. Dimock, "The Place of Gauracandrikā in Bengali Vaiṣṇava Lyrics," JAOS 78 (1958) 153-54.

[2]The edition of the *Bhaktirasāmṛtasindhu* that I have used is that of Haridās Dās, 2nd ed. (Navadvīp: Haribol Kuṭi, 475 Gaurābda = ca. 1958).

[3]For the editions of the *Ujjvalanīlamaṇi* that I have consulted, see the Bibliography. I follow the numbering in the Kāvyamālā edition (Bombay: Nirṇaya Sāgar Press, 1932) (Kāvyamālā 95).

[4]Excellent comprehensive summaries of Rūpa's two works on *bhaktirasa* are found in De, VFM, 170-221.

[5]For a summary of the classical *rasa* theory, as outlined in the *Nāṭyaśāstra* (*Adhyāya*s VI and VII), see S. K. De, *History of Sanskrit Poetics* (hereinafter HSP), 2nd ed. (Calcutta: K. L. Mukhopadhyaya, 1960) II, 16-25. A shorter but highly lucid and penetrating discussion is found in Daniel H.H. Ingalls, trans., *An Anthology of Sanskrit Court Poetry* (hereinafter *Anthology*) (Cambridge, MA: HOS, 1965) 13-16. Chapter VI of the *Nāṭyaśāstra*, together with portions of Abhinavagupta's commentary, is translated by J. L. Masson and M. V. Patwardhan in their *Aesthetic Rapture*, 2 vols. (Poona: Deccan College Postgraduate and Research Institute, 1970). The theory of *rasa* is also expounded in Book IV of the *Daśarūpaka*; see George C. O. Haas, trans., *The Daśarūpa* (New York: Columbia University, 1912). Two recent articles on *rasa*, by Eliot Deutsch and Edwin Gerow, are included in a volume edited by Rachel Van Meter Baumer and James R. Brandon (*Sanskrit Drama in Performance* [Honolulu: The University Press of Hawaii, 1981]), together with two by V. Raghavan and Kapila Vatsyayan that explore the important question of the way in which classical Sanskrit dramas were performed in ancient India.

[6]This analogy, first found in germ in NŚ VI.35, and elaborated by Abhinavagupta in his commentary on NŚ VI.31, is used by Rūpa at BRS II.5.57, where he refers to the mixture as *rasāla*.

[7]*śrīkṛṣṇaviṣayā ratiḥ*, "love that has Kṛṣṇa as its object," BRS II.5.2. Yet, as we shall soon see, love for Rādhā is likewise of great importance for Rūpa.

[8]The eight *rasa*s are listed in NŚ VI.15 and in De, HSP, II, 23. For the ninth, see Masson and Patwardhan, *Śāntarasa and Abhinavagupta's Philosophy of Aesthetics*.

[9]The entire Vraja *līlā* is said to be occurring continually in an unmanifest (*aprakaṭa*) form in the "heavenly" Vṛndāvana. The countless *līlā*s that Kṛṣṇa manifested once sequentially on earth are viewed as going on simultaneously in the various cosmic realms. On the complexities of the relation between the *prakaṭa* and the *aprakaṭa līlā*s in Jīva's exposition, see De, VFM, 333-48.

[10]See Masson and Patwardhan, *Śāntarasa and Abhinavagupta's Philosophy of Aesthetics*, 153-64.

[11]*sāmayika*, BRS II.5.33.

[12]BRS II.5.87. Here and elsewhere we see the primary importance of love in Rūpa's theory; cf. BRS II.5.35.

[13]In the *Ujjvalanīlamaṇi*, Rūpa designates this "the king of the *bhaktirasa*s" (*bhaktirasarāj*) (UNM, *nāyakabhedāḥ* 2.).

[14]*durūhatva*, *rahasyatva*, BRS III.5.2.

[15]De, VFM, 176-77.

[16]Edward C. Dimock, Jr., *The Place of the Hidden Moon* (Chicago: University of Chicago, 1966) 22.

[17]Joseph T. O'Connell, "Social Implications of the Gauḍīya Vaiṣṇava Movement" (unpublished doctoral thesis, Harvard University, 1970) 241-45.

[18]O'Connell mentions the *Prārthana* of Narottama, a disciple of Jīva, as an expression of *mañjarīsādhana* ("Social Implications," 241). In the *Gauragaṇoddeśadīpikā* of Kavikarṇapūra, a work of the first quarter of the seventeenth century, the six Vṛndāvana *gosvāmī*s are identified with six *mañjarī*s, the name of each of which is an abstraction: Rūpa, Lāvaṇya, Rati, Guṇa, Vilāsa, and Rasa. According to De, "of this elaborate scheme there is no trace in the works of the Vṛndāvana Gosvāmins themselves" (VFM, 177 n. 1). For the contrasting practice of Rādhābhāva, see De on Gadādhara Paṇḍita (VFM, 94 n. 2 [from p. 93]). There is, so far as I am aware, no systematic study of the development of the conception of a *mañjarī* or of the practice of *mañjarībhāva*.

[19]Shashibhusan Dasgupta, *Obscure Religious Cults*, 125.

[20]De, VFM, 182.

[21]Both *rāga* and *rāgātmikā* are defined by Rūpa in BRS I.2.71.

[22]*virājatīm abhivyaktām vrajavāsijanādiṣu*
rāgātmikām anusṛtā yā sā rāgānugocyate (BRS I.2.69)

[23]After quoting Jīva's commentary virtually verbatim, with evident approval, Viśvanātha labels the identification of a *sādhaka* aspirant with Nanda *ahaṁgrahopāsana* (a form in which the worshipper identifies himself with the object of his worship, as represented, for example, in the *aham brahmāsmi* formula [BAU I.4.10] of Advaita Vedānta).

[24]Rūpa himself uses the related terms *sādhakarūpa* and *siddharūpa* in BRS I.2.89, but he there indicates that *sevā* is to be performed with *both* forms.

[25]De, VFM, 277ff.

[26]Viśvanātha's commentary on BRS I.2.88.

[27]BRS I.2.86. In the preceding verse, Rūpa uses the adjectival form *lubdha*, "greedy," and in a later passage he uses the still more emphatic compound *gurulubdhatā*, "great desire" (I.3.20). It is striking that greed (*lobha*) and attachment or love (*rāga*), both unequivocally condemned in earlier Indian texts, such as the *Bhagavadgītā* and the Pāli texts of the Theravāda Buddhist canon, are here regarded as highly desirable, indeed, as essential for spiritual progress.

[28]BhP III.1.32, as quoted by Rūpa to illustrate BRS II.2.3.

[29]See Sukumar Sen, *A History of Brajabuli Literature*.

[30]The alternatives that I have surveyed are by no means exhaustive. In his interviews of residents of Braj who regularly attend *rās līlā* performances, Hawley asked them whose part they were accustomed to take as they witnessed these representations. More often than not, they were surprised by the question, and many said that they identified with everyone (personal communication). At the opposite end of the spectrum were the responses of two prominent, highly educated Vaiṣṇavas with whom I spoke extensively in Calcutta: both Prāṇ Kiśor Gosvāmī and Mahanam Brata Brahmachari characterized the process of *sādhana* as taking place in a single *bhāva* over the course of a devotee's entire lifetime.

[31]*nave ratyaṅkure jāte haribhaktasya kasyacit*
vibhāvatvādihetutvam kiñcit tat kāvyanāṭyayoḥ
harer īṣac chrutividhau rasāsvādaḥ satām bhavet
rater eva prabhāvo 'yam hetus teṣāṁ tathākṛtau
(BRS II.5.70-71)

[32]On the basis of such an interpretation of this passage, Prem Latā Sharma has characterized the *Nāṭakacandrikā*, Rūpa's treatise on dramaturgy, as "a manual for the guidance of those who want to depict the deeds of the Lord through drama, for the benefit of novices" ("Studies in Bhaktirasa [Śrī Rūpa Gosvāmī]," unpublished doctoral thesis, Benares Hindu University, 1954, 208).

[33] Rūpa's *stotras*, which number some sixty-four, were gathered by his nephew Jīva into a collection called *Stavamālā*, published in the *Kāvyamālā* series (No. 84). The *Padyāvalī* has been edited by S. K. De (Dacca: Dacca University Oriental Publication Series, 1934).

[34] Rūpa's two *nāṭakas* are included in the *ācārya* course in Gauḍīya Vaiṣṇava *darśana* in Bengal (Dīnśaraṇ Dās, personal communication).

[35] The term *rasika*, derived from *rasa*, refers in classical usage to a person of educated tastes and refined aesthetic sensibility. In a devotional context it designates a type of *bhakta*, one who derives religious inspiration from artistic representations of the Lord's *līlā*.

[36] The phrase Rūpa uses in this verse (I.6) to designate his play is *hariguṇamayī kṛtir iyam*.

[37] The commentator is not named in KM, but in B the commentary is attributed to Viśvanātha Cakravartī, the seventeenth-century commentator on Rūpa's two works on *bhaktirasa*. Viśvanātha is also listed as the author of the commentary in the description of manuscript no. 42112 in *A Descriptive Catalogue of the Sanskrit Manuscripts* (Varanasi: Vārāṇaṣeya Saṁskṛta Viśvavidyālaya, 1964), but Śrīvatsa Goswāmī attributes this identification to the scribe (one Rāmadhana, 1910 v.s. = ca. 1853 A.D.), observing that the commentary itself does not give the name of its author (personal communication).

[38] See Hein, *The Miracle Plays*, 135-36. Intriguing in this connection is Jīva's theoretical discussion of the locus of *rasa:* unlike the classical writers on poetics, he maintains that *rasa* inheres not only in the spectator (*sahṛdaya*), but also in the character (*anukārya*), notably Kṛṣṇa, and also in the actor (*anukartṛ*). Although he is nowhere so explicit, Rūpa would seem to agree.

[39] As I indicated in the Introduction, it is not known whether Rūpa's plays were ever performed in Sanskrit, and it is not even clear that he intended them to be staged.

[40] For a discussion of the biographies of Caitanya and their dates, see De, VFM, 35-63.

[41] See Chapter I, n. 7.

[42] De, VFM, 422ff.

[43] *anarpitacarīm cirāt karuṇayāvatīrṇaḥ kalau*
samarpayitum unnatojjvalarasām svabhaktiśriyam
hariḥ puraṭasundaradyutikadambasaṁdīpitaḥ
sadā hṛdayakandare sphuratu vaḥ sacīnandanaḥ (I.2)

Ujjvala is another name used by Rūpa for *madhura*.

[44]The opening verse of Raghunāthadāsa's *aṣṭaka* on Caitanya narrates this story, attributing Kṛṣṇa's desire to taste his own sweetness to his falling in love with his own image as reflected in a mirror. A variant is found in the third verse of a *caitanyāṣṭaka* of Rūpa, in which it is Kṛṣṇa's longing to experience the sweet feeling of the *gopīs* that led him to steal the golden complexion of Rādhā (De, VFM, 423-25).

[45]See De, VFM, 421-47.

[46]CC III.2.18; cf. II.1.47. The link between Caitanya's ecstatic emotions and the conviction that the names of God, whether recited or sung, have the power to induce the divine presence, is explored in an important article by Norvin Hein ("Caitanya's Ecstasies and the Theology of the Name," in Bardwell L. Smith, ed., *Hinduism: New Essays in the History of Religions* [Leiden: E. J. Brill, 1976]).

[47]E.g., CC II.6.2.

[48]*bahudhābhaktirasābhinarttakaḥ*, Murāri Gupta, *Caitanya-caritāmṛta* 1, as quoted in Bäumer, "*Līlā*," 14 n. 58.

[49]De, VFM, 565; Majumdar, *Caitanya*, 140-41.

[50]De, VFM, 446; Majumdar, *Caitanya*, 143.

[51]CC II.1.136.

[52]CC II.15, as quoted in Hein, "Caitanya's Ecstasies," 109-10. Hein sees this event as Caitanya's participation in a Rāmlīlā that was open to amateurs and presented the events of the Rāmāyaṇa in serial fashion over the course of many days.

[53]CB I.6 (ed. Atulkṛṣṇa Gosvāmī, pp. 283-91) as cited in De, *Bengali Literature in the Nineteenth Century*, 408-9. Cf. Gargi, *Folk Theater of India*, 14-15; Majumdar, *Caitanya*, 147-48. According to De (*Bengali Literature*), the incident is also mentioned in the *Caitanyamaṅgala*; unfortunately, he does not specify which of the two extant works of that name he means see De, VFM, 58-61.

[54]See Chapter I, n. 84. The continuity in this respect between the *Gītagovinda* and a later Bengali work has been observed by Sukumar Sen in his *Chandidas*, in which he maintains that "Jayadeva's poem is a sort of lyric play and so is Chandidas's *Śrīkṛṣṇakīrtan* in a proper estimation" (p. 17).

[55]See the selection translated by Edward C. Dimock, Jr. and Denise Levertov, *In Praise of Krishna: Songs from the Bengali* (New York: Doubleday Anchor, 1967). A collection of *padas* (in Bengali script) has been edited by Sukumar Sen (*Vaiṣṇava-Padāvalī* [New Delhi: Sahitya Akademi, 1971]). The largest and best-known anthology is the late eighteenth-century *Padakalpataru* (available in various editions, e.g. that of Keśav Lāl Rāy, Calcutta, n.d.). The dramatic qualities of temporality and irony in the Hindi poems on the child Krishna

attributed to Sūrdās are explored by Kenneth Bryant in an illuminating study entitled *Poems to the Child-God: Structures and Strategies in the Poetry of Sūrdās* (Berkeley: University of California, 1978) see esp. 35-42.

[56]"Dāmodarastotra" of Satyavrata, in *Bṛhatstotraratnākara*, ed. Rāmāteja Pāṇḍeya (Varanasi: Paṇḍit Pustakālay, 1970) 198 vss. 5-7.

[57]Included in Sen, *Vaiṣṇava-Padāvalī*, 57-58, no. 90. In the Kāvyamālā edition of the *Stavamālā* (Bombay: Nirṇaya Sāgar Press, 1903) (Kāvyamālā 84), the verse is found on page 275, under the general category *rāsalīlāvarṇanam*, as an illustration of the type of heroine called *abhisārikā*.

[58]*śravaṇam nāmacaritaguṇādīnām śrutir bhavet*, BRS I.2.37; cf. I.2.39: *dhyānam rūpaguṇakrīḍāsevādeḥ suṣṭhu cintanam*.

[59]*śrimadbhāgavatārthānām āsvādo rasikaiḥ saha*, BRS I.2.(61). The sixty-four *bhaktyaṅga*s are enumerated initially between I.2.26 and I.2.27, and then given separately and illustrated with verses from the *purāṇa*s and related texts. The editor has numbered them sequentially from one to sixty-four, and put those numbers in parentheses after the *bhaktyaṅga*s in the second, separate listing. Although I have taken this definition from the initial list, I have followed the editor in giving the parenthetical reference.

[60]BRS I.2.(55, 64). 64: *śrīmanmathurāmaṇḍale sthitiḥ*.

[61]*nāmasaṅkīrtanam*, BRS I.2.(63). The practice has come to include singing the name of Rādhā together with that of Kṛṣṇa.

[62]*yathāvaibhavasāmagrīsadgoṣṭhībhir mahotsavaḥ*, BRS I.2.(57).

[63]BRS I.2.(24, 40, 60). 60: *śraddhā viśeṣataḥ prītiḥ śrīmūrter aṅghrisevane*; cf. CC II.22.68.

[64]Vrajamaṇḍala/Brajmandal. Cf. BRS I.2.(64), in which is found the related term *mathurāmaṇḍala*.

[65]This phrase from Eliade seems singularly apt here. See Mircea Eliade, *The Sacred and the Profane* (New York: Harcourt, Brace, 1959) chap. 2.

[66]The term *banjātrā* (Sanskrit *vanayātrā*) means literally "forest journey or pilgrimage."

[67]Hein, *The Miracle Plays*, 159-60.

[68]See Viśvanātha's commentary on BRS I.2.88.

[69]See the summary of Gopāla Bhaṭṭa's *Haribhaktivilāsa* in De, VFM, 448-529, esp. 496.

[70]See De, VFM, 46-47 n. 2, 598-610. The *Smaraṇamaṅgala* attributed to Rūpa, a brief work of eleven verses, is said by

Kṛṣṇadāsa to form the basis for his elaborate *kāvya* (De, VFM, 604). De reconstructs these verses on the basis of a single manuscript, and quotes them in full in VFM (673-75).

[71]See O'Connell, "Social Implications."

[72]*Anubhāvas, sāttvika bhāvas*; see the preceding discussion of Caitanya's emotional expressions.

[73]Mahanam Brata Brahmachari, *Gaurakathā* (Prathama Khaṇḍa) (Calcutta: Mahānām Sampradāy, 1367 Sāl = ca. 1959 A.D.), 55. Dr. Brahmachari uses this example to illustrate the process through which a devotee who tastes with delight the sweetness of Kṛṣṇa (*kṛṣṇamādhurya*) can awaken desire in one who witnesses his joy.

[74]What is at stake here, in my judgment, is not a practical matter, but a metaphysical one. The context of Rūpa's verses on the efficacy of *kāvya* and *nāṭya* is a discussion in which he first refutes the view that the chief cause of the *vibhāvatva* and so forth of Kṛṣṇa and all associated with him is seeing or hearing poetry and drama about the Lord, asserting instead that the essential cause is the power of *rati*, which he describes as *suduṣṭarkamādhuryādbhutasampad*, having the wondrous wealth of inconceivable sweetness. Unlike the *sthāyibhāva* of a mundane drama, *rati* is no ordinary human emotion; it is nothing less than the play (*vilāsa*) of the Lord's *mahāśakti*, identified by Jīva in the commentary as his *hlādinīśakti*, whose essence is inconceivable. It is this wondrous *rati* that makes Kṛṣṇa and the others into *vibhāva*s and so forth and is in turn strengthened by them, just as the ocean nourishes the clouds and is subsequently increased through them (BRS II.5.65-69). Unlike an ordinary human emotion, therefore, *rati* for Kṛṣṇa does not need an aesthetic medium to make it relishable, for it is itself transcendent (*alaukika*) and thus capable of becoming transformed into *rasa* in the heart of a *bhakta* without the aid of poetry or drama. Its very *alaukikatva*, however, makes it capable of transforming the entire life of the *bhakta*, of facilitating for him or her a lifelong participation in the supreme drama, a mode of experience that is simultaneously intensely aesthetic and profoundly religious. On the *alaukikatva* of *rati*, see Uma Ray (*Gauḍīya Vaiṣṇavīya Raser Alaukikatva* [Calcutta: Indian Associates, 1363 Sāl = ca. 1955 A.D.]).

NOTES

CHAPTER III

[1]*kiśorībhujaṅga* (II.52.6). *Bhujaṅga* means "snake" and also "lecherous man." For the citation convention used here, see below, p. 68.

[2]See I.3.6, "*Vidagdhamādhava* composed by you," and I.4, "this composition of mine."

[3]Rūpa, in his role as *sūtradhāra*, says that he was directed to enact the amorous sports of Kṛṣṇa by Lord Śrīśaṅkaradeva (Śiva), a *bhaktāvatāra*. The commentator glosses *bhaktāvatāreṇa bhagavatā śrīśaṅkaradevena* with *brahmakuṇḍatīravartinā gopīśvaranāmnā*, "the one named Gopīśvara, dwelling on the bank of the Brahmakuṇḍa," and then says simply "Śaṅkara," i.e., Śiva. At I.3.3 the text calls the author of the command *jagadguru*, the teacher of the world, which the commentator glosses with "Mahādeva" (Śiva). In the *prastāvanā* of the LM (I.2.2-8), Śiva is likewise represented as commanding Rūpa in a dream, this time to perform the *Lalitamādhava* for the group of Vaiṣṇavas who have assembled on the bank of the Rādhākuṇḍa for the worship of Mount Govardhana at the beginning of the Dīvālī festival.

Taken together with VM I.29--in which Śiva is depicted metaphorically as an ocean that overflows its shores, drawn by the rise of the moon-face of Hari, who is emitting the nectar of the sounds of his flute--these passages seem to represent a consistent perception of Śiva as subordinate to Kṛṣṇa, whose *bhakta*s he serves and whose sweet beauty even he finds irresistible.

The precise significance of *bhaktāvatāra*, as used here by Rūpa, is unclear to me. According to S. K. De, the term is often applied to Caitanya (VFM, 431, 433, 438, 571). Here, however, it is Śiva who is said to be an *avatāra*. Yet it is not obvious in what form Vaiṣṇavas have perceived him as dwelling in Vṛndāvana.

In the third act of Kavikarṇapura's *Caitanyacandrodaya*, in the *garbhāṅka*, or play-within-a-play, Rādhā and her friends are seen gathering flowers for the worship of Gopīśvara Śiva (De, VFM, 571-72).

[4]Bhānutīrtha must have been a pilgrimage place on the Yamunā that was dedicated to the sun (Sūrya, of which Bhānu is a synonym). The significance for the play's main events of the fact that Rādhā was taken there is not clear to me; the name may, however, be related to her worship of Sūrya, which is mentioned at several points in the drama. See especially I.16.

[5]The term *lokottara* means both "transcendent" and "extraordinary." Its ambiguity makes it especially well suited to the context of Kṛṣṇa dramas, where the hero is both: Kṛṣṇa is simultaneously a remarkable youth and the Lord of the Universe.

For the significance of *lokottara* in relation to Rādhā, see Chapter VI, p. 127.

[6]The commentator (at I.14), apparently basing his remark on such passages as VII.1.7, says that Mathurā (the city of King Kaṁsa, which is several miles from the pastoral Vṛndāvana), is the place to which Abhimanyu desires to take Rādhā.

[7]I.15. The word *amṛta*, "nectar," is highly significant for Kṛṣṇa devotion in this aesthetic mode: a central metaphor is that of drinking the sweet nectar that is the sound of Kṛṣṇa's name. For a discussion of this verse, see Chapter VI, p. 122.

[8]As Kṛṣṇa's name is to Rādhā, Rādhā's name is experienced by Kṛṣṇa as sweet. Cf. VI.24 and the lines immediately preceding it (VI.23.42-43), summarized here on p. 60.

[9]See Chapter V, pp. 99-105, for a discussion of Kṛṣṇa's beauty and its significance for devotion in this aesthetic mode.

[10]Sanskrit verses are composed of four *pāda*s, or "quarters," with *caesurae* between the first and second and between the third and fourth, and a longer pause between the second and third.

[11]*tābhir ... adhikakelikalotsukābhiḥ*, "by those ___, exceedingly eager for dalliance/sport."

[12]*ghaṭā*, "number, troop, assemblage," here itself used in the plural: *suhṛdghaṭābhiḥ*.

[13]Balarāma, here simply called Rāma. He later slips away under a pretext when Kṛṣṇa, hearing Rādhā's name from Paurṇamāsī, shows signs of his infatuation. As Kṛṣṇa's elder brother, he would, like Kṛṣṇa's foster parents, be a source of embarrassment to Kṛṣṇa under such circumstances. Like Nanda and Yaśodā, therefore, he does not reappear for the duration of the play.

[14]I.31.21-22. The stage directions here include two of the eight *sāttvika bhāva*s listed in the *Daśarūpaka* (DR 4.7) and other standard works on dramaturgy, *romāñca* (horripilation) and *vepathu* (trembling) (*kampamāna*, 1.22). For a discussion of such dramatic elements and their significance for Rūpa, see Chapter II, p. 43.

[15]Through passages such as this (cf. II.35) are revealed theological and devotional truths. The friends' statement that Kṛṣṇa is only one is reminiscent of the Upaniṣadic passage *ekam eva advitīyam*, "one only, without a second" (*Chāndogya Upaniṣad* VI.2.1), which asserts the uniqueness of *sat*, "being"; the Upaniṣad later identifies *sat* with *ātman*. Here, however, it is a single object of *love* that is revealed. These words come as a supreme consolation to Rādhā, who once again desires to live. Her friends then compare Rādhā to a *campaka* blossom: the purpose of her existence will remain unfulfilled unless Kṛṣṇa (Madhusūdana, also "bee") hovers about her, drinking nectar to his heart's content (II.10).

[16]*Vṛndāvanamadana* (II.11). Madana is Kāmadeva, the inflamer of passions, love itself personified. The Kāma of Vṛndāvana is, of course, Kṛṣṇa. As an adjective, *madana* means "intoxicating, maddening," as well as "delighting, exhilarating." Kṛṣṇa has both effects on the inhabitants of Vṛndāvana.

[17]These events are not described again; Viśākhā says simply "*evam etat*," "it happened in this way," thereby saving the audience from having to listen to a recapitulation of what they have just seen.

[18]The conflict between the auspicious course of righteous conduct (here, *kalyāṇī dharmaśailī*) followed by respectable women and Rādhā's growing passion for Kṛṣṇa is the subject of several verses in the first acts of the drama (I.34, II.14, III.38).

[19]*nāgarendra*, i.e., Kṛṣṇa. See Chapter V, pp. 105-6, for a discussion of *nāgara*. Rūpa here (II.14) plays on the word: the full compound is *paśupanagarīnāgarīnāgarendraḥ*, the prince of *nāgara*s of the *nāgara* women of the city of cowherds.

[20]The word used by Mukharā (II.15), *graha*, "planet," also refers to a class of evil demons that are supposed to seize children and cause convulsions and other maladies. Mukharā calls Rādhā *bālā*, child. Paurṇamāsī makes the former term more specific, saying *aṅganāgraha*, an evil spirit that seizes women (or, referring to Kṛṣṇa, one who "seizes" women by his attractiveness), and likewise refers to Rādhā as *bālā*.

[21]This is indeed the proper cure, of course, but for entirely different reasons!

[22]The term used by Paurṇamāsī is *ātmavidyā*. A somewhat unusual meaning of *vidyā* is "magical skills." Paurṇamāsī does not actually employ such "supernatural" powers in the drama, but she is clearly revered by the other characters.

[23]This is a fundamental and recurrent theme in the drama. See p. 114 for a translation of the beautiful verse (II.17) spoken here by Paurṇamāsī.

[24]*bhāva* (II.18.1). This and the related passage in Act III are discussed in Chapter VII, pp. 133-34.

[25]II.21.1. This is a characteristic metaphor both for Rūpa and for earlier and subsequent Kṛṣṇa poetry. See the Govindadāsa poem translated in Dimock and Levertov, *In Praise of Krishna*, 42.

[26]*Guñjā* is a small shrub bearing red berries that have prominent black spots. The berries are treasured by Kṛṣṇa, who is often depicted wearing a necklace of them, and they, like the bamboo flute and the *kadamba* tree, are the objects of the *gopī*s' jealousy, for they constantly enjoy Kṛṣṇa's company; see II.50 and LM II.21.

[27]II.38. The form of Rādhā's devotion and its significance for Kṛṣṇa *bhakta*s are noted in Chapter VI, p. 122.

[28]The term *raṅgana* is a derivative of *raṅga*, "color; fun, diversion"; I have been unable to find other references to a *raṅgana* garland.

[29]*Tena dhūrtena* (II.44.10), of course, refers to Kṛṣṇa.

[30]For a concise description of the form of worship called *pūjā*, see Thomas J. Hopkins, *The Hindu Religious Tradition* (Encino, CA: Dickenson, 1971) 110-12.

[31]Paurṇamāsī likens Kṛṣṇa's single-minded preoccupation with Rādhā to meditation (*dhyāna*) (III.4). Such comparisons, in the tradition of the *yogaviyoga* verses of classical Sanskrit poetry (see Ingalls, *Anthology*, 231 §5), figure prominently in Rūpa's dramas.

[32]The elders in the cowherd community, such as Jaṭilā, constitute both physical and psychological obstacles to the union of Rādhā and Kṛṣṇa. In verses such as this one (III.9), they are frequently linked with (worldly) *dharma*, which they represent and attempt to enforce. See n. 18 above.

[33]Madhumaṅgala says that he has made a flower bow in order to frighten the cuckoos (III.9.1-3). The flower bow is the weapon of Kāmadeva, who excites passion. The commentator explains that Madhumaṅgala's remark indicates that Kṛṣṇa's verbal opposition should not be taken at face value.

[34]*divicaram ... vidhum*. The verse (III.15) emphasizes Kṛṣṇa's inaccessibility to mortals: as Viṣṇu, he dwells in the heavens, his feet caressed by Lakṣmī. Such passages serve to highlight the wonder of Kṛṣṇa's love for the *gopī*s and, by extension, for all persons.

[35]III.16.6; cf. II.18.1 and n. 24 above.

[36]The *sakhī*s are the intimate companions of the heroine in a Sanskrit drama. See Chapter VII, pp. 134-36, for a discussion of their importance in the *Vidagdhamādhava*.

[37]*narmaśīlam kṛṣṇam* (III.34.7).

[38]Before they leave, Viśākhā, in a significant verse (III.49), enumerates a series of elements in the scene before them, each of which adorns the preceding one. Hari, the ornament of Vṛndāvana, is himself adorned by Rādhā, and she, in turn, is rendered beautiful by her great love.

[39]Yadupati, i.e., Kṛṣṇa. The use of such an epithet, which emphasizes Kṛṣṇa's majesty (*aiśvarya*), accords with the respect (*ādara*) of Candrāvalī and her friends for Kṛṣṇa.

[40]*ādara* (IV.7.2). See preceding note.

[41]This is an instance of *gotraskhalana:* the inadvertent dropping of the name of one's beloved in the presence of a rival.

[42]*nīrādhikā* (IV.14). As an adjective modifying the woods, it means "full of water"; it also means "without Rādhā."

[43]The term that I have translated "anger" is *māna*. See Chapter VIII, pp. 151-52, for an elucidation of this important concept.

[44]Madhumaṅgala is referring to Candrāvalī; Kṛṣṇa understands him to mean Rādhā.

[45]Kṛṣṇa intends *maṅgalabhā rādhikā*, Rādhā with beautiful or auspicious radiance. Madhumaṅgala splits the words as follows: *maṅgala-bhāra-adhikā*, filled with great auspiciousness.

[46]IV.21. The theme of ornaments put on wrong out of eagerness is a common one in love poetry, and especially in poetry about Kṛṣṇa's effect on the *gopī*s. Cf. BhP 10.29.7. Here Lalitā draws the conclusion that Rādhā has utterly forgotten the world. For the comparison between Rādhā and a *yogī*, implied here and stated explicitly elsewhere, see Chapter VI, p. 121.

[47]*kāñcanapratimā iva kathorā* (IV.28.6).

[48]Kṛṣṇa here says "*kesara*," but later indicates that he thought it was a short form of *nāgakesara* by showing Rādhā and Lalitā the *nāgakesara* flowers.

[49]The *añcal* is the end of a sari, which is often extended to receive something.

[50]Kṛṣṇa's subservience to Rādhā is discussed in Chapter VI, p. 124; see IV.41, his elaborate verse declaring that his ten *avatāra*s are likewise in her power.

[51]IV.48. The verse refers to an *alaṁkāra* called *binducyutaka*, in which a word is used a second time, but without its *anusvāra*. Kṛṣṇa says that Rādhā has made his *vaṁśī* (flute) into *vaśī*; i.e., that she has gained control of it. I am indebted to Professor Daniel H. H. Ingalls for this insight.

[52]For a translation of Kṛṣṇa's concluding verse (IV.51), see p. 127 above.

[53]See n. 43 above.

[54]*Abhisāra* means rendezvous or tryst, but it is used with particular reference to a woman who goes out to meet her lover, and who is therefore called an *abhisārikā*.

[55]*tena dhūrtena*, as at II.44.10 (n. 29 above).

[56]V.14. See n. 31 above.

[57]Caṇḍī is a name for the fearsome form of Devī, the consort of Śiva. The adjectival form (*caṇḍa*) means "fierce, violent, impetuous" as well as "passionate, angry, wrathful."

[58]They do not appear on the stage; their voices are heard from the wings.

[59]*kulavṛddhābhīri*. *Ābhīrī* can mean either the wife of a cowherd (*ābhīra*) or a woman of the Ābhīra tribe.

[60]A number of Rādhā-Kṛṣṇa poems take the form of arguments between the *śuka* and the *sārī*.

[61]The names and epithets of Kṛṣṇa that appear most often in the drama are included in the alphabetical list of characters given in the Appendix.

[62]*Śarad*, usually rendered in English as "autumn," is the season immediately following the monsoon rains in North India; it is thus a time of lush green vegetation.

[63]The *rāsa* dance is a circular dance performed by Kṛṣṇa and the *gopī*s. It is described in the *rāsapañcadhyayī* of the *Bhāgavata Purāṇa* (BhP X.33).

[64]VI.8.44. The Sanskrit has *trailokyam*, the three worlds.

[65]This is a common Sanskrit convention: the moon is beautiful in spite of the rabbit-shaped mark; a moon without such a blemish would be incomparably lovely. See Ingalls, *Anthology*, verse 396.

[66]*āḥrtabandhujīvā* (VI.18.14). The commentator glosses this with *madudyānasthabandhujīvapuṣpam hṛtvā* and *āhṛto bandhor mama jīva ātmā yayā tathābhūtā bhūtvā*.

[67]VI.20, which ends: *pathi mādya bhujaṅgatām racaya*. *Mā* can be either a negative with the imperative, or the short form of the accusative *mām*, "me."

[68]This is a variation on the *dānalīlā*, the popular episode in which Kṛṣṇa demands a tax from the *gopī*s as they are taking their curds to market. This theme is represented in medieval Bengali in the *Śrīkṛṣṇakīrtana* attributed to Baḍu Caṇḍīdāsa and in Sanskrit in Rūpa's *Dānakelikaumudī* and Raghunāthadāsa's *Dānakelicintāmaṇi*. Cf. the *Dānalīlā* found as a play within a play in the third act of Kavikarṇapura's *Caitanyacandrodaya*, in which it is flowers, as here, for which payment is demanded (De, VFM, 571-72).

[69]VI.20.20-21. The key word is *saṁgara*, which can mean either battle or union.

[70]*Abhiṣeka* (VI.20.42) means simply "sprinkling," but it is also used more specifically to refer to the bathing of an image or the consecration of a king. *Sveda* (perspiration) is a *sāttvika bhāva*. See n. 14 above.

[71]The term here (VI.20.50, 54-55) that I have translated "worship" is *upāsana*, service, attendance, worship, or religious meditation. Sound and flowers are central elements in *pūjā*, and concentration and wakefulness (vigil) are likewise important forms of religious practice, the first especially in *yoga*, and the second on special days and in fulfillment of particular vows.

[72]VI.24 and Kṛṣṇa's words immediately before the verse.

[73]See especially verse 27, in which the does are described as standing spellbound at the sounds of the flute, with grass half-chewed falling from their mouths.

[74]The term is *kandarpakalāprāgalbhya*, boldness in the art of Kāmadeva. In verse 35, Kṛṣṇa spells out the "damage" inflicted upon him by Rādhā.

[75]*ātmanā kṛtvā param dūṣayitum paṇḍito 'si* (VI.35.1-2).

[76]*Jaṭilā* means "dense" as well as "wearing matted or twisted hair (as an ascetic)." Taken with *sphuṭamañjarībhiḥ* in Madhumaṅgala's verse (VI.36, according to P), it means "heavy with clusters of blossoms" and "bearing matted locks in the form of its clusters of blossoms." The rest of the verse, which Kṛṣṇa hears only after Rādhā and her friends have left, continues the series of comparisons between the *saptaparṇa* trees and devotees of Śiva.

[77]See n. 57 above.

[78]This is the first of a series of deliberate ambiguities that occur throughout the act. Abhimanyu understands *sarvamaṅgala/*-ā to refer to Caṇḍī, as Paurṇamāsī intends him to do; she, of course, is referring to Kṛṣṇa, who is truly the bringer of auspiciousness to all, especially to Rādhā. The ambiguity is made possible by the fact that the term appears in compound (*sarvamaṅgalārādhane*), and it is therefore not possible to determine whether the ending is masculine (-a) or feminine (-ā). See the commentary: *sarvamaṅgalāyāh* (= *devyāḥ*) *sarvamaṅgalasya kṛṣṇasya ca ārādhane*.

[79]*Saubhāgya* is welfare, happiness, and especially the happiness of a married woman whose husband is still living and is not absent from home. *Saubhāgyapūrṇimā* is the full-moon day dedicated to marital happiness.

[80]Karālā uses the phrase *govardhanasya pārśve*, lit., "to Govardhana's side" (VII.6.52).

[81]*svasāram me*, "my sister," but also "my very essence" (i.e., Kṛṣṇa).

[82]Gaurī; see Chapter IV, n. 186.

[83]*lokottara*; see n. 5 above.

[84]A terrible form of Śiva.

[85]By *nātha*, Rādhā means *the* Lord, i.e. Kṛṣṇa, but Abhimanyu naturally understands it to refer to him, her husband.

NOTES

CHAPTER IV

**Rāma's Later History or Uttara-Rāma-charita*, ed. and trans. S. K. Belvalkar (Cambridge: Harvard University, 1915) xvii-xxvii.

[1]Gaurīvihāra, lit., "the play or diversion of Gaurī," i.e., of Kṛṣṇa dressed as Gaurī. For Gaurī, see nn. 18 and 186 below.

[2]This verse illustrates a characteristic pattern, which I have attempted to render intact in the translation: it is made up of three quarters (*pāda*s) consisting of long adjectival compounds, followed by a fourth one containing the subject that these compounds modify. The final *pāda* makes sense of the first three and constitutes a strong ending; in certain verses, such as Madhumaṅgala's humorous one (I.20), the suspense increases with each successive line, until it is resolved in the final one.

[3]The compound Rādhāmādhava, used here, is an old one; see verse 980 in Vidyākara's *Subhāṣitaratnakoṣa*, translated in Ingalls (*Anthology*, 287) for its use by Ḍimboka. In both instances it is in the genitive dual.

[4]I have translated *vidyāmādhurī*, lit., "the sweetness of his learning," simply as "learning." If the second element of the compound is more than purely ornamental, it may convey the connotation that Kaṁsa is being lured by sweet bait. The statement must surely be perceived by the audience or reader as ironic, for Govardhana is typically represented as a boor.

[5]*dhanyānām mūrdhanya* (VII.1.23), lit., "chief of blessed ones." Such vocative expressions, quite common in this as in other Sanskrit dramas, are often awkward to translate into English. See the adjectival vocatives at VII.1.32 (n. 9 below) and VII.1.36, *maṅgalamate*, "well-meaning one."

Viewed from a purely secular vantage point, Paurṇamāsī's term of address to Abhimanyu is ironic, for one whose wife is having a passionate affair with another man would not ordinarily be regarded as fortunate. However, in the Vaiṣṇava view of the *gosvāmī*s, anyone who has direct contact with Rādhā and Kṛṣṇa is unspeakably blessed.

[6]Govinda, "cowherd," is a common name for Kṛṣṇa; see Appendix.

[7]The term is *alpāyus*, "short-lived" (Apte, 157). Manu, using this term at IV.157, states that "a man of bad conduct is ...short-lived" (Bühler tr., SBE, Vol. XXV, p. 153).

[8]Lit., "the flower of your command has been taken on my head" (VII.1.30-31). Even the prose of Rūpa's dramas is highly elaborate in style.

[9]*somānana*. A beautiful or handsome face is often compared to the moon, and to this day mothers in India call their sons "moon."

[10]The commentator explains that *yathārthanāmā* means *gavām vardhanam vṛddhir vartate yasya sa*, "one whose cows increase."

[11]For Caṇḍī, see Chapter III, n. 57.

[12]For the ambiguity employed deliberately here, see Chapter III, n. 78.

[13]The term is *vilāsa*, "sport, play, pastime; amorous pastime, pleasure, dalliance; grace, beauty, elegance, charm." If it is translated "pleasure" or "enjoyment," it permits an ambiguity that seems consonant with the fourth *pāda* of the verse, which I have rendered in the final line of my translation: the joy (*ānanda*, *vilāsa*) is that of Rādhā and Kṛṣṇa, and also that of one who is fortunate enough to witness their rapture. The name of Kṛṣṇa used here is *Kaṁsāri*, "enemy of Kaṁsa."

[14]*śṛṅgāra rasa*. For a discussion of this important concept and its significance for devotion, see Chapter II, p. 28.

[15]*ānanda*; see n. 13 above.

[16]*avātariṣyat*. The associating of "descending" (*ava* + √*tṛ*) into this world with Kṛṣṇa or Viṣṇu is at least as old as the *Bhagavadgītā* (IV.6-8), although neither that verb nor its derivative is used there. The statement that Rādhā too has become incarnate is significant, and reflects more recent conceptual developments. See Chapter VI, pp. 128-29. For a discussion of the name Hari and its significance, see Chapter V, p. 112.

[17]The god of love. The text has *Makarāṅka*, "the one whose emblem is a sea-monster."

[18]In the *Vidagdhamādhava*, Gaurītīrtha is a holy site on which there is a temple to Gaurī, "the fair one," consort of Śiva. It is given in the *Gauḍīya Vaiṣṇava Abhidhān* (Vol. II, p. 1886) as the place where Candrāvalī meets with Kṛṣṇa under the pretext of worshipping Gaurī. A *tīrtha* is a holy place or place of pilgrimage, especially one on the bank of a sacred river; see Diana L. Eck, "India's *Tīrthas:* 'Crossings' in Sacred Geography," *HR* 20/4 (May, 1981) 323-44.

[19]Both P and B have *madhuśriyam* where KM has *madhuraśriyam*, "sweet beauty." The former would seem to be the correct reading; see VII.26.1-2 and n. 78 below.

[20]*padmāvalambikarayā* can mean either "holding a lotus (*padma*) in her hand" or "holding the hand of Padmā."

[21]*Saubhāgya* is welfare, happiness, and especially the happiness of a married woman whose husband is still living and is not absent from home. *Saubhāgyapūrṇimā* is the full-moon day dedicated to marital happiness.

[22]The girlfriends of Rādhā and Candrāvalī; see Chapter III, n. 36.

[23]*candrāvaleḥ*, "of the row of moons" or, according to the commentator, = *candrāvalyāḥ*, "of Candrāvalī."

[24]*candrakamaṇḍalena*, "by its circle of moonlight" or "by the one who has a circle formed by the eye of a peacock feather," i.e., Kṛṣṇa, who wears a peacock-feather crest.

[25]Day lotuses close at nightfall, or, according to Sanskrit poetic convention, when the moon rises.

[26]"*gopīs*" here refers to the girlfriends of Rādhā. The last element is not strictly a pun, as I have rendered it, but a *karmadhāraya tatpuruṣa* compound, lit., "the day lotuses in the form of the faces of the *gopīs* who are blind with pride."

[27]I.e., to meet Kṛṣṇa.

[28]The term used by Lalitā is *daurbhāgya*, the opposite of *saubhāgya*; see n. 21 above.

[29]The commentary has an elaborate discussion of the temporal sequence. The garland was given to Kṛṣṇa on the twelfth day of the lunar month, the day of the *Pavitradhāraṇa* festival. It was seen in Padmā's hair on the very same day, but Paurṇamāsī did not know that this was the garland Rādhā had given to Kṛṣṇa. The next morning Lalitā asked Rādhā about skill in making garlands like the one she had seen, for she wanted to know why Padmā and her friends were so proud. Rādhā said, "That is the garland I gave Kṛṣṇa." Hearing this, Lalitā became very unhappy. That is why she says, "Now I know."

[30]The old female monkey, who figures in Act V and later in the present act.

[31]The two brief lines spoken by Viśākhā (upon entering) and Vṛndā are in P and B but not in KM. They seem essential to the dialogue.

[32]The lord of lotuses (here, *sarojanātha*, VII.6.33) is Surya, the sun conceived as deity.

[33]There is a euphonious internal rhyme in the Sanskrit compound for clove bower: *lavaṅga-kuḍaṅga*. KM and B have what appears to be a wrong reading: *kuḍuṅga* (VII.6.39).

[34]I.e., their presence should not be taken as an indication that Candrāvalī will come.

[35]The elaborate, seemingly unnecessarily wordy phrase used here, *paramautsukyasaṁbhūtena bhuriṇā saṁbhramena saṁbhedite* (VII.6.45-46), may be seen as illustrating Rūpa's sense of the importance of delineating emotion with great precision.

[36]Both P and B have *mānasagaṅgā*, Yamunā, rather than *gaṅgā*, as in KM. The Ganges is some distance from Vṛndāvana. Vṛndā's new plan seems to contradict her previous statement (VII.6.39-40). Perhaps the sight of Padmā and Śaivyā worries her in spite

of her confident response to Lalitā's apprehensive remark (see n. 34 above), and she therefore adopts a more cautious strategy.

[37]The opposition between poison (here, *garala*) and *amṛta*, nectar (given correctly in P and B), is an old one in Indian literature. In the purāṇic accounts of the churning of the ocean, the gods and the demons are trying to get the nectar of immortality (*amṛta* means both "nectar" and "immortal"), and among the things that emerge is the dreadful *kālakūṭa* poison. See *Matsya Purāṇa* 249-50; VP I.9; and J. Bruce Long, "Life Out of Death: A Structural Analysis of the Myth of the 'Churning of the Ocean of Milk,'" in Bardwell L. Smith, ed., *Hinduism: New Essays in the History of Religions*, 171-207; cf. VM II.18.

[38]The form is adjectival: *paṇḍitā* (fem.), "learned; shrewd, clever, skillful."

[39]Most of the women in the drama, with the exception of Paurṇamāsī and Vṛndā, speak in Prakrit. However, they almost always use Sanskrit for verses; in each such case, the stage directions indicate this fact by the term *saṁskṛtena*, which I have rendered "in Sanskrit."

[40]Kṛṣṇacandra, the moon that is Kṛṣṇa. The expression is reminiscent of the name Rāmacandra, a common designation for the hero of the Rāmāyaṇa, distinguished by means of the element *candra* from two other Rāmas, Balarāma and Paraśurāma.

[41]Kātyāyanī is another name for Devī, the consort of Śiva, also called Gaurī, Caṇḍī, etc. In the *Bhāgavata Purāṇa* the *gopī*s observe a vow, usually referred to as *Kātyāyanīvrata*, in order to obtain Kṛṣṇa as their husband (BhP X.22.1-6).

[42]*Pādya* is water for washing the feet of a guest. The full term here is *pādyavidhi*, the practice of giving *pādya*.

[43]Like the term *lokottara* (see Chapter III, n. 5), the term is ambiguous in a significant way: it can mean either "divine" or "wonderful."

[44]Were her lover merely human, these involuntary reactions of Candrāvalī (*romāñca*, *aśru*, *kampa* horripilation, tears, trembling) would be likened simply to gestures of hospitality; for Kṛṣṇa, however, they constitute *pūjā*, worship of the Lord of the universe as an honored guest. For a discussion of Kṛṣṇa's divinity as it is represented in the *Vidagdhamādhava*, see Chapter V, pp. 109-17.

[45]*candramukha*; see n. 9 above.

[46]Padmā is a name of Lakṣmī, the consort of Viṣṇu.

[47]"The one with a lotus in his navel," i.e., Viṣṇu. Here Kṛṣṇa is clearly conscious of his divinity. It is significant that he expresses this consciousness in front of Candrāvalī, and not in front of Rādhā. See Chapter III, n. 39.

[48]This would be remarkable; see n. 25 above.

[49]Saṅkarṣana, "the ploughing one," is a name of Balarāma. In the ancient Pañcarātra system, Saṅkarṣana is one of the four *vyūhas* or "forms" of Vāsudeva. For *tīrtha*, see n. 18 above.

[50]The word *aghamathana*, "destroyer of sins (*agha*)," is also a name for Kṛṣṇa, who is the slayer of the demon Agha.

[51]The term *rasa* here means both "water" and "poetic mood," that which is tasted in genuine aesthetic experience. The commentator glosses it with *śṛṅgārādirasa*, "*śṛṅgāra rasa* and the others."

[52]The cowherd village in which Kṛṣṇa grew up.

[53]*Mitra* means "the sun" and also "a friend." In the second sense it here refers to Kṛṣṇa.

[54]The word used here for lotus, *padminī*, also designates a member of a class of women. The commentator explains that Śaivyā is referring to Kṛṣṇa's favoring of Rādhā and her friends (lit., "by increasing the *saubhāgya* of Rādhā's coterie").

[55]I.e., Govardhana; see the commentary.

[56]The commentator gives the following explanation: "It is well known that Lakṣmī does not remain in a forest of lotuses (*padmavana*) at night. The alternative meaning is as follows: Why is Candrāvalī not taken out for *abhisāra* [with Kṛṣṇa] at nightfall?"

[57]The commentator identifies the creepers as the other *gopī*s and the jasmine as Candrāvalī; the verse, he says, asserts the superiority of her love.

[58]Lit., "by bards (*bandi*) in the form of buzzing bees."

[59]The commentator gives a hidden meaning as follows: "Although I am the refuge of all, I appear near to you." Such emphasis on Kṛṣṇa's *aiśvarya* would be appropriate with Candrāvalī; see Chapter III, n. 39.

[60]Candrāvalī's assertion (*lalitā vṛndāvanalakṣmī*) serves as a hint presaging the entrance of Lalitā and Vṛndā. Such hints are common in Rūpa's as in other Sanskrit dramas.

[61]The commentator explains that the vessel is heavy because the *ghṛtasneha* (*ghī*-love) it contains is made of respect (*ādara*). The term *gaurava*, used in the verse, means both "weight, heaviness" and "respect." For *ādara*, see Chapter III, n. 39. Rūpa himself makes the distinction between *ghṛtasneha* and *madhusneha* in speaking of the love of Candrāvalī and Rādhā in his *Ujjvalanīlamaṇi*. See Chapter VII, pp.

[62]*anurāgabhaṭa*; the commentator glosses this with *madhusneha*; see preceding note.

[63]I.e., Kṛṣṇa.

[64]The sense of the verse is that Rādhā's love is so intense that there is no room for respect (*gaurava*) in it; see n. 61 above.

[65]The doe Raṅginī /Rādhā.

[66]The commentator says, "How much more for Rādhā herself!"

[67]The commentator explains *madonnata*, "puffed up with pride (*mada*)," as follows: *mada*, which gives me supreme pleasure, arises because they have *madhusneha*, which is a superb magnet (for attracting me); see n. 61 above.

[68]Commentary: "According to the treatises on astronomy, Anurādhā is supposed to rise immediately after Viśākhā." Rādhā is another name for the constellation Viśākhā.

[69]The word for lake is *sarasī* (fem.), rather than the more usual *saras* (neut.). The commentator offers the following interpretation: "Even though you are not summoned by Kṛṣṇa, you go and offer your love to him; this does not give him pleasure, but annoys him. Rādhā and her friends are not like this: again and again Krsna goes to Radha for the attainment of his greatest joy."

[70]P gives this Prakrit verse to Lalitā. This seems strange, for it would then come under the stage direction *saṁskṛtena*, "in Sanskrit," which follows Lalitā's name. Moreover, Lalitā would hardly call Śaivyā "my wise friend," except perhaps ironically. B agrees with KM in assigning the verse to Padmā.

[71]The commentator says, "*paurāṇikā*s," the authors of the *purāṇa*s.

[72]Māpati, the husband (*pati*) of Lakṣmī (Mā), is here substituted for Mādhava, Kṛṣṇa, which is etymologically a derivative of *madhu*, spring, but may also be split Mā-dhava, the husband (*dhava*) of Lakṣmī.

[73]*Śatacandra* means "bearing a hundred moons."

[74]Rādhāmādhava is an old compound going back at least to the tenth century A.D.; see n. 3 above.

[75]*Vaiśākhā* is the name of the second lunar month.

[76]I.e., Kṛṣṇa. It is noteworthy that *rasa* is here used in the plural.

[77]This is precisely the opposite of what is the case.

78 The temporal setting for this act is the rainy season. The commentary introducing the act states that Rūpa is here revealing the *līlā* that begins on the full moon day of Śrāvan, and the opening verse is clearly describing the transformation of the forest by the monsoon rains. However, at Kṛṣṇa's request, Vṛndā has decked Gaurītīrtha with vernal loveliness, causing spring flowers to blossom (see VII.4). It is the fragrance of this artificially induced spring to which Kṛṣṇa is referring.

It is not clear to me why Rūpa introduces this change of season. Perhaps it is because it facilitates puns on Kṛṣṇa's name, such as the one found in v. 27 (see n. 79 below). It may also be part of the oral tradition that Rūpa inherits. Jayadeva's *Gītagovinda*, for example, is set in the springtime. However, the change of season may also be more integral to Rūpa's design: Vṛndā's clothing of Gaurītīrtha in spring beauty provides a parallel in the realm of nature to Kṛṣṇa's disguise, and it serves to blur further the line between reality and illusion.

79 *Mādhava*, a common name for Kṛṣṇa, may also designate the spring season, more often called *madhu*. It is masculine in either case; hence the "his" in the last line of my translation refers both to spring and to Kṛṣṇa.

80 *vallī* (fem.): lit., "vine"; fig., "woman." Cf. v. 28, in which is found the image, frequent in Sanskrit poetry, of the (feminine) vine clinging to the (masculine) tree, and II.47, which contains a striking variation.

81 *Mādhavī* is a vine with white fragrant flowers that blooms in the spring. The commentary says that *mādhavī* refers simultaneously to the creeper of that name and to *Rādhā* (the latter, presumably, because of her close association with Mādhava, i.e., Kṛṣṇa).

82 *vighneśajananī*, "the mother of the Lord of obstacles (Gaṇeśa)," i.e., Śiva's consort, who is called by various names, including Caṇḍī, Gaurī, Devī. For Caṇḍī, see Chapter III, n. 57; for Gaurī, see n. 186 below. Devī simply means "the Goddess."

83 The word *karālā* is a hint that signals the arrival of the grandmother of Candrāvalī. For jasmine as a metaphor for Candrāvalī, see VM VII.15. The *tamāla* tree is closely associated with Kṛṣṇa, in part, presumably, because of its black trunk, which resembles his body; cf. VM III.44.38-43 and v. 45.

84 This is a rather free rendering of an obscure line. *Caṇḍāla*s are untouchables because they handle dead bodies. Karālā is not actually a member of the *Caṇḍāla* caste.

85 *bhujaṅgatva*, lit., "snake-ness," "snake-like nature." The commentator glosses it with *kāmukatva*, "lustfulness"; see Chapter III, n. 1.

[86]*Śyāmala*, the epithet used here to address Kṛṣṇa, a variant of a more common name of his, Śyāma, participates in the darkness imagery that Rūpa has Karālā exploit in her angry accusations.

[87]Kṛṣṇa here expresses his insolence by the use of the diminutive as well as by his impertinent question.

[88]I.e., Nanda, Kṛṣṇa's foster father.

[89]The commentary contains the following elaboration: "When your bad conduct is proclaimed in the royal assembly, and the king's men--unable to find you because you will have disappeared into the forest out of fear of the king's punishment--bring your father before the court, he will be overcome with grief and shame to think that he has such an ill-behaved son."

[90]The commentator explains that *sādhvasam gataḥ*, "became frightened," can alternatively be split *sādhu asaṁgataḥ*, "not well united." The double meaning allows Kṛṣṇa to tell the truth in a concealed way: at the same time that he confesses his desire to Candrāvalī, he conveys to Karālā the virtual opposite of what is the case.

[91]The word is *ucchiṣṭa*, the leavings of a meal, which are considered ritually impure. In *bhakti*, this convention is deliberately reversed, for the devotees eat as *prasāda* ("grace") that which has been offered to the deity. Karālā's attitude typifies that of the unenlightened and indifferent worldling, who has no taste for *bhakti*. The use of *tṛṣṇā*, thirst, is noteworthy here. For a discussion of the significance of this central metaphor, see Chapter II, pp. 37-38.

[92]The cardinal directions are feminine, and each has a (male) deity as her lord; cf. III.37.

[93]The implied meaning is given by the commentator.

[94]As the commentator points out, *jīvananātha*, "the lord of (her) life," is (metaphysically speaking) Kṛṣṇa. Thus at this deeper level, Lalitā's implication is wholly true: Candrāvalī *is* devoted to Kṛṣṇa.

[95]I.e., Govardhana.

[96]*kuñjakuṭumbinī*, lit., "housewife of the bowers."

[97]I.e., Rādhā; see n. 79 above.

[98]Brahmā is renowned for his eloquence; his consort is Sarasvatī, goddess of speech and learning. *Saubhāgya*, "luck in love," here refers to good fortune in a devotional sense. See n. 21 above.

[99]According to the account in the *Matsya Purāṇa* (250, esp. 3-4), both Lakṣmī and the *kaustubha* gem were produced from the

churning of the ocean. The gem is often referred to as adorning the chest of Viṣṇu (see BhP X.3.9). In the present verse, the *kadamba* blossoms are said to usurp its function, and indeed to surpass it in splendor; Rūpa is here following the tradition of verses that extol the beauty of Kṛṣṇa's natural forest ornaments.

100 *Praṇaya* is the comfortable, abiding love of long familiarity. If the term here refers to Rādhā's feeling for Kṛṣṇa, the verse expresses the wonder of her friends at this extraordinary love, which enhances her beauty (see VM III.49). It seems more likely, however, that it refers to their great love for her; the third and fourth *pāda*s of the verse then parallel VII.33d; see n. 105 below.

101 The entire verse plays on the words *kamala* (lotus) and Kamalā (Lakṣmī). Lakṣmī is the ultimate embodiment of beauty; here even *her* loveliness is said to be surpassed by that of Rādhā. For the theological concomitants of this fact, see UNM (*Haripriyāprakaraṇam*, 38) and the discussion of Jīva's *Prītisandarbha* in De (VFM, 400).

102 I take here the reading of P and B (*gandhaphalikā*), which follows naturally from Vṛndā's presentation to Kṛṣṇa of the *campaka* blossoms from Rādhā at VII.29.37-38; see n. 105 below.

103 The word *karambita*, "set, inlaid," suggests that the flute has been lovingly placed in Kṛṣṇa's hand, perhaps by his foster mother Yaśodā, who is mentioned in the last *pāda* of the verse (see n. 105 below). The suggestion of the dressing and adorning of the image in *pūjā* is very strong here. In *pūjā*, the *bhakta* may be seen as responsible for the beauty of the image in two senses: the literal one (as here with Yaśodā) and a spiritual one, for it is the intensity of the *bhakta*'s devotion that renders the image uniquely beautiful to him or her. (To an outsider, the same image might seem ordinary, or even garish.) Cf. LM I.26.

104 *candrikā*, lit., "moonlight." In its masculine form (*candraka*), it means the moon, and also the eye in a peacock's tail; see n. 24 above. The image may be a deliberate setting parallel of Kṛṣṇa, who bears on his head the moon in the form of the eye in his peacock-feather crest, with Śiva, who wears the crescent moon in his matted locks.

105 Yaśodā's *vātsalyalakṣmīrasa* is described as *mūrta*, "embodied" or "incarnate." *Mūrta* also means "hard" or "solid," and may here be consciously juxtaposed with *rasa*, "liquid extract," to create an apparent paradox. The noun form *mūrti* is discussed in n. 136 below.

There are at least two senses in which Kṛṣṇa may be said to be the embodiment of Yaśodā's *vātsalya*. The commentator explains that his unsurpassed beauty is a result of Yaśodā's fondling. This may be understood quite literally, for example, as asserting that Yaśodā lovingly put the *tilaka* on Kṛṣṇa's forehead. With this interpretation, however, one has difficulty accounting for the *campaka* blossoms adorning his ears, for

Kṛṣṇa has presumably not been home since Vṛndā gave him this gift from Rādhā. The reading of KM (*puṣpakalikā*) appears to provide a way out of this dilemma.

One may, however, read the verse on a metaphysical level, in the light of Gauḍīya Vaiṣṇava interpretations of the intimate interdependence of Kṛṣṇa and his *bhakta*s. As is suggested even more clearly in LM I.26, Kṛṣṇa's sublime beauty may be seen as the reflex, or obverse, of his devotees' love; see n. 103 above.

The commentator gives the sense (*bhāva*) of the verse as follows: "Ah, what a (marvellous) fruition of her destiny (*bhāgyaparipāka*)!" Understood in this way, the verse expresses wonder at the incomparable good fortune of Yaśodā, and may therefore be viewed in the context of the class of verses that express wonder, often mixed with envy, toward such natural objects as the bamboo flute that is constantly fondled and kissed by Kṛṣṇa (IV.7), or the *guñjā* garland that resides perpetually on his chest (LM II.21). Cf. VM VII.30, which describes the *kadamba* tree that serves Kṛṣṇa continually (*sevā*) by offering him its blossoms for his garlands in what may be interpreted as a form of *pūjā*; cf. n. 44 above.

106 *kṛṣṇa-mudira*, "black cloud/cloud in the form of Kṛṣṇa." Peacocks dance in the rainy season, which is heralded by the approach of dark rainclouds. The single-minded devotion of Kṛṣṇa's peacock toward him, and its rejoicing in his presence, may serve as a model for the devotee, although neither the main point of the verse nor its tone is a didactic one. The attitude is one of rejoicing in *bhakti* wherever it is found. It is significant that the form of devotion described here is that of spontaneous *dancing*.

107 *paramā śobhā*, lit. "supreme beauty." Here something wholly ordinary, the staff used to drive the cows, is transformed through its association with Kṛṣṇa into an aesthetic object. It is striking that it is superseded, not by something else of wholly utilitarian value, but by the sounds of Kṛṣṇa's flute, which lure the cows because of their extraordinary *beauty*.

108 Kṛṣṇa. I leave untranslated *parama*, "most excellent, best," an adjective modifying Madhusūdana, for it seems superfluous in the context of the verse.

109 *parimala*. Kṛṣṇa's body is sometimes referred to as exuding a wondrous fragrance.

110 The term *harimūrti* has strong devotional overtones, combining as it does the name Hari (see Chapter V, p. 112) with the religiously significant term *mūrti*. For the latter, see n. 136 below.

111 As a noun, *vāmā* refers to a woman, especially a lovely woman; as an adjective, however, it can mean either adverse, contrary, perverse, or lovely, charming. Both adjectival senses are appropriate here, and the Sanskrit pregnantly conveys both simultaneously.

[112] *līlākamala*. In classical Sanskrit literature, ladies of the court are described as carrying lotuses for play.

[113] *murabhid*, lit., "breaker of Mura" (see Appendix).

[114] The term is *pragalbha*, which means bold, daring, mature, skillful, audacious. The feminine nominal form (*pragalbhā*) refers to a representative of a class of women. Apte cites the *Sāhityadarpaṇa* and summarizes as follows: "A bold or mature woman, one of the classes of heroines in poetic composition; she is versed in all kinds of caresses, lofty of demeanour, possessed of no great modesty; of mature age, and ruling her husband." In his *Ujjvalanīlamaṇi*, Rūpa follows the classical writers on aesthetics in distinguishing three classes of *nāyikās*, *mugdhā* (innocent and artless), *madhyā* (intermediate), and *pragalbhā* (mature and bold). Rādhā is a *madhyā nāyikā*, combining as she does the qualities of the other two; UNM, *Nāyikābhedāḥ*, 10ff.

[115] The commentator glosses *nairañjanya* first with *brahmatva* and then with *kajjalarāgaśūnyatva:* literally, it means the state of being free from collyrium; more figuratively, it connotes the state of being unstained, pure. The primary causal relation is that of Rādhā's flowing tears to the effacing of the collyrium earlier applied to her eyes. However, a connection may also be perceived on the metaphysical level; one of the most common images in *advaita* philosophy for the soul's becoming *brahman* is that of a drop of spray sinking back into the ocean, with which it has ever been essentially one. Eyes suffused with (salty) tears may serve to evoke this image.

[116] *Rāgitā*, an abstract noun derived from *rāgin*, "possessing *rāga*," means both redness and passion.

[117] *saṅgin*. The commentator does not gloss this term.

[118] The term *yoga* refers both to the discipline of that name, which has as its goal *kaivalya* (isolation), and to union, which is its etymological meaning (from √*yuj*, "join, unite").

[119] *mumukṣā*, the desire for *mokṣa* (freedom, release); for a knot, this would mean the wish to become untied (see the commentary).

[120] The term is *vidagdha*, which may simply mean "clever, artful," or "lovely, charming," as well as "experienced." For a fuller discussion of this term, see Chapter V, pp. 106-7.

[121] The commentator says that *medhya* (pure) means devoid of the fault of lust (*kāma*).

[122] An important antecedent to this verse is the passage in the *Harivaṁśa* in which Nanda, having freed his foster son from the mortar to which he is tied, after Kṛṣṇa has pulled down with it a pair of *arjuna* trees, holds him in his lap for a long time and cannot get enough of looking at him. It is striking

that it is the same root (√*tṛp*, become satisfied) that is used both in VM VII.41 and in this passage in the *Harivaṁśa*. (HV 51.34 and the half-*śloka* found after that verse in some manuscripts; see the note on that verse found on p. 349 of the critical edition.)

[123]For *nāgara*, see Chapter V, pp. 105-6.

[124]The term used here by Rūpa is *maṇḍapa*; see n. 125 below.

[125]The Sanskrit is *mandira*, dwelling, house, place, but also temple; *mandir* is, in fact, the most common Hindi word for temple. Rūpa's choice of this word, together with his use, in the preceding line, of *maṇḍapa* (bower, pavilion, hall, especially a hall forming part of a temple complex) rather than such neutral words as *kuñja* (bower), which he uses elsewhere, may well be deliberate: as the temporary abode of Rādhā and Kṛṣṇa, and more particularly as the locus of their wondrous love-making, the bower of creepers is a holy place, consecrated by the sacred union of the Lord of the universe and his eternal consort. Such words with religious connotations, together with verses of a clearly devotional nature, such as VII.41, may serve to remind the devotee of the transcendent dimension of what, to the uninitiated, might appear to be purely secular love scenes.

[126]I differ here from the commentator, who takes *tāratarala* to mean pearls and diamonds.

[127]*murabhid*, as at VII.38; see n. 113 above.

[128]*sindūra*, red lead. In Hindi, the term refers to the red powder put in the part in a married woman's hair as well as on images of Hanumān and Gaṇeśa.

[129]The final line presents an apparent paradox: to an ordinary worldling a disheveled, withered heap of flower-petals would not appear lovely. Its beauty to the devotee lies in its adornment--one could even say consecration--by the colored powder, lac, saffron paste, and perspiration from the bodies of Rādhā and Kṛṣṇa; see v. 46 below, and n. 125 above. Compare also the eagerness of the devotees in VM I.3, who roll in the dust that has been touched by Kṛṣṇa's feet.

[130]These words are not in the text, but the sense of the verse demands something of the sort. See the commentary: *idānīm eva bālikā āsīt, idānīm eva pravaratarunyabhūd iti bhāvaḥ*, "just now she was a little girl, and now [suddenly] she has become an excellent young woman." The first half of the verse, together with her wonder at Rādhā's transformation, is a beautiful illustration of Vṛndā's *vātsalya-bhāva*, or feeling of tender motherly affection for Rādhā. Vṛndā's emotion is parallel in some respects to that of Yaśodā for Kṛṣṇa, expressed, for example, at VM I.20.6-7, where she says that he is still an infant, and described by Nanda in the following verse (I.21). The juxtaposition with *mādhurya* is made there as well, by means of Madhumaṅgala's humorous verse (I.20) and his subsequent aside to Kṛṣṇa (I.20.8-9).

[131]The commentator asks, "From what *guru*?" The implied answer is, "From Krsna, the *guru* of the universe."

[132]*pravaravibhramakauśala*, lit., "skill in excellent amorous play." *Vibhrama* means error, confusion, illusion, as well as love-play. Is it possible that a metaphysical illusion is being hinted at here, consonant with the paradox of reversal in the final *pāda*?

[133]As Lord of the universe, Kṛṣṇa is invincible (the term used here is *ajita*), yet paradoxically he is conquered by Rādhā.

[134]*Anagha*, lit., "sinless, faultless, pure," is an epithet of Viṣṇu used here by Rūpa in part because of its similarity in sound to *jaghana*, thigh, which follows it immediately in the third *pāda* of the verse.

[135]In this verse Rādhā is portrayed as a *svādhīnabhartṛkā*, a woman who has her lover wholly in her control; see UNM, *Nāyikābhedāḥ*, 90-92.

[136]*samṛddhā mūrtiḥ*. The term *mūrti*, which simply means "form," may well have been chosen by Rūpa because of its religious connotations: in a devotional context it signifies an embodiment of divinity in some person or object, especially an image.

[137]The final *pāda* is a striking example of Rūpa's use of alliteration: *samṛddhā me medhām madhu-mathana-mūrtir madayati*. Such playing with sounds, increasingly common in late Sanskrit poetry, here gains new significance: far from being sheer pedantry, these playful verse-forms may be seen as yet another manifestation of the *līlā* of Kṛṣṇa and his close associates in Vṛndāvana.

As in verse 43 above, there is here, in the final *pāda*, a reversal of what one would expect from a mundane perspective: Kṛṣṇa appears even more beautiful in his disheveled condition, because of the signs of his love-making with Rādhā. A striking parallel to this paradox of Kṛṣṇa's unkempt beauty is found in BhP X.8.23, in which is described the mud-besmeared splendor of the infants Kṛṣṇa and Balarāma (*paṅkāṅgarāgarucirau*). In both cases it is his unfettered play (*līlā*), whether his aimless crawling in the dust during infancy or his subsequent unrestrained love-making in the bowers, that renders Kṛṣṇa surpassingly beautiful.

[138]According to Sanskrit poetic convention, the eyes of a beautiful woman are so long that they appear to extend to her ears. The sense here is that they themselves serve as dark ornaments, making water-lily earrings unnecessary.

[139]Rūpa seems to imply a comparison by his use of the words *mukta* and *atimukta:* Kṛṣṇa is contemplated by (mere) *mukta*s (liberated souls), whereas Rādhā deserves to be served by *atimukta*s. The commentator glosses *atimuktāḥ* with *atiśayamuktāḥ*, superior liberated ones, those who have attained the highest

liberation, as well as with *mādhavīpuṣpāṇi*, *mādhavī* blossoms. In strict *advaita* tradition, of course, there could be no such distinction, for Advaitins recognize no gradations of *mokṣa*. Kṛṣṇa is here adorning Rādhā, indicating in this manner his subservience to her.

[140]A *yāma* is a three-hour period; thus there are eight *yāma*s in twenty-four hours.

[141]The commentator glosses *yauvana*, "youth, prime," with *vistāra*, "breadth, magnitude." The force of the rains is greater in the early part of the monsoon season. The signs of approaching rain, so welcome to humans and especially to united lovers, distress the cows, who do not relish being drenched in a downpour.

[142]*vinoda*, a term akin to *līlā*, "play." From a metaphysical standpoint, this may be said to be Kṛṣṇa's sole purpose for being born on earth. In the *Ujjvalanīlamaṇi*, for example, Kṛṣṇa is described as having become incarnate in order to taste the essence of *rasa* (*rasaniryāsasvādārtham avatāriṇi*, UNM, *Nāyakabhedāḥ*, 18).

[143]A pretended *gotraskhalana*; see Chapter III, n. 41.

[144]*priye candrānane* (as if justifying his earlier "mistake").

[145]The stage direction here is *apavārya*, "aside," speaking in a way that indicates that only one person, here Vṛndā, is supposed to hear.

[146]*madhu*; see n. 147 below. The word *madhu* could also mean "spring" here; see nn. 78 and 79 above.

[147]*madhura*. The image is that of a meal, which concludes with a sweet course.

[148]The commentator identifies the voice as that of the female monkey: "Through the voice of Kakkhaṭikā it is insinuated that the friends of Candrāvalī are hidden (nearby)."

[149]*Sārasī*, "female crane," presumably the pet of Candrāvalī or perhaps of one of her friends.

[150]Two technical terms are used in this first compound describing Kṛṣṇa, *sūtradhāra* (stage manager) and *nāṭaka* (drama).

[151]*nāṭaka*; see n. 150 above and the Introduction, n. 5.

[152]The double meaning here suggests the direct causal relation between the two alternatives: by luring women to fall in love with someone so deceitful, Kṛṣṇa's flute causes them unbearable anguish.

[153]I.e., he is subject to Candrāvalī's beck and call.

[154]*vidagdha*; see n. 120 above.

[155]*vallabhakṛṣṇasāra*.

[156]The audience or reader would take delight in the inadvertent complicity of Candrāvalī's coterie; see VII.6.65-66. Madhumaṅgala is a brahman, and would presumably have been engaged by Padmā in his official capacity.

[157]*gotraskhalita*; see Chapter III, n. 41.

[158](Bala)rāma's younger brother is, of course, Kṛṣṇa. See Chapter III, n. 13.

[159]The spring season has been brought to Gaurītīrtha by Vṛndā; it is apparently not in evidence elsewhere in Vṛndāvana.

[160]*caṇḍālī*; see n. 84 above.

[161]Both *audāsya* and *nirdvandva* have positive religious connotations: the first means indifference, for example, to the things of the world, and the second, as used in the *Bhagavadgītā* (e.g., at 2.45) refers to the yogic goal of indifference to the pairs of opposites (hot and cold, pleasure and pain, etc.).

The third *pāda* is ambiguous. It can mean either "Mukunda has become indifferent toward the hosts of beautiful women," i.e., because he longs for Rādhā alone, or "toward you," as Vṛndā clearly intends Rādhā to understand it. It is interesting that Rādhā does not become nearly so distressed as she did upon receiving similar news in the earlier acts, e.g., at II. 41-47. Her confidence in Kṛṣṇa's love for her seems to have grown, even though her initial reaction to his deliberate *gotraskhalana* is one of jealous anger.

[162]*Mohana*, a frequent epithet of Kṛṣṇa, has both positive and negative connotations. As used by Rādhā and her friends, it means "fascinating, enrapturing, enchanting"; in Jaṭilā's usage, however, it means "perplexing, deluding, infatuating," qualities that she fears in Kṛṣṇa; see Chapter V, pp. 101-3.

[163]Lit., "knowledge or magical skill associated with the bowers," a wholly appropriate designation for Kṛṣṇa.

[164]Lalitā, Vṛndā, and Rādhā; the Sanskrit has *tisraḥ*.

[165]*bhāṇḍīradevatā*. *Bhāṇḍīra* is a name for the Indian fig tree.

[166]I.e., Kṛṣṇa. The commentator glosses *svasāram me* as follows: *svasāram bhaginīm. vastutas tu svasya mama sāram kṛṣṇam*.

[167]*Mantra* may also mean a charm.

[168]The complete image used in the prose is that of a casket containing the jewels that are Kṛṣṇa's most intimate secrets.

[169]The presence of Kṛṣṇa's peacock Tāṇḍavika signals Jaṭilā that he must be there. The *vāhana* or animal mount of the Goddess is a lion. What Jaṭilā is referring to here is presumably a stone carving of Gaurī's lion.

[170]*lokottara*; see Chapter III, n. 5.

[171]The commentator glosses *yāmi* as follows: *he bhagini. pakṣe he kulanāri*. If one takes the second meaning (virtuous woman), Kṛṣṇa's words are wholly in accord with reality.

[172]*citram*. The sense of wonder is a central element in Kṛṣṇa devotion. See BhP X.6.31; X.7.19, 30, 37; X.9.17, etc.; VM II.13.17; VII.44, etc.; and the discussion of this theme in Chapter IX, pp. 182-83.

[173]I.e., Kṛṣṇa, the *nāgara* of the bowers.

[174]*kas tam jano jānāti*. This is a virtual quotation of Rādhā's question to Lalitā at VI.33.5: *kā khalu tam jānāti*. The question accords with metaphysical truth: no one knows the Lord of the universe in all his fullness. It would seem that Rūpa is concerned to emphasize this point. Kṛṣṇa's repetition of Rādhā's earlier question may also be intended as a hint to her of his identity--a hint that she misses, at least temporarily, but that the audience or reader may enjoy.

[175]The verse is somewhat obscure, and the commentator is utterly silent. *Pārada* means mercury (quicksilver). The second meaning given in Apte for Mukunda, the name for Kṛṣṇa (or Viṣṇu) used by Vṛndā in the preceding verse (VII.52), is also quicksilver. In reference to Kṛṣṇa, *tāpyamānaḥ kṛśānunā* could mean suffering because of the fire (of separation). However, the sense of the verse is that Kṛṣṇa has been transformed through his disguise, which Rādhā must penetrate in order to perceive his true identity. Mercury is of central importance in alchemy, and one of the ways in which this metal was purified for medicinal and magical purposes was by reducing it to ashes. See Prafulla Chandra Ray, *History of Chemistry in Ancient and Medieval India* (Calcutta: Indian Chemical Society, 1956). It is also striking that a commonly used synonym for mercury (as given in *Amarakośa* and *Śabdakalpadruma*) is *rasa*, a term that is found in the titles of numerous alchemical works. In her quest of Kṛṣṇa, Rādhā is indeed seeking *rasa*, although not in the alchemists' sense.

[176]This is typical of the teasing verses exchanged by Kṛṣṇa, Rādhā, and their friends earlier in the play; cf. IV. 31-33.

[177]The commentator glosses *gokularāmāpreyasi* as follows: *he gokularāmāṇām preyasi, pakṣe gokularāmāḥ preyasyo yasya kṛṣṇasya*.

[178]This direction is given in P and B but omitted in KM, which assigns the following lines to Viśākhā. They seem to be more properly attributed to Rādhā, who would be heard from the wings.

[179] *prasāda*, often translated "grace."

[180] For *līlā*, see Chapter I, n. 11.

[181] Kṛṣṇa is called *mohana*, e.g., at VII.52.1 (see n. 162 above). *Mohinī* means a fascinating woman; it is the name of the form assumed by Viṣṇu during the churning of the ocean, by means of which he cheated the demons of the *amṛta*, the nectar of immortality (VP I.9: Wilson, trans., *Vishñu Puráña*, p. 66 and n. 8, pp. 66-67).

[182] I.e., without Kṛṣṇa.

[183] *Gaurī*; see n. 186 below.

[184] *lokottara*; see Chapter III, n. 5.

[185] The term used by Abhimanyu (VII.53.39) is *daṇḍavatpraṇāma*, a word used by Gauḍīya Vaiṣṇavas to refer to a central ritual act, that of prostrating fully, as before an image (of Kṛṣṇa, or of Kṛṣṇa with Rādhā).

[186] The term *Gaurī*, which Kṛṣṇa uses here, may be a proper name, one of many names for the benign form of the consort of Śiva, or it may simply mean a fair woman. Kṛṣṇa was apparently not intending to disguise himself as the Goddess; the term he uses in declaring his intention is *varavarṇinī*, "fair woman" (VII.50.17). It is the juxtaposition of his presence in the temple, Rādhā's "prostration" (in reality, fainting from shock) at Jaṭilā's and Abhimanyu's arrival, their response, and his extraordinary beauty, that brings about his identification with Gaurī. Yet Rādhā calls him *Devī* at VII.53.31, just before Jaṭilā and Abhimanyu burst in upon them. The situation seems to develop gradually.

[187] *Mānin* can mean either "proud" or "honored."

[188] A terrible form of Śiva.

[189] *saharṣam*, lit., "with delight."

[190] *ballavīkuladevatā*. I take *kula* here simply as a pluralizer; otherwise the compound would mean "tutelary deity of the *gopīs*." Rādhā's address is consonant with reality: Kṛṣṇa is indeed the deity adored by all the *gopīs*.

[191] Like her address to Kṛṣṇa (see preceding note), Rādhā's words of praise and her request accord with the true nature of things: as Lord of the universe, Kṛṣṇa is indeed omnipotent, and it is Rādhā's perpetual desire that she never be separated from her true Lord, i.e., Kṛṣṇa.

[192] *navabhakti*, lit., "new devotion." *Bhakti* is also spoken of as *navadhā*, or ninefold. Here, however, it is the perpetual freshness of Rādhā's devotion that Kṛṣṇa praises.

[193] Here as elsewhere in the dramas two ideals, that of the *yogī* (here, *vaśin*), one whose passions are under his control, and that of the *bhakta*, whose ardent passion is directed toward the Lord, are contrasted. Not even the most highly disciplined sage can forge bonds of devotion strong enough to contain Kṛṣṇa; cf. II.17.

[194] The verb *ā √rādh*, used in a nominal form here and in the imperative in Abhimanyu's next lines (VII.57.3), means "propitiate, conciliate, please," as well as "honor, worship, respect." Thus it is sufficiently ambiguous to embrace the complexity of Rādhā's attitudes and actions toward Kṛṣṇa at the same time that it conveys to Jaṭilā and Abhimanyu a more conventional sense of worship.

[195] *bhaktajanavatsala*. The Goddess is frequently addressed as "Mother"; Kṛṣṇa, on the other hand, is regarded as a child. If the compound be taken as a *bahuvrīhi*, "receiving affection (*vatsala* = *vātsalya*) from your devotees," it may be seen as an address appropriate to Kṛṣṇa, although this is not what Abhimanyu intends.

[196] *gokulanandinī*. See the discussion of Rādhā-Kṛṣṇa parallels in Chapter VI, pp. 123-25.

[197] It is noteworthy that Rūpa here uses the name *Hari* in a context that is clearly one of worship.

[198] *gaurāṅgī*, "of fair limbs." Is Rūpa here deliberately laying the groundwork for the identification of Caitanya, called Gaurāṅga, with Kṛṣṇa? Or perhaps he is expressing, wholly unselfconsciously, his own perception of Caitanya as Kṛṣṇa. Alternatively, his use of the term here may be simply coincidental.

[199] *Nikuñjakuladevatā* is ambiguous: although *devatā* is grammatically feminine, a deity referred to by that term may be either masculine or feminine.

[200] *Aṅgarāga* may mean either complexion (lit., "the color of the limbs") or unguent. Here it seems to refer to Kṛṣṇa's artificially applied golden color.

[201] Paurṇamāsī's choice of this way of addressing Kṛṣṇa is consonant with her own feelings of maternal affection for him and serves to evoke *vātsalya bhāva*.

[202] Lit., "I have surely been made one whose birth has not been in vain." This line suggests that the purpose of existence for human devotees is service to Rādhā and Kṛṣṇa and the vision of their sublime love. For a discussion of Paurṇamāsī and Vṛndā as models of *bhakti*, see Chapter VII.

[203] *kelivibhrama*. For *vibhrama*, see n. 132 above.

[204] *madhuriman*; see Chapter V, p. 104. It is noteworthy that the same term is used in the opening verse of the drama. The synonymous term *mādhurī* occurs far more frequently (e.g., in VII.61).

[205] Kṛṣṇa's sports in Gokula are described as *pure* nectar (*nirmalasudhā*). The commentator does not discuss the significance of the term *nirmala* here, as he does that of *medhya* at VII.41 (see n. 121 above). It seems likely, however, that Rūpa's use of this term in the final verse of the drama is meant to emphasize the unique nature of the love of Kṛṣṇa and the *gopīs*, especially its distinction from ordinary passion.

NOTES

CHAPTER V

[1]*Abhinavabhāratī* (Vol. II, p. 412), as cited by K. C. Pandey in his *Indian Aesthetics*, 2nd ed. (Varanasi: Chowkhamba, 1959) 443, and quoted by him on p. 689.

[2]Cf. VII.30 and 33.

[3]*harinmaṇimanoharadyutibhir ujjvalāṅgo hariḥ*. The term *ujjvala* is of particular significance: it means shining, luminous, as well as beautiful, and it is used by Rūpa as an alternative designation for *madhura bhaktirasa* (as a masculine noun, it means love, passion). The next two verses are likewise descriptions of beauty: Kṛṣṇa's (I.18) compares the herd of gleaming white cows to the heavenly Ganges, and Nanda's (I.19) extols the splendor of the cowherd village. Thus not only Kṛṣṇa himself, but also the setting for his *līlā*, is presented by Rūpa as strikingly beautiful. Cf. I.3, V.38, and VII.1 for descriptions of the special charms of Vṛndāvana and the delight that it affords to all the senses.

[4]E.g., VI.23 and prose immediately following; VI.28. Cf. the pun in VII.6 (explained in Chapter IV, n. 29) and the reference to the moon in Kṛṣṇa's hairknot in VII.33 (Chapter IV, n. 117). At least two verses refer to its falling or being scattered by Rādhā in the course of their lovemaking (VI.35 and VII.46).

[5]E.g., at III.16 and IV.36. The flowers are identified as *kadamba*s in VII.30 and 33. Like his crest, his garland is referred to (in VI.35) as a victim of Rādhā's passion.

[6]II.50. Decorations painted on his body with mineral dyes are also referred to several times, e.g., at IV.36 and V.5.

[7]*kalevaradyotihṛtākṣitandraḥ* (VII.9).

[8]E.g., V.10. At III.12.2, he is called Śyāmasundara, "the one with dark beauty," and the name Kṛṣṇa itself means "the black one."

[9]In addition to the epithet Kṛṣṇacandra, "the moon in the form of Kṛṣṇa" (or, paradoxically, "the black moon") found, e.g., at IV.6 and VII.9 (see Chapter IV, n. 47), there are at least three others that use the word *candra*, "moon": *nandanayanendīvaracandra* (I.14.23-24) "moon for the water-lily eyes of Nanda," and two, *candramukha* (I.31.15; III.21.8) and *candrānana* (I.31.11, III.9.4), that mean "moon-faced." Kṛṣṇa is elsewhere described as having a face like the moon, e.g., at I.21 (*mukhendu*) and at V.7 (*induvadana*). The comparison implies both beauty and luster.

[10] In Act VII, both Rādhā (VII.23.3) and Lalitā (VII.31.2) refer to Kṛṣṇa as *kamalekṣaṇa*, "lotus-eyed (one)," and Vṛndā subsequently uses the synonymous epithet *khañjekṣaṇa* (VII.51. 20-21). In Act V, Paurṇamāsī first refers to Kṛṣṇa as *puṇḍarīkākṣa*, "lotus-eyed (one)" (V.17.59), and later addresses him by that name (V.41.1). There are other variants, such as *vanajekṣaṇa* (V.46).

[11] In Act IV, Rādhā refers specifically to the rays emitted from Kṛṣṇa's nails (*nakharadyotinikaraiḥ*, IV.23), and his shining forehead is singled out for comment in VII.33, but his general refulgence is also repeatedly commented upon. See n. 7 above and n. 12 below. In the first act of the *Lalitamādhava*, Rādhā, catching a glimpse of Kṛṣṇa, expresses her wonder at his brilliance and attractive power by means of a complex conceit that ends with the image of a pasture filled with emeralds (LM I.52).

[12] *ujjvalatā* (VI.30.11); see n. 3 above.

[13] *śyāmalacandrikā* (II.4); cf. LM I.26.

[14] E.g., at I.31.42, II.35.5, II.8.18, III.10.2, III.21.10, IV.8.4; and V.52 (in KM). On the distinction between static and dynamic beauty, see Daniel H. H. Ingalls, "Words for Beauty in Classical Sanskrit Poetry," *Indological Studies in Honor of W. Norman Brown* (New Haven: American Oriental Society, 1962) 106 (3.14).

[15] E.g., in the long genitive compound modifying Mādhavasya in VI.16, *navamanasijalīlābhrāntanetrāntabhājaḥ*, "his eyes dancing in the playful movements of new love." Cf. Jaṭilā's apprehensiveness because Kṛṣṇa is "making his eyes dance" (*naṭayan netratribhāgam*) upon the *gopīs* (II.53). Cf. II.12, II.14.

[16] E.g., at VI.29, *ibhavaragāmī*, and VII.9, where his sportive gait is said to be even more beautiful than that of an elephant. According to Sanskrit poetic convention, the gait of a powerful man or a lovely woman is like the graceful, fluid motion of an elephant.

[17] E.g., at VI.21, where he is called *taralaballavakuñjara*, "capricious elephant among the cowherds," at VI.2.30-31, where Viśākhā refers to him as that *gandhakalabhendra*, "prince of rutting elephants," and at II.27, where Madhumaṅgala calls him *vṛndāvanakuharalīlākalabha*, "elephant who sports in the depths of Vṛndāvana."

[18] *madayati mama medhām mādhurī mādhavasya* (VI.16d). Compare this line with VII.46d, given in Chapter IV, n. 137.

[19] IV.2. Cf. LM II.31, in which Paurṇamāsī says of Kṛṣṇa after he has slain the demon Śaṅkhacūḍa *madhuripur ayam akṣṇor modam āviṣkaroti*, "This enemy of Madhu is giving delight to (my) eyes." Her description of Kṛṣṇa after his combat, in the first

three *pādas*, is strongly reminiscent of Vṛndā's description of his disheveled condition after his lovemaking with Rādhā (VM VII.46).

[20]These stage directions are so common that it is pointless to enumerate all the occurrences. *Saharṣam* is found, for example, at VII.34.3, giving Vṛndā's response to seeing Kṛṣṇa, whom she describes in vs. 35, and also at VII.8.3, and *sānandam* is found at II.47.14.

[21]II.12.1; III.22.2; III.36.1; III.46.4; IV.2.7; VII.52.12.

[22]IV.35. At II.35.5, Lalitā uses the adjective *sarvagokulasukhakārin*, "the giver of happiness to all of Gokula," to describe Kṛṣṇa.

[23]E.g., I.31.38; II.47.5 (*trailokyamohana*, used as an adjective rather than an epithet); II.52.2; V.31.1. In II.13, Nāndīmukhī speaks of Kṛṣṇa's *mohanatva* (enchanting power). As a masculine noun, *mohana* is an epithet of Śiva, and also the name of one of Kāmadeva's five arrows; as a neuter noun, it has, among others, the meaning "seduction, temptation."

[24]E.g., *vrajasundarīgaṇamanomāṇikyahārī* (IV.3); *nikhilabhuvanacetohāriṇī vidyā* (VI.28). For Kṛṣṇa's overpowering quality, see II.1.2, where the word *vikrānta* (conquered, overcome) is used in reference to the effect of Kṛṣṇa's seductive ways upon Rādhā.

[25]In IV.3, Vṛndā, speaking from the wings, refers to Rādhā's condition as *duranta unmāda*, "incurable madness." In the *Ujjvalanīlamaṇi*, Rūpa gives *unmāda* as the eighth of the ten states of fully developed *pūrvarāga* (UNM, *śṛṅgārabhedaḥ* 38-39). He also gives *divyonmāda*, "divine madness," as the final characteristic of *modana adhirūḍha mahābhāva* (UNM, *sthāyibhāvaprakaraṇam* 174ff.).

[26]The word *nāda*, which Rādhā uses here, has metaphysical overtones; in *yoga* it signifies the nasal sound represented by a semicircle, and one of the *yoga upaniṣads* is entitled the *Nādabindūpaniṣad*. For the religious significance of the term as attested by treatises on music, see my article, "On Practicing Religiously: Music as Sacred in India," in Joyce Irwin, ed., *Sacred Sound: Music in Religious Thought and Practice* (*JAAR* Thematic Studies, Vol. 50, No. 1, 1983).

[27]I.35.1-3. *Nāgara* is discussed below. *Mantra* here means a powerful incantation or spell; cf. V.17, and Chapter IX, p. 180.

[28]Verse IV.35, uttered by Rādhā immediately after Kṛṣṇa mistakenly gives her his flute, enumerates this and others of its effects on the *gopīs*.

[29]I.33.6-7; I.35.2-3; V.26 (*viśvamohana*). Cf. VII.8.2-3, where Rādhā describes herself as so stupefied (*mohitā*) by the sound that she is unable to ascertain the direction from which it has come.

[30] *yuvatimānaghanasya taskarī*, "thief of the pride of young women," V.22.

[31] VI.12. See VII.50.7-8 and Chapter IV, n. 152.

[32] VI.8.10-11. Cf. III.24; VII.36. A substantial section of Rūpa's *Ujjvalanīlamaṇi* is devoted to types of *dūtī* and of message. See De, VFM, 209-10.

[33] I.22. Each of these is known for its cooling properties. In Sanskrit literature, written in the context of the Indian climate, it is invariably coolness of touch, rather than warmth, that is praised.

[34] At the beginning of the play, Rūpa, in his role as *sūtradhāra*, gives an elaborate description of Kṛṣṇa in accordance with the four unique qualities enumerated in the *Bhaktirasāmṛtasindhu*. He there (VM I.2.5-6) describes Kṛṣṇa as the chief teacher of the accomplishments of learning the art of perfect flute playing.

[35] In II.14, Rādhā calls Kṛṣṇa *dṛgbhaṅgīparimalakalākarmaṭha*, proficient in the art of casting sidelong glances.

[36] IV.11.1. Although Padmā's comment forms part of a playful exchange, it accords with religious truth. In his *Bhaktirasāmṛtasindhu*, Rūpa enumerates sixty-four qualities of Kṛṣṇa, some of which involve dexterity and artistic accomplishment (BRS II.1.19-27).

[37] Its derivative *nāgaraka*, in addition to its adjectival senses of "clever, shrewd, cunning" (Apte lists *vidagdha* as a synonym), is used as a noun to designate a thief. This Kṛṣṇa surely is: a thief of butter, of the *gopī*s' clothes, and ultimately of love. See Hawley, *Krishna, the Butter Thief*.

[38] See the *Lalitamādhava*, especially the response of Kṛṣṇa to the portrayal of "Mādhava," the Kṛṣṇa of Vṛndāvana, in the play-within-a-play in Act IV. Rūpa makes this point at various places in that drama as well as in his theoretical writings; see BRS II.1.104-106. For the superiority of Kṛṣṇa's natural forest ornaments to precious jewels (even a heavenly one, the magnificent *kaustubha* gem), see the verse on the *kadamba* tree in the concluding act (VII.30).

[39] The reference given by the *GVA* is *Bṛhadbhāgavatāmṛta* 2.6.111. The general dictionary definition of *vidagdha* shares with that of *nāgara* the element of cleverness, as well as such negative connotations as those expressed in the English terms "shrewd" and "crafty"; *vidagdha*, however, may also mean "lovely" or "charming." See Ingalls, "Words for Beauty," 97. As a noun, it may signify a wise or learned man or a libertine. In the *Bhaktirasāmṛtasindhu*, *vidagdha* is included in the list of Kṛṣṇa's sixty-four *guṇa*s, and defined as *kalāvilāsadigdhātman*, expert in the arts and in dalliance (BRS II.1.54).

[40]E.g., in VM II.11, where Nāndīmukhī calls Rādhā *mugdhe* and says that she is unacquainted with the fullness of mature love (*vaidagdhī*, a derivative of *vidagdha*). The two words occur in direct succession. For uses of *mugdha* in classical Sanskrit poetry, see Ingalls, "Words for Beauty," 95-97.

[41]IV.49.14. Cf. II.53 and IV.50 (*caṭula*); II.5 (*caṭula-dhīḥ*); IV.32, 39.

[42]*karpūrāvalī*, IV.33.14. The word *candra*, usually "moon," can also mean camphor (*karpūra*).

[43]UNM, *śṛṅgārabhedāḥ* 1-3; see Chapter VIII.

[44]Epithets like *capala* ("fickle one") may likewise be interpreted as indicating the elusiveness of the Lord: one cannot pin him down, any more than the *gopīs* can pin down Kṛṣṇa.

[45]Act IV. Cf. BhP X.33, the description of the circular *rāsa* dance, in which Kṛṣṇa multiplies his form so that each *gopī* may have him at her side.

[46]See J.S.M. Hooper, *Hymns of the Āḻvārs* (Calcutta: Association Press, 1929), especially the hymns of Periyaḻvar. See also K. C. Varadachari, *Alvars of South India* (Bombay: Bharatiya Vidya Bhavan, 1966).

[47]See H. W. Schomerus, *Der Çaiva-Siddhanta* (Leipzig, 1912), and V. A. Devasenapathy, *Of Human Bondage and Divine Grace* (Annamalainagar: Annamalai University, 1963), especially Lecture I.

[48]II.9.1-2; IV.6.8-9; VI.2.5. Cf. the synonymous term *gokulapurandaranandana*, IV.38; cf. *bhartṛdāraka*, III.21.11.

[49]Viṣṇu-Kṛṣṇa is called *puruṣottama* from the *Mahābhārata* onward. For an early record containing that name, see S. C. Mukherji, *A Study of Vaiṣṇavism in Ancient and Medieval Bengal*, 21.

[50]Connotations of divinity may not be wholly lacking even in such an ostensibly secular context. The line between the divine and the human is not sharp in India, and such figures as the king, the *guru*, the husband, the wife, are all regarded as in some sense divine.

[51]Such ambiguity accords with the ambivalent status of *māyā* and *prakṛti* in Indian thought: both are understood to be simultaneously concealing and revealing, binding and liberating.

[52]As further evidence for this assertion one could cite the fact that Hari, unlike Mukunda and Kṛṣṇa, is always found in the drama in the third person; it is never, so far as I am aware, used there as a vocative.

[53]Gonda, *Aspects of Early Viṣṇuism*, 107.

54 Gonda, *Viṣṇuism and Śivaism*, 17.

55 I.1, I.2; cf. I.4, I.6.

56 After writing this chapter, I was happy to have my impression confirmed with relation to an earlier text in Barbara Miller's introduction to her translation of the *Gīta-govinda:* she finds cosmic overtones in Jayadeva's use of the name Hari (*Love Song*, 20).

57 See Chapter IV, n. 191. Kṛṣṇa's inability to rectify the situation after Madhumaṅgala's bungling is one of many instances in which omnipotence on a metaphysical plane, to which Rādhā refers here, is not exercised by Kṛṣṇa within the framework of the drama.

58 See Chapter III, n. 5.

59 IV.20.2-3. The lines contain a pun: *guṇa* means thread as well as quality. For *māna*, see pp. 151-52 below.

60 *muktavibhramaguṇagrāma* (V.5d). Kṛṣṇa's confusion is emphasized by the use of another adjective, *ghūrṇitamanas*, "his mind whirling."

61 For an enumeration of Kṛṣṇa's sixty-four *guṇas*, see BRS II.1.19-102. Rūpa maintains that even seemingly inconsistent qualities can coexist in Kṛṣṇa (II.1.119).

62 I.27-33. In the *Bhāgavata*, Śiva is represented as a servant of Kṛṣṇa (X.10.37), and he and Lakṣmī are said to worship Kṛṣṇa's feet (X.44.13). In the *Bhaktirasāmṛtasindhu*, Brahmā, Śiva, and Indra are specifically named among the *dāsas* or servants of Kṛṣṇa (BRS III.2.15).

63 IV.31. Cf. BhP X.1.22; *Saddharmapuṇḍarīka*, Chapter V, as, for example, in the translation of H. Kern, Vol. XXI of "The Sacred Books of the East" (Oxford: Clarendon, 1884); *Buddhacarita* I.69-75, especially 73, in the translation of E. H. Johnston (Delhi: Motilal Banarsidass, 1972 [1st ed., Lahore, 1936]).

64 II.47.5. Cf. BhP X.29.40, in which Kṛṣṇa's beauty (*rūpa*) is called *trailokyasaubhaga*, the joy (or wealth) of the three worlds.

65 *eka evaiṣa mahānāgaraḥ kṛṣṇaḥ*, II.9.3. For a parallel Upaniṣadic passage, see Chapter III, n. 15.

66 VII.52.53. See Chapter IV, n. 174.

67 *sa tu kamalayā lālitapadaḥ*, III.15. This is a virtual quotation of a compound in BhP X.15.19: *ramālālitapādapallavaḥ*. Both verses play upon the paradox of Kṛṣṇa's simultaneous divinity and humanity.

68 Padmā is another name of Lakṣmī, the consort of Viṣṇu.

69 VII.10.10-11. Viṣṇu is characteristi the *purāṇas* and represented in sculpture as serpent Śeṣa and with a lotus growing out of which sits Brahmā, the creator.

70 VI.19. Cf. VI.26, in which Lalitā use According to the purāṇic accounts, Viṣṇu, in gigantic boar, rescued the earth from the cosm another deliberate reference to Viṣṇu, see IV.

71 These include *yadupati*, *gokulapati*, *pun* *svāmin*, *bhagavat*, *deva*.

72 See Chapter II.

73 All three examples given in the precedin cases in point.

74 The term "epiphany," which is so apt for Sanskrit literature on the cowherd Krishna, was by Professor Ingalls; see the introduction to his (p. 29). The term is also used to good effect by in his work on the child-Krishna poems of Sūrdās, after the completion of my thesis. Bryant sugges audience of the poems, like that of the *Bhāgavata* led to share to some degree in the temporary amnes characters in the narrative; see his *Poems to the* especially pp. 35-51.

NOTES

CHAPTER VI

[1]I.1, translated on p. 36 above. Cf. I.6, in which Rūpa describes his play as composed of the *guṇa*s of Hari.

[2]When they are mentioned, it is often in very general terms. In IV.21, for example, the purpose of Lalitā's enumeration of the adornments that Rādhā has put on wrong is not to describe Rādhā's physical appearance per se, but to reveal her confused emotional state as she prepares to meet Kṛṣṇa. Cf. VII.47, which serves primarily to reveal Kṛṣṇa's feelings.

[3]E.g., I.33; IV.22.

[4]Such comparisons occur throughout the play, e.g., at V.14, VI.25, VI.31.4, and VII.55. The superiority of Rādhā's face is declared in V.20, V.49, and VI.14. Straightforward similes are instances of an extremely common Sanskrit figure of speech termed *upamā*; those in which Rādhā surpasses the term of comparison are examples of the figure known as *atiśayokti*. See Gerow, *A Glossary of Indian Figures of Speech*.

[5]Described by Kṛṣṇa in II.51 and VI.17 and by others in III.42, VI.17, and VI.22. In each instance it is the effect of Rādhā's grace and coquetry on Kṛṣṇa that is the main point of the passage. Like Kṛṣṇa's beauty, therefore, Rādhā's loveliness is significant largely because of its power.

[6]It is significant that this term and such closely related words for sweetness as *madhuriman* and *mādhurya*, which are often used in reference to Kṛṣṇa, are here and elsewhere used of Rādhā, especially by Kṛṣṇa (II.30.3, 45.1; IV.15, 46; LM I.54).

[7]II.31.4. In the general verse that he gives in support of his inference, Kṛṣṇa uses the phrase *paramo 'nubhāva*, "supreme greatness."

[8]Cf. III.49, in which it is Rādhā's love that is said to adorn her.

[9]Viśākhā at III.12.1-2 refers to her *rāgasya gariman*, "the greatness of [her] redness/love," by which even Śyāmasundara ("the beautiful black one") is made red/loving (*rakta*).

[10]See I.14.27-28 for Nāndīmukhī's description of the signs of Rādhā's intense emotion, which she terms *atibhūmim gata*, "become exceedingly great."

[11]*vātula*, II.0.11; cf. II.5. In seeing Kṛṣṇa everywhere, Rādhā is perceiving metaphysical truth.

[12]Rādhā uses the word *durūha*, "hard to comprehend" (II.1.8; cf. II.4) and Paurṇamāsī uses the synonymous terms *durvibodha* (II.16.3) and *durgama* (II.17.2). In II.18, Paurṇamāsī maintains that only one who has experienced such love for Kṛṣṇa "knows its tortuous and sweet steps."

[13]I.16. The fact that the *prema* of Rādhā and the other *gopīs* for Kṛṣṇa arises naturally is of crucial importance for Rūpa. Nāndīmukhī reiterates the point immediately, using the term *svābhāvika*, "innate, natural," with specific reference to Rādhā's love. She proceeds to qualify that statement somewhat, however, pointing out that the cleverness of Rādhā's friends serves as an excitant (*uddīpanam*). For the use of the term *sahaja* among *sahajiyā* Vaiṣṇavas, see Dimock (*The Place of the Hidden Moon*, 35-36, 42).

[14]Translated above on p. 114.

[15]VI.21. The last two words of the verse, *jagad vismṛtam*, "the world forgotten," succinctly express a central goal of *yoga*, total obliviousness to the mundane realm.

[16]II.47.9. The stage directions (II.47.10) instruct the actor or actress to enact *dhyāna* (meditation). *Dhyāna* is a central term in *yoga*; see Mircea Eliade, *Yoga: Immortality and Freedom*, 2nd ed. (Princeton: Princeton University, 1969) 71-73.

[17]II.47. The *tamāla* is black, like Kṛṣṇa, and is thus closely associated with him. Rādhā's wish presupposes the conventional imagery of classical Sanskrit poetry, in which the (female) creeper and the (male) tree around which it is entwined represent the loving couple.

[18]III.16. Cf. III.41 for the expression of a parallel desire by Kṛṣṇa.

[19]In his *Bhaktirasāmṛtasindhu*, Rūpa lists three activities connected with the name of the Lord among the *aṅgas* of *vaidhī bhakti: japa* (repeated utterance), *gīta* (singing), and *saṅkīrtan* (communal chanting) (BRS I.2 [32-34]). See Norvin Hein, "Caitanya's Ecstasies and the Theology of the Name," in Bardwell L. Smith, ed., *Hinduism*.

[20]III.4; III.8.14-15; V.14. Cf. II.24.

[21]II.48. The terms *jīvitapati* and the virtually synonymous *prāṇanātha* are reminiscent of several of the names of Viṣṇu enumerated, for example, at MBh 13.149, notably *jīvana*, *prāṇa*, *prāṇadā*, and *praṇabhṛt* (Gonda, *Aspects of Early Viṣṇuism*, 18). In the *Vidagdhamādhava*, however, such terms assume a new significance, for the context is not a metaphysical one, but an emotional one of love and longing.

[22]II.46.1. At LM IV.34.1, Mādhava (Kṛṣṇa in the play-within-a-play) likewise refers to Rādhā as a life-giving herb (*jīvitauṣadhi*); and a closely parallel expression by Rādhā is found at LM III.25, in which she refers to Kṛṣṇa as *jīvarakṣauṣadhinidhi*, the repository of the herbs that sustain life.

[23] *prāṇās tvam asi rādhike*, V.31. Cf. VI.18.14, in which Kṛṣṇa, punning on another name for the *bandhūka* flowers that Rādhā has picked, asks Rādhā how she can leave, taking the life of (her) friend, i.e., his life (*āhṛtabandhujīvā*).

[24] VI.8.44. Viśākhā here calls Rādhā *premodbhrānte*, "you who are mad with love." Paradoxically, it is this "demented" condition that allows her to perceive metaphysical truth.

[25] Cf. LM II.33.3, in which Mukharā (or Lalitā, in KM), punning on Rādhā's name, says to Kṛṣṇa after his valiant slaying of Śaṅkhacūḍa, "O hero, fortunately your worshipper (*ārādhikā*) has been saved."

[26] IV.46; the description is Kṛṣṇa's own. See VI.20.53-55 (discussed in n. 71 to Chapter III): Madhumaṅgala there playfully interprets the nocturnal vigil that he and Kṛṣṇa keep, while waiting for Rādhā, as a form of worship (*upāsana*).

[27] See I.20.6-7. In the *Lalitamādhava*, Yaśodā herself expresses *vātsalya* toward Rādhā, whom she terms *vatsā laghvī*, "my dear little child," comparing her to Kṛṣṇa in the delight that seeing her gives. Paurṇamāsī replies that all the inhabitants of Gokula feel a comparable delight (LM I.42.15-19).

[28] At Rādhā's first tryst, Viśākhā, addressing Kṛṣṇa, characterizes her as the goddess Shyness herself incarnate (III. 40.1-2).

[29] See note 34 below.

[30] Compare Rādhā's own words at V.7 with Kṛṣṇa's description of the expressions of her conflicting feelings in IV.51, translated below.

[31] IV.51. The term that I translate "love" is *praṇaya*, the comfortable affection of long familiarity. Rādhikā is a diminutive employed frequently throughout the drama; I use it here for metrical purposes. Cf. V.44 and VII.50, in which Kṛṣṇa describes in turn Rādhā's agitation and her anger, both of which render her still more beautiful in his eyes.

[32] E.g., by Madhumaṅgala at VI.20.50.

[33] Both in the *Bhāgavata Purāṇa* (e.g., at X.35.12) and in Rūpa's *Bhaktirasāmṛtasindhu* (e.g., at I.2.79), the *gopīs* are referred to as *vrajadevyaḥ*, "queens/goddesses of Vraja." Thus the use of the term *devī* in relation to Rādhā is not in itself sufficient to set her apart from the other *gopīs*.

[34] *mahiman* is used by Kṛṣṇa at II.31.4. At III.12.1, Viśākhā, responding to Rādhā's expression of anguish, addresses her as *avijñātanijamāhātmya*, "you who fail to recognize your own greatness."

[35] See nn. 9 and 12 above.

[36]See Chapter I, n. 43.

[37]On Rādhā as Kṛṣṇa's *hlādinī śakti*, see De, VFM, 279-81.

[38]On *sahajiyā* Vaiṣṇavas, see Dimock, *The Place of the Hidden Moon*.

[39]In the *Ujjvalanīlamaṇi*, Rādhā's love is termed *mahābhāva*, "great emotion."

[40]A revised form of this chapter, based on further study of the *Lalitamādhava*, is found in John Stratton Hawley and Donna Marie Wulff, eds., *The Divine Consort: Rādhā and the Goddesses of India* (Berkeley: Berkeley Religious Studies Series, 1982) 27-41. The remaining essays in the first half of the volume explore different aspects of the figure of Rādhā as she is presented in Sanskrit and vernacular literature; those in the second half examine other female deities.

NOTES

CHAPTER VII

[1]In his *Bhaktirasāmṛtasindhu*, following certain of the classical theorists, Rūpa distinguishes two fundamental types of *vibhāva*s (causal factors): *ālambana vibhāva*s (substantial causes), including Kṛṣṇa and his *bhakta*s, and *uddīpana vibhāva*s (excitants), including his lovely qualities, his embellishments, and his flute.

[2]See Chapter II, pp. 26, 28.

[3]For *yogamāyā*, the delusive energy of Viṣṇu, see BhP X. 29.1. Cf. BhP X.1.25, where this principle is personified as *viṣṇor māyā bhagavatī*.

[4]On *svakīyā* and *parakīyā rati*, see De, VFM, 204-6, 348-51; Dimock, *The Place of the Hidden Moon*, 200-14.

[5]LM III.2; cf. LM III.56. A general characterization of Vṛndā is found in VM V.2.

[6]Vṛndā expresses a similar sentiment in VII.41.

[7]DR II.13; Lévi, *Le Thêatre Indien*, 123, 358.

[8]Lévi, *Le Thêatre Indien*, 358.

[9]E.g., that of Vāsavadattā to Sāgarikā in Harṣa's *Ratnāvalī*.

[10]See Chapter III, n. 39. Rūpa's emphasis on Candrāvalī's *ādara* may be seen most clearly from his discussion of *ghṛtasneha* in the *Ujjvalanīlamaṇi* (see below), in which he uses the term four times in three verses, twice qualifying it with adjectives that mean great or deep. In the third of these verses he describes *ādara* as arising from *gaurava*, "respect," a term that the commentators explain as a sense of Kṛṣṇa's greatness.

[11]IV.12.5-6. A recent expression of a similar sentiment is found in the *pravacan* of a *līlā* enacted in Brindavan. There Kṛṣṇa explains that although he has many names, one in particular is especially dear to his heart: *mākhan cor*, "butter thief." The reason for his choice is not far to seek: other names presuppose respect and thus distance, whereas an insult like *mākhan cor* necessarily signifies intimacy. See Hawley, *Krishna, the Butter Thief*, 184-86.

[12]UNM, *sthāyibhāvaprakaraṇam* 79-83.

[13]Jīva Gosvāmī and Viśvanātha Cakravartī.

[14]UNM, *sthāyibhāvaprakaraṇam* 84-85.

[15]UNM, *sthāyibhāvaprakaraṇam* 87. Rūpa defines *māna* somewhat differently in his discussion of forms of *vipralambha śṛṅgāra*. See Chapter VIII, 293-95.

[16]UNM, *sthāyibhāvaprakaraṇam* 89-127.

[17]UNM, *yūtheśvarībhedāḥ* 1-6.

[18]UNM, *sthāyibhāvaprakaraṇam* 56.

[19]E.g., in his commentary on UNM, *sthāyibhāvaprakaraṇam* 82.

[20]*kuṭilā*, II.15.7. Might this line be the source for the character named Kuṭilā, the sister of Jaṭilā in the folk legend summarized by Chaṭṭopādhyāy (*The Yatras*, 13-14); see Chapter I, n. 66. It is, of course, also possible that Rūpa has borrowed the adjective from the name of the character.

[21]Like Kaṁsa in the *Bhāgavata* account, she thinks continually of Kṛṣṇa, and this constant preoccupation, though it be for the wrong reasons, may itself be regarded as a form of devotion.

[22]It is noteworthy in this connection that Rūpa states emphatically in the *Bhaktirasāmṛtasindhu* that the slightest mixture of *śṛṅgāra* with *vatsala* produces an extremely disagreeable result (BRS IV.8.33).

NOTES

CHAPTER VIII

[1]E.g., the *Naṭyaśāstra* and the *Sāhityadarpaṇa*. The *Daśarūpaka*, by contrast, distinguishes three varieties, *ayoga*, *viprayoga*, and *sambhoga*, the first two of which taken together include three of the four types of *vipralambha* enumerated by Rūpa. See DR IV.58-78 and Haas's notes, especially on verses 58 and 65.

[2]*yūnor ayuktayor bhāvo yuktayor vātha yo mithaḥ*
abhīṣṭaliṅganādīnām anavāptau prakṛṣyate
sa vipralambho vijñeyaḥ sambhogonnatikārakaḥ (1-2)

The arabic numerals in this chapter all designate verses in the *śṛṅgārabhedāḥ* section of the *Ujjvalanīlamaṇi*.

[3]*ratir yā saṇgamāt pūrvam darśaṇaśravaṇādijā*
tayor unmīlati prājñaiḥ pūrvarāgaḥ sa ucyate (5)

[4]Rūpa differentiates *prauḍha* ("mature") *pūrvarāga* from two less developed varieites (17).

[5]II.17, translated above on p. 114.

[6]*mṛtyu* (in the Kāvyamālā edition, *mṛti*) literally means "death." Rūpa's definition is given in verse 42.

[7]Although Kṛṣṇa appears first in the *Vidagdhamādhava*, Rādhā's *pūrvarāga* is earlier described by Nāndīmukhī, in the prologue, and it is her response to Kṛṣṇa's name, the sound of his flute, and his picture to which the last scene in Act I and the first portion of Act II are devoted.

[8]Bengali Vaiṣṇava poets have taken special delight in this form of *vipralambha*, perhaps because it is a singularly apt metaphor to represent the soul's longing for the Lord; Vaiṣṇava anthologies contain many charming verses on different aspects of this theme.

[9]*dāmpatyor bhāva ekatra sator apy anuraktayoḥ*
svābhīṣṭāśleṣavīkṣādinirodhī māna ucyate (68)

Although it has its effects on the hero, *māna* is almost always considered to be an emotion of the heroine; I therefore take *dāmpatyor* as part of the locative absolute with *sator anuraktayoḥ*, rather than as a genitive modifying *bhāva*, as Jīva seems to take it. DR IV.66, however, clearly defines *praṇayamāna* as an emotion of both, and Dhanika's commentary gives an example of the hero's *māna* as well as one in which the emotion is shared by hero and heroine (Haas, *Daśarūpa*, 135).

[10]I.e., of "caused" (*sahetu*) *māna*.

[11]See De (VFM, 218 n. 1), who notes in addition to the ingredients that I have mentioned "an element of *chalanā*, an indefinable playfulness, which is wayward and yet alluring."

[12]Chapter VI, p. 127.

[13]*priyasya sannikarṣe 'pi premotkarṣasvabhāvataḥ*
yā viśleṣadhiyārtis tat premavaicittyam ucyate (134)

[14]Dimock, apparently taking De's use of the word "apprehension" (VFM, 218) to signify apprehensiveness rather than an awareness (here, false), defines *premavaicittya* as "the pain that is aroused in the heart of one who truly loves even when close to the beloved, at the realization that even in union is potential separation" (*The Place of the Hidden Moon*, 24). Yet he includes in his selection of songs a beautiful verse of Vogindadāsa that illustrates Rūpa's definition perfectly (Dimock and Levertov, tr., *In Praise of Krishna: Songs from the Bengali*, 23).

[15]*pūrvasaṅgatayor yūnor bhavet deśāntarādibhiḥ*
vyavadhānam tu yat prājñaiḥ sa pravāsa itīryate (139)

[16]These include *udvega*, *jāgarya* (*jāgara*), *tānava*, *vyādhi*, *unmāda*, *moha*, and *mṛtyu*

[17]Rūpa is clearly not thinking of dramas here, for such explicit actions would never be represented in a traditional Indian performance. See n. 30 below.

[18]For more circumscribed uses of the term *narma*, see DR I.57; II.79.

[19]See De, VFM, 592. By judging Rūpa's dramas solely in accordance with Western literary canons, De seems utterly to have missed both their profound devotional significance and their considerable literary charm.

[20]See Chapter VI, pp. 121-22.

[21]III.25-27. Viśākhā's enumeration of the indications of Rādhā's eagerness and confusion (III.25) and her earlier verse describing to Kṛṣṇa the signs of Rādhā's love (III.23) illustrate the next category.

[22]It is important to note that recurrent situations manifesting emotion are not limited to the portions of the drama representing *vipralambha*. One characteristic element found in several scenes of union is a verbal contest among Rādhā, Kṛṣṇa, (e.g., III.8.1-17). Like the more serious scenes of separation and mutual longing, such teasing arguments emphasize the depth of their love.

[23]Chapter VI, pp. 123-24.

[24]UNM, *sthāyibhāvaprakaraṇam* 202.

[25]In the light of this judgment I would qualify Hein's emphasis on the didactic value of the *rās līlās* (see Hein, *The Miracle Plays*, e.g., p. 13). Although the plays clearly serve this function, it is not their primary role in Vaiṣṇava devotional life.

[26]See Chapter IV, n. 106.

[27]For *rasika*, see Chapter II, n. 35.

[28]At some point in our reading of the *Vidagdhamādhava* together, I commented to Dr. Prem Lata Sharma about its unusual length. Her response was memorable: she replied that for Vaiṣṇavas, who want the *līlā* to go on before them forever (cf. VII.41), 263 pages is nothing!

[29]Cf. BhP X.2.6-12.

[30]This convention reflects ancient Indian sensibilities that persist to the present day.

[31]For *śleṣa*, see SD X.58ab, and P. V. Kane's notes, pp. 182-88 in *The Sâhityadarpana of Viśvanâtha Kavirâja* (Bombay: Oriental Publishing Co., 1910); cf. Edwin Gerow, *A Glossary of Indian Figures of Speech* (The Hague: Mouton, 1971) 288-94.

[32]For *viṣama*, "incongruity" (typically of cause and effect), a figure of which Rūpa is especially fond, see SD 69cd-71ab, and Kane's notes, pp. 234-36; cf. Gerow, *A Glossary of Indian Figures of Speech*, 275-76. For *virodha*, "contradiction," called elsewhere *virodhābhāsa*, "apparent contradiction," see SD X.68-69ab, and Kane's notes, pp. 226-31. Kane explains that the contradiction must always be explicable; if it is final, it is termed a fault (*doṣa*). Gerow, drawing on earlier writers, distinguishes *virodha* from *virodhābhāsa* (*A Glossary of Indian Figures of Speech*, 265-69).

[33]See Chapter IV, n. 137.

[34]The main figure of speech in the verse is *śleṣa*.

[35]The adjective describing the *mantra* and the sound in these two similar verses, *viṣama*, is simultaneously the name of the figure of speech being employed: in both cases the cause of the sound is something good, whereas the effect is disturbing.

[36]I.25; I.35 (translated above on p. 102); IV.12; IV.35.

[37]E.g., III.42; VII.44. Other verses expressing Rādhā's incongruous feats of conquest include IV.34, IV.36, and VI.21.

[38]For lists of the sources quoted by Rūpa in his two chief theoretical works, see De, VFM, 201-3, 220-21.

[39]The second act of the *Lalitamādhava* includes one such episode, that in which Kṛṣṇa slays the demon Śaṅkhacūḍa (BhP X.34).

[40]Indeed, the author is outspokenly critical of the arrogance of the unnamed favorite, whom he terms *dṛptā*, "proud" (X.30.38).

[41]The understanding of *māyā* in the *Bhāgavata* is somewhat different from that of the school of Śaṅkara: it may be rendered "delusive energy," but it is here a blessed delusion with which the Lord draws his *bhakta*s to himself. For *yogamāyā*, see Chapter VII, n. 3.

[42]BhP X.9.9; cf. BhP X.9.21. Compare VM II.17 and III.17.

[43]X.44.14-16. The first of these verses is a striking parallel to the envy verses in Rūpa's dramas.

[44]See Chapter I, n. 84.

[45]In addition to the *Gītagovinda*, these include the Bengali *pada*s of Chandidās and the Brajabuli lyrics of Vidyāpati. For translations of selections from these poets, see Deben Bhattacharya, tr., *Love Songs of Chandidās* (London: George Allen and Unwin, 1967) and W. G. Archer, ed., *Love Songs of Vidyāpati* (London: George Allen and Unwin, 1963).

NOTES

CHAPTER IX

[1]The term *saulabhya*, "accessibility," is central to the theology of the Srī Vaiṣṇava *sampradāya*, the South Indian school that is based on the teachings of Rāmānuja. The tension between the Lord's *saulabhya* and his *paratva*, his "otherness" or transcendence, is closely parallel to that between *mādhurya* and *aiśvarya* as explored in the Bengal school. On the former, see John B. Carman, *The Theology of Rāmānuja* (New Haven: Yale University Press, 1974) 77-87.

[2]Umā Ray, with whom I read Rūpa's theoretical works in Calcutta, went still farther and asserted that one should not even imagine oneself to be a *mañjarī*, but rather a servant of a *mañjarī*. If one envisions the Vraja *līlā* as a series of concentric circles with Rādhā and Kṛṣṇa in the innermost one, such servants of *mañjarī*s would occupy the fourth one, three full steps removed from the loving couple.

[3]Professor Chakravarty's use of the term "seriousness" is striking: like the moral earnestness of earlier interpreters of this tradition, such seriousness contrasts tellingly with the *narma* or playful humor that is such an essential element in the *līlā*.

[4]Janardan Chakravarty, personal communication. The source of the quotation is unknown to me. A Bengali version of the statement is found in the *Caitanyacaritāmṛta* of Kṛṣṇadāsa: *jīver svarūp hay kṛṣṇer nityadās* (CC II.20.108 according to the Gauḍīya Maṭh numbering; ed. Atulkṛṣṇa Gosvāmī, p. 208).

[5]In the *Bhaktirasāmṛtasindhu* (II.1.104-106), Kṛṣṇa is said to be threefold, according to the degree to which his attributes (*guṇa*s) are manifest: he is *pūrṇa* ("complete") in Dvaraka, *pūrṇatara* ("more complete") in Mathurā, and *pūrṇatama* ("most complete") in Gokula, the cowherd village in the region known as Vraja.

[6]Sukumar Sen, personal communication.

[7]*Saṁkṣipta bhāgavatāmṛta* 2, as summarized in De, VFM, 252.

[8]John S. Hawley, *At Play with Krishna*, 51.

[9]I explore Abhinavagupta's treatment of *rasa*, together with that of Rūpa, in an article entitled "*Rasa* as a Religious Category: Aesthetics and Supreme Realization in Medieval India," *Jaar*, forthcoming.

[10]Sylvain Lévi, *Le Théatre Indien*, 20; De, VFM, 429-30, 577, 593.

[11]Rabindranath Tagore, *Hungry Stones and Other Stories* (London: Macmillan, 1966) 3-25.

[12]Tridib Ghosh, personal communication.

[13]See Gerardus van der Leeuw, *Sacred and Profane Beauty: The Holy in Art* (New York: Holt, Rinehart, and Winston, 1963) 268-71; John W. Dixon, Jr., "Art as the Making of the World: Outline of Method in the Criticism of Religion and Art," *JAAR* 51/1 (March, 1983) 15-36, esp. 23.

[14]This assumption is expressed explicitly by William James in *The Varieties of Religious Experience* (London: Longmans, Green, 1902) 12, note.

[15]James also espouses a view reminiscent of this attitude; see *The Varieties*, 37-38.

GLOSSARY

The pages cited at the end of an entry indicate where in the work the term is more fully discussed.

abhisāra — the act of a heroine in "venturing forth" to a designated spot for a rendezvous with her lover

ādara — respectful affection; the characteristic feature of the love between Kṛṣṇa and Candrāvalī (pp. 139 and 245 n. 10)

aiśvarya — lordly majesty, the powerful, awe-inspiring aspects of a deity. In Gauḍīya Vaiṣṇava tradition this complex of Kṛṣṇa's attributes is regarded as veiled by his lovable "sweetness" (*mādhurya*) (pp. 99 and 109-17).

ārati — a graceful ritual in which lamps or candles are waved in circular patterns before an object or person perceived as divine

avatāra — "descent"; one of several (classically, ten) forms assumed by Viṣṇu, in which he effects the welfare of the world and protects his devotees; chief among these is Kṛṣṇa (pp. 8 and 189 n. 7).

bhakta — devotee

bhakti — loving devotion

bhaktirasa — Rūpa's designation of what he considers the highest form of the religious life: devotion realized as aesthetic experience (pp. 26-28).

bhāva — emotion, emotional state; in classical aesthetic theory, such stable and transitory emotions, together with their expressions, serve as the "ingredients" of one or another of the eight *rasa*s, modes of aesthetic experience regarded as universal (pp. 26-28)

brahman — ultimate reality, the impersonal essence of the universe

Caitanya — ecstatic mystic saint of Bengal (1486-1533), regarded by his followers, who comprise the Gauḍīya Vaiṣṇava sect, as an incarnation of Rādhā and Kṛṣṇa

darśan	"seeing, beholding"; the religious act of beholding an image or other embodiment of divinity
dāsya bhāva	servitude as a mode of relation between devotee and deity (pp. 27-28)
dharma	action in accordance with duty, as determined by one's caste and stage of life; such duties are codified in brahmanical treatises called *dharmaśāstra*s; also the cosmic order itself, especially as reflected in these codes of conduct
gandharva	one of a class of heavenly musicians
Gauḍīya	of or pertaining to Gauḍa (Bengal), Bengali (p. 187 n. 1)
Gauḍīya Sampradāya	Bengali Vaiṣṇava sect, the members of which look to the sixteenth-century ecstatic mystic Caitanya as their founder and spiritual leader (p. 187 n. 1)
gopī	cowherd woman of Vraja
gosvāmī	"owner of cows"; a title of respect applied initially to the six learned disciples of Caitanya who lived in Vṛndāvana and wrote the most authoritative treatises of the Gauḍīya Vaiṣṇava school (p. 188 n. 12)
jīva	the individual soul
kāvya	Sanskrit court poetry, a highly ornamented style employing complex meters
līlā	play, in most of its major English senses, including child's play, love play, and dramatic representation. In Vaiṣṇava theology, the term most often designates the actions of Kṛṣṇa, Rādhā, and the other inhabitants of the blessed land of Vraja (pp. 9-10 and 190 n. 11).
madhura bhaktirasa	the transfiguration of *śṛṅgāra rasa*, the aesthetic mode of erotic love, in a devotional context: Rūpa's designation for the love between the *gopī*s--especially Rādhā--and Kṛṣṇa (p. 28)
madhurā rati	erotic love, the fundamental emotion (*sthāyibhāva*) of *madhura bhaktirasa*, the devotional mode exemplified by the *gopī*s, especially Rādhā, in their love for Kṛṣṇa (p. 28)

mādhurya	"sweetness," the term for the aggregate of Kṛṣṇa's charming, endearing qualities; erotic love as a mode of relation (*bhāva*) between devotee and deity (pp. 99-110)
māna	a complex of emotions, including hurt, jealousy, anger, and deep yearning, aroused in a heroine by her lover's infidelity (pp. 151-52)
mañjarī	young female maidservant of one of the friends of Rādhā, privileged because of her innocence to witness the lovemaking of Rādhā and Kṛṣṇa (p. 29)
mañjarībhāva	the fundamental emotional state of a *mañjarī*; the devotional mode exemplified by a *mañjarī* (p. 174)
mañjarīsādhana	the practice of assuming in one's devotional life the role of a *mañjarī* (p. 29)
māyā	the mysterious, creative power of a deity; the universe, conceived in certain Hindu schools, notably Advaita Vedānta, as deluding, but represented in the *Bhāgavata Purāṇa* and other theistic works as revelatory of divinity
mokṣa	release, liberation from *saṁsāra*, the ceaseless round of death and rebirth
nāgara	"city dweller"; sophisticate, rogue, lover: en epithet of Kṛṣṇa (pp. 105-6)
nāṭaka	the full-length dramatic form regarded as the most basic and highest type of Sanskrit drama (p. 187 n. 5)
nāndī	benedictory verse at the opening of a drama
pada	a verse in the concentrated form characteristic of medieval Bengali and Brajabuli lyrics (p. 197 n. 1)
pāda	a quarter of a verse
prastāvanā	prologue of a drama
pūjā	a ritual in which one offers food, flowers, and other expressions of hospitality to a deity or deities, treating them as honored guests
purāṇa	"ancient"; one of a class of medieval Sanskrit texts that recount stories of gods and heroes

pūrvarāga	the first phase of love, spanning the period from the dawning of love (the term literally means "first redness") to the first full union (pp. 150-51)
rāgānugā bhakti	Rūpa's designation for the higher form of devotion in which one emulates the love of one or another of the close associates of Kṛṣṇa (pp. 30-34)
rasa	flavor, taste, liquid extract; in classical aesthetic theory, one of eight "moods" or modes of aesthetic experience that were considered universal (pp. 25-26)
rasika	connoisseur, person of refined aesthetic sensibility (p. 200 n. 35)
rati	love, sexual desire; for Rūpa, love for Kṛṣṇa, the fundamental emotion (*sthāyibhāva*) of each of the five primary *bhaktirasa*s (p. 26)
sakhī	girl friend of the heroine or of her rival; here, primarily applied to the friends of Rādhā, and secondarily, to those of Candrāvalī (pp. 134-36)
sakhībhāva	the fundamental emotional state of a friend of Rādhā; the devotional mode exemplified by Rādhā's close friends (pp. 29-30)
sakhya bhāva	friendship as a mode of relation between devotee and deity (p. 28)
śakti	energy, power, especially the creative energy that generates and continues to activate the universe; conceived as female and and often represented as the consort of a male deity or as the dynamic, independent Goddess. Rādhā is understood by Jīva Gosvāmī and other Vaiṣṇava theologians to be the *hlādinī śakti* ("blissful energy") of Kṛṣṇa (p. 193 n. 43).
sambhoga, *sambhoga śṛṅgāra*	love in union
saṁsāra	the mundane world, the arena of birth, death, and rebirth; the cyclic process of transmigration
saṅkīrtan	communal chanting and singing, especially of the names and auspicious qualities of Kṛṣṇa and Rādhā

śṛṅgāra	erotic love; the *rasa* of erotic love, the first and most important of the eight *rasa*s of the classical theory, as enumerated in the *Nāṭyaśāstra* attributed to Bharata (p. 28)
sthāyibhāva	fundamental emotion; in classical aesthetic theory, the unifying emotional theme of a drama (pp. 26-27)
sūtradhāra	stage manager
svarūp	"own form," the very form of Kṛṣṇa and Rādhā as manifested in the persons of the young *brahman* boys who assume these roles for the enaction of the *rās līlā*s (pp. 19-20)
tamāla	a black tree associated with Kṛṣṇa because its dark trunk resembles his slender form
ujjvala	"shining, beautiful"; Rupa's designation for *madhura bhaktirasa*
vaidhī bhakti	Rūpa's designation for devotion that follows the injunctions found in religious texts (p. 30)
Vaiṣṇava	pertaining to Viṣṇu/Kṛṣṇa; a devotee of Viṣṇu/Kṛṣṇa, often together with his consort
vātsalya bhāva	parental affection as a mode of relation between devotee and deity (p. 28)
vipralambha, *vipralambha śṛṅgāra*	love in separation
Vraja	"cowherd settlement"; the place of Kṛṣṇa's childhood and youth (p. 189 n. 3)
Vṛndāvana	"the forest of basil," the place of Kṛṣṇa's childhood and youth, and especially the site of his clandestine meetings with Rādhā and the other *gopī*s (pp. 187 n. 1 and 189 n. 3)

BIBLIOGRAPHY

I. Works in Indian Languages

Bhāgavata Purāṇa, with Bhāgavatamāhātmya, & Bhāgavatacūrṇika summary. Bombay: Veṅkaṭeśvara Press, 1867 samvat = ca. 1810.

Bhaktivinod Thākur. *Jaivadharma* Mayapur: Śrī Caitanya Math, 1378 Baṅgābda = ca. 1970.

Bharata, *Nāṭyaśāstra* with the Abhinavabhāratī commentary of Abhinavagupta. Edited by Madhusūdan Śāstrī. Vārāṇasī: Kāshī Hindu Viśvavidyālaya, 2028 saṁvat = ca. 1971.

Brahmachari, Mahanam Brata. *Gaurakathā* (Prathama Khaṇḍa), Third Edition. Calcutta: Mahānām Sampradāy, 1379 Sāl = ca. 1971.

Bṛhatstotraratnākara. Edited by Ramtej Pāṇḍey. Vārāṇasī: Paṇḍit Pustakālay, 1970.

Dās, Haridās. *Gauḍīya Vaiṣṇava Sāhitya*, Second Edition. Navadvīp: Haribol Kuṭī, 483 Gaurābda = ca. 1966.

Harivaṁśa. Edited by Parashuram Lakshman Vaidya. Poona: Bhandarkar Oriental Research Institute, 1969.

Harṣa. *Ratnāvalī*, with the commentary of Govinda. Edited by Kāshīnāth Pāṇḍurang Parab. Bombay: Nirṇaya Sāgar Press, 1895.

Kālidāsa. *The Abhijñāna-śākuntala*, with the commentary Arthadyotanikā of Rāghava Bhaṭṭa, Twelfth Edition. Edited by Nārāyaṇ Rām. Bombay: Nirṇaya Sāgar Press, 1958.

Kālidāsa, *Kumārasambhava*. Edited and translated by M. R. Kale. Delhi: Motilal Banarsidass, 1967.

Kṛṣṇadāsa Kavirāja. *Caitanyacaritāmṛta*, Fourth Edition. Edited by Atulkṛṣṇa Gosvāmī. Calcutta: Naṭavar Cakravartī, 1333 Baṅgābda = ca. 1925.

________. *Caitanyacaritāmṛta*. Edited By Sukumar Sen. New Delhi: Sāhitya Akademi, 1963.

Mammaṭa. *Kāvyaprakāśa*, with the commentary Bālabodhinī of V. A. Jhalakikar, Sixth Edition. Poona: Bhandarkar Oriental Research Institute, 1950.

Padakalpataru. Edited by Śiśir Kumār Ghoṣ. Calcutta: Keśav Lāl Rāy, n.d.

Ray, Umā. *Gauḍīya Vaiṣṇavīya Raser Alaukikatva*. Calcutta: Indian Associates, 1363 Sal = ca. 1955.

Rūpa, Gosvāmī. *Bhaktirasāmṛtasindhu*, with the commentaries of Jīva Gosvāmī, Mukundadāsa Gosvāmī, and Viśvanātha Cakravartī, Second Edition. Edited by Haridās Dās. Navadvīp: Haribol Kuṭī, 475 Gaurābda = ca. 1961. (Original edition 462 Gaurābda = ca. 1948.)

________. *Dānakelikaumudī*. (*Bhāṇikā*) Edited by Purīdās. Mymensingh: Śacīnātha Rāyachaudhurī, 1947.

________. *Lalitamādhavanāṭakam*, with a commentary, Second Edition. Edited with a Bengali translation of Rāmanārāyaṇa Vidyāratna. Murśidābad: Rāmanārāyaṇa Vidyāratna, 1309 Sāl = ca. 1901. (Original edition 1288 Sāl = ca. 1880.)

________. *Lalitamādhava-nāṭakam*. Edited by Purīdās. Mymensingh: Śacīnātha Rāyachaudhurī, 1947.

________. *Lalitamādhava-nāṭaka*, with the Commentary of Nārāyaṇa. Edited with Introduction and critical notes by Bābūlāl Śukla. Kashi Sanskrit Series 190. Varanasi: Chowkhamba Sanskrit Series Office, 1969.

________. *Nāṭakacandrikā*. Edited by Purīdās. Mymensingh: Śacīnātha Rāyachaudhurī, 1948.

________. *Nāṭakacandrikā of Srī Rūpa Goswāmin*. Edited with the Prakāśa Hindi commentary and critical notes by Bābūlāl Śukla. Chowkhamba Sanskrit Series 97. Varanasi: Chowkhamba Sanskrit Series Office, 1964.

________. *Padyāvalī*. Edited by S. K. De. Dacca: Dacca University Oriental Publication Series, 1934.

________. *Stavamālā*. Edited by Jīva Gosvāmī. Kavyamala 84. Bombay: Nirnaya Sāgar Press, 1903.

________. *Ujjvalanīlamaṇi*. With the commentaries Locanarocanī of Jīva Gosvāmī and Ānandacandrikā of Viśvanātha Cakravarti. Edited with a Bengali translation by Rāmanārāyaṇa Vidyāratna. Second Edition. Murśidābād: Rāmanārāyaṇa Vidyāratna, 1295 Sāl = ca. 1887.

________. *The Ujjwalanīlamaṇi by Shrī Rūpagoswāmī*, with the commentaries of Jīvagoswāmī and Vishvanātha Chakravarty. Edited by Durgaprasād and Wāsudev Laxman. Second Edition. Kāvyamālā 95. Bombay: Nirṇaya Sāgar Press, 1932.

________. *Ujjvalanīlamaṇi*. Edited by Purīdās. Mymensingh: Śacīnātha Rāyacaudhurī, 1946.

________. *Ujjvalanīlamaṇi*, with the commentary Svātmapramodinī of Viṣṇudāsa Gosvāmī and the Bengali translation of Haridās Dās. Edited by Kānāilāl Adhikārī. Navadvīp: Haribol Kuṭī, 478 Gaurābda = ca. 1964.

Rūpa Gosvāmī. *Vidagdhamādhavanāṭakam*, with the commentary of Viśvanātha Cakravartī, the Bengali Padāvalī of Yadunandana, and the Bengali translation of Rāmanārāyaṇa Vidyāratna, Second Edition. Murśidābād: Rāmanārāyaṇa Vidyāratna, 1307 Sāl = ca. 1899.

________. *The Vidagdha-mādhava of Śrī Rūpadeva Gosvāmī*, with a commentary. Edited by Bhavadatta Śāstrī and Kāsīnāth Pāṇḍurang Parab. Kāvyamālā 81. Second Edition. Bombay: Nirṇaya Sāgar Press, 1937. (Original edition, 1903.)

________. *Vidagdhamādhava-nāṭakam*. Edited by Purīdās. Mymensingh: Śacīnātha Rāyachaudhurī, 1947.

________. *Vidagdhamādhava*, with the commentary of Viśvanātha Cakravartī. Edited and translated by Satyendranāth Basu. Calcutta: Basumatī Sāhitya Mandir, n.d.

Sen, Sukumar. *Bāṅgālā Sāhityer Itihās*, Vol. 1, Fifth Edition. Calcutta: Eastern Publishers, 1970.

________, ed. *Vaiṣṇava-Padāvalī*, Second Edition. New Delhi: Sahitya Akademi, 1971. (Original edition, 1957).

Siṁha, Śukdeb. *Srīrūp O Padāvalīsāhitya*. Calcutta: Bharati Book Stall, 1967.

Subhāṣitaratnakoṣa, compiled by Vidyākara. Edited by D. D. Kosambi and V. V. Gokhale. Harvard Oriental Series, Vol. 42. Cambridge, MA: Harvard University Press, 1957.

Viṣṇu Purāṇa, with the commentary Vaiṣṇavākūṭacandrikā. Bombay: Gopāla Nārāyaṇa and Co. Śaka 1824 = ca. 1902.

Viśvanātha Cakravartī. *Rāgavartmacandrikā*. Edited and translated by Prāṇkiśor Gosvāmī. Calcutta: Vinodakiśor Gosvāmī, 1372 Sāl = ca. 1964.

Viśvanātha Kavirāja. *Sāhityadarpaṇa*, with the commentary Lakṣmī by Kṛṣṇamohan Śāstrī. Kāshī Sanskrit Series. Banaras: Chowkhamba Sanskrit Series Office, 1955.

II. Works in European Languages

Antoine, Robert. "Greek Tragedy and Sanskrit Drama." *Jadavpur Journal of Comparative Literature* 8 (1968) 21-49.

Archer, W. G. *The Loves of Krishna in Indian Painting and Poetry*. London: George Allen and Unwin, 1957.

________, ed. *Love Songs of Vidyāpati*. Translated by Deben Bhattacharya. London: George Allen and Unwin, 1963.

Bäumer, Bettina. "*Līlā*." Unpublished paper, n.d.

________. "Schöpfung als Spiel: Der Begriff *līlā* im Hinduismus, seine philosophische und theologische Bedeutung." Ph.D. dissertation, München: Ludwig-Maximilians-Universität, 1969.

Baumer, Rachel van M. and James R. Brandon, eds. *Sanskrit Drama in Performance*. Honolulu: University Press of Hawaii, 1981.

Belvalkar, Shripad Krishna, ed. and tr. *Rāma's Later History or Uttara-Rāma-charita; An Ancient Hindu Drama by Bhavabhūti*. Harvard Oriental Series, Vol. 21. Cambridge, MA: Harvard University Press, 1915.

Bhandarkar, R. G. *Vaiṣṇavism, Śaivism and Minor Religious Systems*. Strassburg: Grundriss der indo-arischen Philologie und Altertumskunde, III/6, 1913.

Bhattacharya, Deben, tr. *Love Songs of Chandidās*. London: George Allen and Unwin, 1967.

Bhaṭṭacharya, Siddheśvara. *The Philosophy of the Śrīmad-Bhāgavata*. 2 vols. Santiniketan: Visva-Bharati (Ranajit Ray), 1960-62.

Bhavnani, Enakshi. *The Dance in India*. Bombay: D. B. Taraporevala, 1965.

Bon, B. H. "Drama." *Indian Philosophy and Culture*, Vrindaban, 11/4 (1966) 1-11.

Brahmachari, Mahanam Brata. *The Philosophy of Śrī Jīva Goswāmī*. Chicago: The Institute of Oriental Students for the Study of Human Relations, 1937.

Brown, Cheever Mackenzie. *God as Mother: A Feminine Theology in India; An Historical and Theological Study of the Brahmavaivarta Purāṇa*. Hartford, VT: Claude Stark, 1974.

Bryant, Kenneth. *Poems to the Child-God: Structures and Strategies in the Poetry of Sūrdās*. Berkeley/Los Angeles: University of California Press, 1978.

Bühler, G., tr. *The Laws of Manu*. Sacred Books of the East, Vol. 25. Delhi: Motilal Banarsidass, 1970. (First published 1886.)

Caland, W. "Een onbekend Indisch Tooneelstuk (Gopālakeli-candrikā). Tekst met Inleiding door W. Caland," *Verhandelingen der Koninklijke Akademie van Wetenschappen te Amsterdam*, Afdeeling Letterkunde, N. R. deel XVII, No. 3 (1917).

Carman, John B. *The Theology of Ramānuja; An Essay in Interreligious Understanding*. New Haven: Yale University, 1974.

Chakravarti, Monmohan. "Uriya Inscriptions of the 15th and 16th Centuries." *Journal of the Asiatic Society of Bengal* 62, pt. 1 (1894) 88-104.

Chakravarti, Sudhindra Chandra. *Philosophical Foundation of Bengal Vaiṣṇavism*. Calcutta: Academic Publishers, 1969.

Chatterji, Suniti Kumar, et al. *Indian Drama*. Delhi: Ministry of Information and Broadcasting, 1956.

Chaṭṭopādhyāya, Niśikānta. *The Yātrās: Or the Popular Dramas of Bengal*. Calcutta: Granthan, 1976.

Coomaraswamy, Ananda K. "Lila." *Journal of the American Oriental Society* 61 (1941) 98-101.

Dasgupta, Shashibhusan. *Obscure Religious Cults*, Third Edition. Calcutta: K. L. Mukhopadhyay, 1962.

________, and De, S. K. *A History of Sanskrit Literature: Classical Period*, Vol. 1. Calcutta: University of Calcutta, 1947.

De, S. K. *Bengali Literature in the Nineteenth Century*, Second Edition. Calcutta: K. L. Mukhopadhyay, 1962.

________. *Bengal's Contribution to Sanskrit Literature and Studies in Bengal Vaiṣṇavism*. Calcutta: K. L. Mukhopadhyay, 1960. (First published 1943 and 1934 respectively.)

________. *Early History of the Vaiṣṇava Faith and Movement in Bengal*, Second Edition. Calcutta: K. L. Mukhopadhyay, 1961.

________. *History of Sanskrit Poetics*, Second Edition. 2 vols. Calcutta: K. L. Mukhopadhyay, 1960.

Devadhar, C. R., ed. and tr. *Dramas of Kālidāsa*. Delhi: Motilal Banarsidass, 1966.

Devasenapathy, V. A. *Of Human Bondage and Divine Grace*. Annamalainagar: Annamalai University, 1963.

Dhavamony, Mariasusai. *Love of God according to Śaiva Siddhānta*. London: Oxford University Press, 1971.

Dimock, Edward C., Jr., tr. *Caitanyacaritāmṛta*. Harvard Oriental Series. Cambridge, MA: Harvard University Press, forthcoming.

________. "The Place of Gauracandrikā in Bengali Vaiṣṇava Lyrics." *Journal of the American Oriental Society* 78 (1958) 153-69.

________. *The Place of the Hidden Moon: Erotic Mysticism in the Vaiṣṇava-sahajiyā Cult of Bengal*. Chicago: University of Chicago Press, 1966.

________, and Levertov, Denise. *In Praise of Krishna: Songs from the Bengali*. New York: Doubleday Anchor, 1967.

Dimock, Edward C., et al. *The Literatures of India*. Chicago: University of Chicago Press, 1974.

Dixon, John W., Jr. "Art as the Making of the World: Outline of Method in the Criticism of Religion and Art." *Journal of the American Academy of Religion* 51/1 (March, 1983) 15-36.

Eck, Diana L. "India's *tīrthas* 'Crossings' in Sacred Geography." *History of Religions* 20/4 (May, 1981) 323-44.

Edgerton, Franklin, tr. *The Bhagavad Gītā*. 2 vols. Harvard Oriental Series, Vols. 38 and 39. Cambridge, MA: Harvard University Press, 1944.

Eidlitz, Walther. *Kṛṣṇa-Caitanya; Sein Leben und Seine Lehre*. Stockholm: Almqvist & Wiksell, 1968.

Eliade, Mircea. *The Sacred and the Profane*. Translated by W. R. Trask. New York: Harcourt, Brace, 1959.

________. *Yoga: Immortality and Freedom*, Second Edition. Translated by W. R. Trask. Princeton: Princeton University Press, 1969.

Eliot, Sir Charles. *Hinduism and Buddhism: An Historical Sketch*. 3 vols. London: Routledge & Kegan Paul, 1921. (Reprinted, 1968.)

Farquhar, J. N. *An Outline of the Religious Literature of India*. Delhi: Motilal Banarsidass, 1967. (First published 1920.)

Gail, Adalbert. *Bhakti im Bhāgavatapurāṇa*. Wiesbaden: Otto Harrassowitz, 1969.

Gargi, Balwant. *Folk Theater of India*. Seattle: University of Washington Press, 1966.

Gerow, Edwin. *A Glossary of Indian Figures of Speech*. The Hague: Mouton, 1971.

Ghosh, Manomohan. *Contributions to the History of the Hindu Drama*. Calcutta: K. L. Mukhopadhyay, 1958.

Gonda, Jan. *Aspects of Early Viṣṇuism*, Second Edition. Delhi: Motilal Banarsidass, 1969.

________. *Ursprung und Wesen des Indischen Dramas*. Acta Orientalia 19. Leiden, 1943.

________. *Viṣṇuism and Śivaism: A Comparison*. London: The Athlone Press, 1970.

Goswami, Asha. "Rādhā." *Journal of the Department of Sanskrit*, University of Delhi 1/2 (1972) 34-44.

Goswami, C. L., tr. *Srīmad Bhāgavata Mahāpurāṇa*. 2 vols. Gorakhpur: Motilal Jalan, 1971.

Growse, F. S. *Mathurā: A District Memoir*, Third Edition. Allahabad: North-Western Provinces Government Press, 1883.

Guha, Abhaykumar. "Rasa-cult in the Chaitanya Charitāmṛta." *Sir Asutosh Mookerjee Silver Jubilee Volumes*, Vol. 3, Pt. 3, 368-88. Calcutta: Calcutta University Press, 1927.

Guha-Thakurta, P. *The Bengali Drama*. London: Kegan Paul, Trench, Trubner, 1930.

Haas, George C. O., tr. *The Daśarūpa*. New York: Columbia University Press, 1912.

Hawley, John Stratton. *At Play with Krishna: Pilgrimage Dramas from Brindavan*. Princeton: Princeton University Press, 1981.

________. "The Butter Thief." Unpublished Ph.D. dissertation, Harvard University, 1977.

________. *Krishna, the Butter Thief*. Princeton: Princeton University Press, 1983.

________, and Donna Marie Wulff, eds. *The Divine Consort: Rādhā and the Goddesses of India*. Berkeley: Berkeley Religious Studies Series, 1982.

Hein, Norvin. "Caitanya's Ecstasies and the Theology of the Name." Bardwell L. Smith, ed., *Hinduism: New Essays in the History of Religions*, pp. 15-32. Leiden: E. J. Brill, 1976.

________. *The Miracle Plays of Mathurā*. New Haven: Yale University Press, 1972.

Hopkins, Thomas J. *The Hindu Religious Tradition*. Encino, CA: Dickenson, 1971.

Hooper, J.S.M. *Hymns of the Āḻvārs*. Calcutta: Association Press, 1929.

Hospital, Clifford George. "The Marvellous Acts of God: A Study in the *Bhāgavata Purāṇa*." Unpublished Ph.D. dissertation, Harvard University, 1973.

Hudson, Dennis. "Bathing in Kṛṣṇa: A Study in the Theology of Refuge." Unpublished paper, 1976.

Hume, Robert Ernest, tr. *The Thirteen Principal Upanishads*, Second Edition. London: Oxford University Press, 1931.

Ingalls, Daniel H. H., tr. *An Anthology of Sanskrit Court Poetry*. Harvard Oriental Series, Vol. 44. Cambridge, MA: Harvard University Press, 1965.

________. "The Harivaṃśa as a Mahākāvya." In *Mélanges d'Indianisme à la Mémoire de Louis Renou*. Paris: E. de Boccard, 1968.

Ingalls, Daniel H. H. "Words for Beauty in Classical Sanskrit Poetry." In Ernest Bender, ed., *Indological Studies in Honor of W. Norman Brown*. New Haven: American Oriental Society, 1962.

Iyer, K. Bharatha. *Kathakali: The Sacred Dance-Drama of Malabar*. London: Luzac, 1955.

Jaiswal, Suvira. *The Origin and Development of Vaiṣṇavism*. Delhi: Munshiram Manoharlal, 1967.

James, William. *The Varieties of Religious Experience*. London: Longmans, Green, 1902.

Johnston, E. H. *The Buddhacarita or Acts of the Buddha*. Delhi: Motilal Banarsidass, 1972. (First published 1936.)

Joshi, Rasik Vihari. *Le Rituel de la Dévotion Kṛṣṇaïte*. Pondicherry: Institut Français d'Indologie, 1959.

Kane, Pandurang Vaman. *History of Sanskrit Poetics*, Third Edition. Delhi: Motilal Banarsidass, 1961.

________. Introduction and notes to *The Sáhityadarpana of Viśvanátha Kavirája*. Bombay: Oriental Publishing, 1910.

Keith, A. Berriedale. *The Sanskrit Drama*. London: Oxford University, 1924.

Kennedy, Melville T. *The Chaitanya Movement*. Calcutta: Association Press, 1925.

Kern, H., tr. *Saddharma-Puṇḍarīka or the Lotus of the True Law*. The Sacred Books of the East, Vol. 21. New York: Dover, 1963. (First published, 1884.)

Keyt, George, tr. *Sri Jayadeva's Gīta-Govinda; The Loves of Kṛṣṇa and Rādhā*. Bombay: Kutab-Popular, 1947.

Kinsley, David R. "The Divine Player: A Study of Kṛṣṇa-līlā." Unpublished Ph.D. dissertation, University of Chicago, 1970.

________. *The Sword and the Flute*. Berkeley: University of California Press, 1975.

________. "Without Kṛṣṇa There Is No Song." *History of Religions* 12/2 (1972) 149-80.

Konow, Sten. *Das Indische Drama*. Berlin: Walter de Gruyter, 1920.

________. *The Indian Drama*. Trans. S. N. Ghosal. Calcutta: General Printers and Publishers, 1969.

Krishnamachariar, M. *History of Classical Sanskrit Literature*, Third Edition. Delhi: Motilal Banarsidass, 1974.

Kunbae, Bak. *Bhasa's Bālacarita*. Delhi: Meharchand Lachhmandas, 1968.

Lévi, Sylvain. *Le Théâtre Indien*. Paris: Collège de France, 1963. (First published, 1890.)

Long, J. Bruce. "Life out of Death: A Structural Analysis of the Myth of the 'Churning of the Ocean of Milk.'" Bardwell L. Smith, ed., *Hinduism: New Essays in the History History of Religions*, pp. 171-207. Leiden: E. J. Brill, 1976.

Macnicol, Nicol. *Indian Theism from the Vedic to the Muhammadan Period*. Delhi: Munshiram Manoharlal, 1968. (First published, 1915.)

Majumdar, A. K. *Caitanya, His Life and Doctrine: A Study in Vaiṣṇavism*. Bombay: Bharatiya Vidya Bhavan, 1969.

Majumdar, Bimanbehari. *Kṛṣṇa in History and Legend*. Calcutta: University of Calcutta, 1969.

Masson, J. L., and Kosambi, D. D. *The Avimāraka*. Delhi: Motilal Banarsidass, 1970.

Masson, J. L., and Patwardhan, M. V. *Aesthetic Rapture*. 2 vols. Poona: Deccan College Postgraduate and Research Institute, 1970.

________. *Śāntarasa and Abhinavagupta's Philosophy of Aesthetics*. Poona: Bhandarkar Oriental Research Institute, 1969.

Mathur, J. C. *Drama in Rural India*. New York: Asia Publishing House, 1964.

Miller, Barbara Stoler, ed. and tr. *Love Song of the Dark Lord: Jayadeva's Gītagovinda*. New York: Columbia University, 1977.

________. "Rādhā: Consort of Kṛṣṇa's Vernal Passion." *Journal of the American Oriental Society* 95 (1975) 655-71.

Mukherji, S. C. *A Study of Vaiṣṇavism in Ancient and Medieval Bengal*. Calcutta: Punthi Pustak, 1966.

O'Connell, Joseph T. "Social Implications of the Gauḍīya Vaiṣṇava Movement." Unpublished Ph.D. dissertation, Harvard University, 1970.

O'Flaherty, Wendy Doniger. *Asceticism and Eroticism in the Mythology of Śiva*. London: Oxford University Press, 1973.

Pandey, K. C. *Comparative Aesthetics*, Vol. 1: *Indian Aesthetics*, Second Edition. Varanasi: Chowkhamba (Sanskrit Series), 1959.

Radhakrishnan, S., ed. *The Principal Upaniṣads*. London: George Allen and Unwin, 1953.

Raghavan, V. "Concept of Beauty." *Vedanta Kesari* 46/4 (1959) 181-84.

Ray, Kumudranjan, ed. *Viswanatha's Sahityadarpana*, Second Edition, Vol. 2. Calcutta: Sanskrita Pustak Bhandar, n.d.

Ray, Prafulla Chandra. *History of Chemistry in Ancient and Medieval India*. Calcutta: Indian Chemical Society, 1956.

Renou, Louis, and Fillozat, Jean. *L'Inde Classique; Manuel des Études Indiennes*. 2 vols. Paris: Payot, 1947-49.

Sanyal, J. M., tr. *The Srimad-Bhagvatam of Krishna-Dwaipayana Vyasa*, Second Edition. 2 vols. New Delhi: Munshiram Manoharlal, 1973. (Original edition in 5 vols., 1929.)

Śastri, S. V., ed. *Matsya Puranam*. Delhi: Oriental Publishers, 1972.

Saunders, Virginia. "Portrait Painting as a Dramatic Device in Sanskrit Plays." *Journal of the American Oriental Society* 39, Pt. 5 (1919) 299-302.

Schomerus, H. W. *Der Çaiva-Siddhanta*. Leipzig, 1912.

Sen, Dineschandra. "Domestic Element in the Popular Creeds of Bengal." *Sir Asutosh Mookerjee Silver Jubilee Volumes*, Vol. 3, Pt. 1, 155-76. Calcutta: Calcutta University, 1922.

Sen, Dinesh Chandra. *History of Bengali Language and Literature*. Calcutta: University of Calcutta, 1954.

Sen, Sukumar. *Chandidas*. New Delhi: Sahitya Akademi, 1971.

________. *History of Bengali Literature*, Second Edition. New Delhi: Sahitya Akademi, 1971.

________. *A History of Brajabuli Literature*. Calcutta: University of Calcutta, 1935.

Sharma, Prem Lata. "Studies in Bhaktirasa (Śrī Rūpa Gosvāmī)." Unpublished Ph.D. dissertation, Banaras Hindu University, 1954.

Singer, Milton, ed. *Krishna: Myths, Rites, and Attitudes*. Honolulu: East-West Center Press, 1966.

Sitaram, K. N. "Dramatic Representations of South India." *Journal of the Royal Asiatic Society* (1924) 229-37.

Smith, Wilfred Cantwell. *The Meaning and End of Religion*. New York: Macmillan, 1963.

Solomon, Ted J. "Early Vaiṣṇava Bhakti and its Autochthonous Heritage." *History of Religions* 10/1 (1970) 32-48.

Spinks, Walter M. *Krishnamandala; A Devotional Theme in Indian Art*. Ann Arbor, MI: Center for South and Southeast Asian Studies, The University of Michigan, 1971.

Tagore, Rabindranath. *Hungry Stones and Other Stories*. London: Macmillan, 1966.

Temple, Sir Richard Carnac. *The Legends of the Panjab*. 3 vols. Bombay: Education Society's Press, 1884-1901.

van Buitenen, J.A.B., tr. *Tales of Ancient India*. Chicago: University of Chicago Press, 1959.

_______, tr. *Two Plays of Ancient India*. New York: Columbia University Press, 1968.

Varadachari, K. C. *Āḻvārs of South India*. Bombay: Bharatiya Vidya Bhavan, 1966.

Vatsyayan, Kapila. *Classical Indian Dance in Literature and the Arts*. New Delhi: Sangeet Natak Akademi, 1968.

Vaudeville, Charlotte. "Evolution of Love-symbolism in Bhagavatism." *Journal of the American Oriental Society* 82, Pt. 1 (1962) 31-40.

White, Charles. "Kṛṣṇa as Divine Child." *History of Religions* 10/2 (1970) 156-77.

Wilson, F., ed. and tr. *The Bilvamaṅgalastava*. Leiden: E. J. Brill, 1973.

Wilson, Frances, ed. *The Love of Krishna; The Kṛṣṇakarṇāmṛta of Līlāśuka Bilvamaṅgala*. Philadelphia: University of Pennsylvania Press, 1975.

Wilson, H. H. *Select Specimens of the Theatre of the Hindus*, Third Edition. London: Trubner, 1871.

_______, tr. *The Vishnu Purana*. Calcutta: Punthi Pustak, 1961. (First published, 1840.)

Winternitz, M. *A History of Indian Literature*, Vol. 3, Fasc. 1: *Ornate Poetry*. Translated by H. Kohn. Calcutta: Calcutta University Press, 1959.

_______. *A History of Indian Literature*, Vol. 3, Part I: *Classical Sanskrit Literature*, Second Edition. Translated by Subhadra Jha. Delhi: Motilal Banarsidass, 1977.

_______. "Kṛṣṇa-Dramen." *Zeitschrift der deutschen morgenländischen Gesellschaft* 74/1 (1920) 118-44.

Wulff, Donna Marie. "On Practicing Religiously: Music as Sacred in India." Joyce Irwin, ed., *Sacred Sound: Music in Religious Thought and Practice. Journal of the American Academy of Religion*, Thematic Studies 50/1 (February, 1984) 149-72.

________. "*Rasa* as a Religious Category: Aesthetics and Supreme Realization in Medieval India." *Journal of the American Academy of Religion*, forthcoming.

van der Leeuw, Gerardus. *Sacred and Profane Beauty: The Holy in Art*. Translated by David E. Green. New York: Holt, Rinehart and Winston, 1963.

Zaehner, R. C., tr. *The Bhagavad-Gita*, with a Commentary based on the original sources. London: Oxford University Press, 1969.

________. *Hinduism*. London: Oxford University Press, 1962.

Zimmer, Heinrich. *Myths and Symbols in Indian Art and Civilization*. Edited by Joseph Campbell. New York: Pantheon, 1946.